Father Martin D'Arcy

Father Martin D'Arcy

Philosopher of Christian Love

H.J.A. Sire

First published in 1997

Gracewing
Fowler Wright Books
2 Southern Ave, Leominster
Herefordshire HR6 0QF

© H.J.A. Sire

ISBN 0 85244 439 7

Typesetting by Action Typesetting Ltd,
Gloucester, GL1 1SP

Printed by Cromwell Press,
Broughton Grifford Wiltshire SN12 8PH

Contents

List of Illustrations

15. The chapel at Wardour Castle.
16. Fr D'Arcy sets the *ton* at Santa Monica, 1960s, with Mrs (Pat) Anderson.
(ii) Fr D'Arcy's eightieth birthday party at 21 (New York). From left to right: Evelyn Johnson, Fr D'Arcy, Jane Engelhard, the Duke of Windsor, Maria Shrady, Viscount Margesson, Mrs Edmund Wilson, Senator Mansfield; (in front) Phyllis McGinley and Dan McKeon.

Copyright Acknowledgments

Preface

It is now twenty years since the death of Fr Martin D'Arcy. The other English Jesuits who played a comparable role in the life of their Church during this century – Bernard Vaughan, Charles Plater, Cyril Martindale – all had Jesuit biographers appointed and their Lives published immediately after their deaths. When Fr D'Arcy died in 1976 that honour was not extended to him; and yet his career deserved to be recorded on wider grounds than those of his predecessors. More than any of them he transcended the limits of clerical life and claims a place in such worlds as those of art connoisseurship, of literary circles between the wars, and a particular period and flowering of American Catholicism. In his writings he also interpreted a school of thought more distinctive and more delicate than the apologetics of most of the leading English Catholic figures of the past.

Permission to examine certain classes of documents relating to Fr D'Arcy's life – notably the letters written to him by his numerous friends, and the records of his Provincialship – has been refused by the English Jesuit Province on the grounds that an official biographer may be appointed in the future. It is much to be hoped that this will happen, since the use of those sources will enable the writer to fill certain inevitable gaps in the present study: perhaps to give a more intimate picture of Fr D'Arcy's friendships and especially of his earlier years, and to arrive at a more rounded judgment of his achievements and failures as English Provincial. In the mean time that limitation has imposed certain points of perspective from which his life had to be viewed. It was remarked of Fr D'Arcy that though he had a great gift for friendship his genius avoided intimacy. That trait, together with the darkness of the family background, has produced a more superficial or external picture than a biographer would ideally like to give of his subject; perhaps that would have been in accord with the wishes of a priest who so made his own the Jesuit ideal of a self-abnegating ministry. Added to this has been the impossibility of recovering the voice and presence of a man whose characteristic achievement was in the personal impact he made on people. Only someone who knew Fr D'Arcy in his prime would be able to convey the flavour of his talk, and perhaps also the quality of his spiritual direction and the inspiration of his thought communicated face to face.

It is a pity that no-one thus qualified has undertaken to write this biography, whether spontaneously or under commission; but the longer the task is left the more second-hand will the narrative be.

The research and writing of this book have been funded by the exceptional generosity of the late Mr Joseph Fattorini and another friend of Fr Martin D'Arcy's, and I would like to express my keen gratitude to both of them for making it possible. My thanks are due to those who helped me with the research, especially to Fr Geoffrey Holt, formerly Archivist of the English Jesuit Province, who put himself and the Farm Street archives at my disposal over a period of several weeks, and to the Master of Campion Hall, Fr Joseph Munitiz, who offered me the hospitality of his House and whose punctual and efficient response to all my requests has greatly smoothed my path. I would also like to thank the friends of Fr D'Arcy who have shared their memories with me: the Earl of Longford, the Earl of Oxford and Asquith, Lady Helen Asquith, Lord Hailsham, Mgr Alfred Gilbey, Sir Isaiah Berlin, the Hon. Mrs C.E. Fremantle, Fr Philip Caraman, Fr John Coventry, Fr Deryck Hanshell, Fr Vincent Bywater, Fr Cyril Barrett, the late Mr Thomas Burns, Fr Francis Sweeney, Fr Donald Rowe, Fr Ronald Tacelli, Mrs Frederick Shrady, Mrs Barrett McDonnell, Mr William S. Abell, and Mr Matthew Murray. Miss Zita Kelly's genealogical help as a cousin of Fr D'Arcy's has been invaluable to me. My thanks are also due to Mr Claude Blair, Mr Julian Bell, Mr Geoffrey Lewis and Mr Nigel Nicholson for supplying me with documents and other information, and to Mr Auberon Waugh for permission to quote extracts from Evelyn Waugh's writings. I would like finally to extend my thanks and apologies to any who have helped me with the research and whom I may have omitted to mention.

For the benefit of readers unfamiliar with some of the settings of Fr D'Arcy's life, the Notes include not only references but explanations of abbreviations, biographical details of people alluded to and other supplementary information.

Skeleton Pedigree of
Father Martin D'Arcy

The estate owned by members of the family is shown in *italics*; the estate of the families to which their wives belonged is shown in brackets.

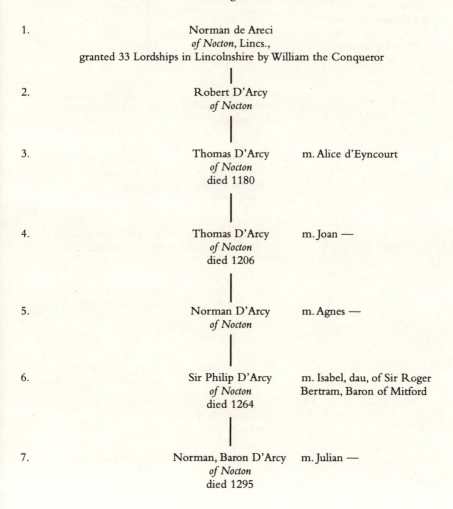

1. **Norman de Areci**
    of Nocton, Lincs.,
    granted 33 Lordships in Lincolnshire by William the Conqueror

2. **Robert D'Arcy**
    of Nocton

3. **Thomas D'Arcy**   m. Alice d'Eyncourt
    of Nocton
    died 1180

4. **Thomas D'Arcy**   m. Joan —
    of Nocton
    died 1206

5. **Norman D'Arcy**   m. Agnes —
    of Nocton

6. **Sir Philip D'Arcy**   m. Isabel, dau, of Sir Roger
    of Nocton   Bertram, Baron of Mitford
    died 1264

7. **Norman, Baron D'Arcy**   m. Julian —
    of Nocton
    died 1295

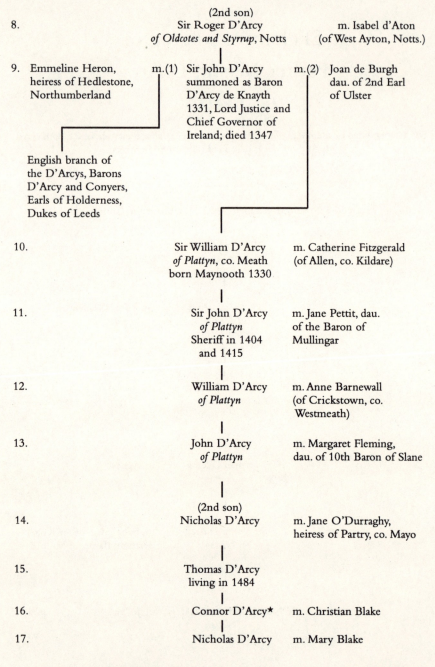

8.
(2nd son)
Sir Roger D'Arcy
of Oldcotes and Styrrup, Notts
m. Isabel d'Aton
(of West Ayton, Notts.)

9. Emmeline Heron,
heiress of Hedlestone,
Northumberland
m.(1) Sir John D'Arcy
summoned as Baron
D'Arcy de Knayth
1331, Lord Justice and
Chief Governor of
Ireland; died 1347
m.(2) Joan de Burgh
dau. of 2nd Earl
of Ulster

English branch of
the D'Arcys, Barons
D'Arcy and Conyers,
Earls of Holderness,
Dukes of Leeds

10. Sir William D'Arcy
of Plattyn, co. Meath
born Maynooth 1330
m. Catherine Fitzgerald
(of Allen, co. Kildare)

11. Sir John D'Arcy
of Plattyn
Sheriff in 1404
and 1415
m. Jane Pettit, dau.
of the Baron of
Mullingar

12. William D'Arcy
of Plattyn
m. Anne Barnewall
(of Crickstown, co.
Westmeath)

13. John D'Arcy
of Plattyn
m. Margaret Fleming,
dau. of 10th Baron of Slane

14. (2nd son)
Nicholas D'Arcy
m. Jane O'Durraghy,
heiress of Partry, co. Mayo

15. Thomas D'Arcy
living in 1484

16. Connor D'Arcy★ m. Christian Blake

17. Nicholas D'Arcy m. Mary Blake

★ He appears in printed pedigrees as Conyers D'Arcy, but this is probably a later misreading in the light of the English Conyers D'Arcy, Baron D'Arcy and Conyers.

18.   **Sir James (Riveagh) D'Arcy**   m. Elizabeth Martin
                                   of Kiltullagh, co. Galway
                             Lord President of Connaught
                        and Governor of Galway died 1603

(3rd son)   (7th son)

19. James D'Arcy   m. Mary Skerrett   Patrick D'Arcy (1598–1668)
    (moved to Lisbon)   Leader of the Confederate
                                  Catholics of Ireland

20. John D'Arcy   m. Anastace Blake (of Dunmenure, co. Mayo)
    of Gorteen, co. Mayo

21. Patrick D'Arcy   m. Margery French (of   James   Francis
    of Gorteen   Abbert, co. Galway)   killed at   ancestor of the
                                      Athlone 1691 Counts D'Arcy

                                               Jacobite officers

22. John D'Arcy   m.   Anastace Daly (of
    of Gorteen   Calla, co. Galway)
    died 1747   Thomas ffrench of
                                   Castle ffrench, co. Galway

(4th son)   (4th or 5th dau.)   Sir Charles   m.   Rose, 1st
23. Nicholas D'Arcy m.   Catherine? ffrench   ffrench, Bt   Baroness ffrench
    died before 1780

                    Edmund Kelly of Ballyforan m. Claire ffrench

24. Anthony D'Arcy m.   Clara Kelly, heiress of Ballyforan   Barons
    died 1815   died 1823   ffrench

25. Nicholas D'Arcy m.   Teresa Burke (of Springfield, co. Tipperary)
    of Ballyforan, co. Roscommon
    1801–1868

                            Peter Keegan J.P.

(3rd son)
26. Martin Valentine D'Arcy   m.   Madoline Mary Keegan
    1845–1917   1855–1935

27. Edmund Conyers D'Arcy SJ   Martin Cyril D'Arcy SJ
    1885–1967   1888–1976

Chapter One

Childhood and Schooling

Some genealogists have traced the D'Arcy lineage to William Count of Arques, a younger son of Richard, fourth Duke of Normandy. According to this view the earliest recorded ancestor of Fr Martin D'Arcy would be the father of the first Duke of Normandy, the Viking Rögnwald, who led a life undistinguished by Christian love in the middle of the ninth century. Other authorities maintain that when Noah was loading the Ark he called out, 'All aboard, and don't forget the D'Arcy pedigree!'

The more humdrum scholarship of today finds the origin of the D'Arcy line in Norman de Areci (a son of William Count of Arques according to the first theory), who held thirty-three manors in Lincolnshire by the grant of William the Conqueror.[1] Skipping lightly over the next eight generations we come to Sir John Darcy (the spelling of the family name remains fluid until the eighteenth century), who was summoned as Lord Darcy de Knayth in 1331. He married successively an English and an Irish wife and by them founded the English and the Irish branches of his family.

Among the English Darcys we find Thomas Lord Darcy, who spoke out in Parliament against Henry VIII's divorce from Catherine of Aragon and was executed for failing to suppress the Pilgrimage of Grace, with which he sympathised. Despite this promising start, the English Darcys later became Protestants and thus opened their way to the highest honours. The seventeenth century brings us to Conyers Darcy, whose right to the baronies of Darcy and Conyers was recognised in 1641. His descendants became Earls of Holderness, and the fourth Earl was a minister in the cabinet of Henry Pelham, whose brother the Duke of Newcastle was glad, from the humble standpoint of a newly-minted duke, to observe of him: 'He has no pride about him, though a D'Arcy.'[2] The Dukes of Leeds, descended from the family in the female line, assumed the name of D'Arcy to add distinction to their own.

Turning to the Irish line we find, nine generations on from the first Lord Darcy de Knayth, Sir James D'Arcy, known to the Irish as Riveagh, who was a man of some note in County Galway in the reign of Queen Elizabeth. His third son, James, went to live in Lisbon, at that time part of the Spanish empire, and prospered there. His fortune bought the estate of

1

Gorteen in County Mayo, where his descendants built a large house. As Catholics, the D'Arcys of Gorteen supported James II, and a younger son, Francis, founded the Jacobite branch of the family in France, who received the title of Count. In the 1930s we find Fr Martin D'Arcy celebrating the weddings and funerals of their descendants, who were by then living in England.

An eighteenth-century younger son of the Gorteen line, Francis D'Arcy, married a lady of the ffrench family, soon to be ennobled.[3] His son Anthony, who was brought up at Castle ffrench, made an advantageous marriage to his cousin, Clara Kelly, who inherited the estate of Ballyforan in County Roscommon. The Kellys had been at Ballyforan since the seventeenth century and were a Protestant family, but one supposes that Clara had been brought up a Catholic by her mother, who was a ffrench. Her son Nicholas inherited the estate in 1823, shortly after he came of age.

The D'Arcys at this time and place seem to have suffered from a generalised dottiness, as one can see from the case of a relation who, to put in their place some parvenus who had established themselves ostentatiously in her neighbourhood, resolved to give a grand ball for all the people *comme il fallait* of her circle. When the night came her house was empty since she had forgotten to send out the invitations. Fr Martin D'Arcy told the anecdote to Evelyn Waugh, who worked it into his short story *Bella Fleace Gave a Party*.[4] Nicholas D'Arcy was evidently a full participant in these peculiarities; he showed himself quite incapable of managing his estate and had to sell Ballyforan back to the Kellys. After trying to run a hotel in Dublin he retired to London, where he died in 1868.

Of Nicholas's six children, the eldest son broke with his father and went to live in the United States, where Fr D'Arcy discovered descendants in the 1960s.[5] Two of the daughters married two promising young lawyers, Patrick Coll and Joseph Walton.* Whatever the extent of their father's ruin the younger D'Arcys were protected from penury by their mother's family, the Burkes of Springfield and Dalkey, who owned the Shelbourne Hotel and were prominent in Dublin society.

It was the youngest son, Martin Valentine D'Arcy, born in 1845, who seems to have fared worst financially of the six children. He moved with his father to London, and after leaving school he worked as a clerk for six years. No doubt he shared the conviction of his race that a D'Arcy was necessarily an aristocrat whatever his worldly circumstances, but he

---

* The Rt Hon. Sir Patrick Coll, KCB (1839–1917), Chief Crown Solicitor for Ireland from 1888, Irish Privy Councillor from 1905; and Sir Joseph Walton (1845–1910), Chairman of the General Council of the Bar 1899–1901 and then a judge.

would have to work hard to make that rank visible. Whether he was able to save out of his earnings or whether some money became available on his father's death, in 1869 he found it possible to return to Dublin to study law for two years at the King's Inns. He then entered himself on the books of the Middle Temple to prepare for the English Bar, but again the need to earn his living prevented him from continuing with his studies. A teaching post which he held in a London school at this time gained him the testimonial that 'his high character, gentlemanly bearing, and professional ability as a teacher would render his appointment to a Mastership an advantage to any school.' [6] At last from 1875 he was able to keep his terms uninterruptedly, and he was called to the Bar in 1878.

Throughout his career Valentine D'Arcy was to lean on the genial aid of his brother-in-law, Joseph Walton, who was by now well established as a barrister at Liverpool. It was this which led D'Arcy to start practising on the Northern Circuit, but in 1880 he received an appointment as a parliamentary draftsman. Perhaps on the strength of this he got married the same year to Madoline Mary Keegan, the daughter of a well-to-do Belfast wine merchant who, though a Catholic, had the talent to win acceptance in that Protestant city, both socially and as a Justice of the Peace. By her marriage settlement Madoline Keegan had £200 a year, which must have been an important contribution to the D'Arcy economy throughout her married life. Madoline had two sisters living in Ireland and two in England, of whom one became the Prioress of a Carmelite convent in Wells and the other lived at Wimbledon, married to a member of an old English Catholic family, William Eyre.

Valentine and Madoline D'Arcy had two sons born in the next two years, but they both died when only a few years old. Two more sons followed, Edmund Conyers, born in 1885, and Martin Cyril, born on June 15th 1888. The family custom was to use the second Christian name, and Martin D'Arcy will be referred to as Cyril until his reception as a Jesuit, after which the more formal appellation prescribed by his birth certificate took priority in common use. Conyers continued to be known by that name throughout his life.

After three years as a parliamentary draftsman, Mr D'Arcy had been appointed electoral agent to Lord Weymouth, the heir to the Marquess of Bath, and, though Conyers was born in London, by 1888 the D'Arcys had moved to Bath, where the youngest son was born in a house adjoining the Cleveland Bridge. From the back door an ill-guarded little Cyril might have rolled fifty yards down a grassy slope into the River Avon.

Mr D'Arcy's work was to manage his employer's affairs in the marginal constituency of Frome, which Lord Weymouth contested unsuccessfully in 1885 and 1892 and successfully in 1886 and 1895 (exactly in line with overall Conservative fortunes in those general elections). The constituency included mining villages which were strongly Liberal, and Mr D'Arcy found himself having to fight elections almost literally, facing crowds of stone-throwing miners armed only with a walking-stick. His thrills were cut short by his dismissal about 1892.[7] One might think that the loss of the seat in that year had something to do with it, but apparently his patron had accused him of trying to further his own political ambitions. What this means presumably is that Lord Weymouth suspected him of wanting to succeed to the constituency when he himself went to the Lords (which he did in 1896, his younger brother replacing him as parliamentary candidate). The suspicion seems a very plausible one; even for a man without political interests, a seat in Parliament was a huge advantage to a lawyer's practice and was a sure avenue to the Bench. To be electoral agent to a nobleman who would soon be succeeding to a peerage was an ideal way of getting one's foot into a constituency. It seems clumsy of Valentine D'Arcy, however, to have made his intentions apparent, and worse than clumsy to allow the discovery to lead to a breach – he is said to have ordered Lord Weymouth out of the room on hearing the accusation.

We seem here to see the same erratic behaviour that had been his father's downfall. Valentine D'Arcy, although, in his son's words, 'very free with those lower in station and in consequence much liked by them', evidently had an exaggerated sense of what was due to his name. On one occasion a few years later, when the family were on holiday in Kingstown, Mrs D'Arcy pointed out a man who had just walked past them as the Earl of Kenmare, the grandest Catholic nobleman in Ireland, a venerable figure who had held the offices of Lord Chamberlain and Comptroller of the Household; her husband had to be restrained from going after Lord Kenmare and striking him for daring to pass a lady without saluting her. Yet the only reason Mrs D'Arcy knew Lord Kenmare was that her sister's husband was his land agent. With this incident in view we may surmise that in his earlier clash with the peerage Mr D'Arcy had taken offence at Lord Weymouth's failure to see that a D'Arcy was at least as worthy as a Thynne of a seat in the legislature.

Thus Valentine D'Arcy found himself, in his late forties, having to pick up the threads of his legal career, at an age when most of his contemporaries had a quarter of a century's practice under their belts. Once again he turned to Joseph Walton, whose career was now reaching its peak; he became leading Counsel to the Jockey Club in 1894, Recorder of Wigan the following year, and Chairman of the General Council of the Bar in 1899. Through his help, Valentine D'Arcy was able to re-establish himself in the Northern Circuit. The D'Arcys seem to have left Bath in November 1894[8] and for a time they lived at Blackburn, while Mr D'Arcy pursued unrewarding briefs in the local courts, but by 1900 his work and residence were in Liverpool. In competition however with younger men such as F.E. Smith, Gordon Hewart and Rigby Swift,[9] who at this time were forming an exceptionally brilliant group on the Northern Circuit, he failed to make headway. He was never able to take silk, and in 1904 he accepted a post as Revising Barrister, with the task of revising electoral lists in the Liverpool area at a modest but secure salary. While his relationship with Joseph Walton (who was raised to the Bench and knighted in 1901) enabled him to rub shoulders with the leading men of his profession and to move in the *première société* of Catholic Liverpool, success by his own merits eluded him.

As both the D'Arcy brothers became priests, they kept little in the way of early documents, and there are no family survivors to give their memories, with the consequence that the evidence for Cyril D'Arcy's childhood comes largely from his own reminiscences in old age. He lamented that his mother 'shut herself up desperately'[10] when they moved north. Perhaps it was not so much the geography as the knowledge that her husband had thrown away a golden opportunity. When they reached Blackburn, Conyers was sent to the Jesuit school of Stonyhurst, just a few miles away, and Cyril was left at home by himself. He grew up without friends, until at the age of eight he was himself sent to board at Bishop's Court, a small dame's school recently opened near Liverpool. In the mean time he had led 'a very lonely life ... reading and reading and reading and creating a world of my own of imagination'[11] – so much so that when he made his first friend at school he recounted to him as his own experiences the stories he had read in *Boxiana*, a collection of pugilistic tales.

In September 1898 Cyril followed Conyers to Stonyhurst, where he was to spend fifteen of the next twenty-six years of his life. He went first to the preparatory school, Hodder Place, where some fifty of the smaller boys were taught. His class-fellows included the younger son of Oscar Wilde, Vyvyan Holland (his mother had changed their name after Wilde's disgrace), whose memoirs provide a parallel source for these years.

At ten years old Cyril was young for his class – Vyvyan Holland was nearly two years older, and this accounts for a difference of experience between them. For Holland, Stonyhurst was a relief from the bullying he had known at other schools, but Cyril D'Arcy was small and puny for his age and he suffered terribly. It was a peculiarity of Stonyhurst that, with fees less than half those charged by establishments like Eton and Harrow, it drew its pupils from a much wider social range than the ordinary public schools. A consequence was that, besides a clientele who took for granted schooling from eight to eighteen, it catered for a number of well-meaning folk who hoped that three or four years at the famous Jesuit school – starting with scanty mental or social preparation at twelve or thirteen – would turn their sons into first-rate Catholics. Perhaps that happened in the long run, but in the mean time they were more in evidence as overgrown louts who vented their shortcomings on their weaker companions. As this rougher element tended to leave early, however, it was a common Stonyhurst experience, which Cyril D'Arcy shared, to find the last years in the school more civilised than the early struggles. It may be significant that his closest Stonyhurst friend in later life, Basil Gurrin, only entered his class in the second-last year.

The headmaster of Hodder was Fr Francis Cassidy, the first of a number of admirable Irish Jesuits who were to figure in D'Arcy's career, a man who made of native charm a veritable apostolate. Fr Martindale described the honeyed guile by which he would 'ask advice, and after warmly applauding suggestions quite alien to his intentions, proceeded to modify them, with the utmost grace and simplicity, till they harmonised at every point with his original scheme.' The same invisible craft characterised his government of small boys. He had a knack of making each boy feel himself a favourite. In a thousand cosy little ways he made religious practice part of the domestic life of the school. He had recently introduced the Apostleship of Prayer, which fostered devotion to the Sacred Heart, and had built a Lourdes Grotto, with a pond in front of it known as the 'Apostleship Pond' A boy who was at the school in the nineties was to write: 'As for our faith he imbued us with it – unlectured, unforced, never screwed into us. It would not be easy to find phrases to describe the holy yet homely atmosphere he achieved for our First Communions.'[12] Vyvyan Holland, who made his First Communion with Cyril D'Arcy on June 1st 1899, describes the effect on a boy of more unsettled experience: 'The First Communicants went into retreat for two or three days to get into the right frame of mind. The emotional strain of the moment of receiving Communion was almost unbearably ecstatic, and the feeling of holiness which it gave one persisted through the day. I felt safe, sanctified, and with one foot firmly on the path that leads to salvation.'[13]

Of his life at home Fr D'Arcy recalled, 'With the early losses in their minds we were very dear to our parents'; but he felt an undeclared preference on his father's part for Conyers, who was brilliant, energetic, and it must be said rather overbearing to his frail younger brother. At thirteen Conyers won a Stonyhurst scholarship and was already in the third-highest class in the school – and at the head of it moreover; he was also a notable actor and cricketer. One has the impression of Cyril as a rather strange little boy, his head full of stories from his books, and perhaps ill-behaved at school, for one of his few references to the delightful Fr Cassidy was to record a veiled threat of birching he received from him. As for Liverpool, Cyril never liked it, and indeed he had little opportunity to do so, since the holidays from Stonyhurst were only three weeks at Christmas and seven in the summer; at Easter the boys stayed at school until 1905. What he most looked forward to was going in the summer to Killarney, where his uncle Maurice Downey managed the vast estate of the Earl of Kenmare.

Mr D'Arcy's violent impulse towards that nobleman for ignoring a lady may be called paranoid, but it was indicative of the high standards of etiquette insisted on in the D'Arcy household. In later years Fr D'Arcy's exquisite manners were to be part of the winning impression he made on those he met. Another advantage Cyril derived from his father was in his excellent library, where, he says, 'I soaked myself in the story of the Crusades and then in the myths of the Holy Grail.' His heroes were Sir Lancelot, the thirteenth-century crusader William Longsword, and Edward the Black Prince. Cervantes added another touch to the romanticism of this boy whose own family history – though left very vague at this time by his father's reserve – stretched back to the times of those exploits. The world of ancient chivalry was a refuge from the hardships of school life, which did not abate when, after a year at Hodder, he moved up to Stonyhurst College.

The choice of Stonyhurst for the D'Arcy boys was a natural one, even apart from its proximity. Joseph Walton had been a prize pupil, and sent seven sons there, of whom the youngest, Joseph, was the same age as Conyers. The college which Cyril entered in 1899 was physically speaking almost the creation of a cousin and namesake of his uncle William Eyre, one of the most distinguished English Jesuits of the nineteenth century, who as Rector from 1879 to 1885 had not merely directed most of its rebuilding but largely financed it with a princely gift from his inheritance. The core of the building was the Elizabethan house which the Jesuits had taken over a century previously, once the home of the great Catholic Lancashire family of Shireburn, which had become extinct in the person of Mary Duchess of Norfolk in 1754.

In its academic past too, Stonyhurst epitomised the Recusant tradition of English Catholicism. The college had been founded at St Omers in the Spanish Netherlands in 1593, and for two centuries it was one of the two principal schools to which British Catholics sent their sons to evade the prohibition on Catholic education in their own country; in 1794 the advance of the French revolutionary armies provided the incentive for its move to Stonyhurst. By the time St Omers had been in existence for forty years it was a college of two hundred boys – virtually the same number that Stonyhurst had at the beginning of the twentieth century – and its organisation had reached a system of such efficiency that it served as a model to which the college could return after vicissitudes both in its Continental days and after its move to Stonyhurst. When Fr John Gerard produced the centenary history of Stonyhurst in 1894 he was able to quote descriptions of seventeenth-century St Omers and remark how Stonyhurst men could see in them 'their familiar customs thus pictured to the life, as though no centuries had rolled between.' Although Stonyhurst, from such different beginnings, had taken its place in the ranks of the public schools, it had so far resisted almost completely the pressure to conform to their model. The methods that had nurtured heroic missionaries and staunch laymen in penal days were the same which made a precious contribution to nineteenth and early twentieth-century English Catholicism.

Instead of separate houses and house-masters Stonyhurst had three groups called Playrooms (the name was used for both the division and its place of recreation) arranged on a horizontal principle. Third Playroom was for the youngest boys (and Cyril D'Arcy, entering the college at just eleven years old, was not untypically young); one was promoted to Second Playroom more or less on attaining puberty; First Playroom, or Higher Line as it was more usually called, contained the three highest classes, generally boys of fifteen and upwards, though Conyers D'Arcy was academically precocious enough to reach it when only twelve. Communication between boys of different Playrooms was forbidden, especially between Higher and Lower Lines. The system was designed to prevent sexual corruption or bullying of younger boys by older ones, though as Cyril D'Arcy's experience showed it was useless against bullying within one age-group.

Each Playroom had assigned to it a Prefect, not a senior boy but a member of the Jesuit staff, who had no teaching duties and whose sole charge was to supervise the boys outside class hours. The bounds of the building itself and the playground were rigorously enforced, and there was therefore much closer control than at public schools where boys were allowed to wander about the streets of some neighbouring town. Any Stonyhurst boy would have declared, and the authorities would have encouraged the notion, that discipline was strict and all-seeing (even the myth that a Prefect patrolled the dormitories at night was left conveniently flourishing). Outsiders had an idea of the Jesuit schools as operating a fanatical and foreign system, but their practice had been formed by generations of wholly English figures who from their own schooldays knew both the dodges and when not to notice them. As the Prefects did not teach they were chosen from among the less intellectual Jesuits; the two First Prefects who formed the character of their office, Fr Thomas Kay (1869–88) and Fr James Robinson (1888–1906) were both plain blunt Lancashiremen renowned for their indisposition to stand anything resembling nonsense. The product of this system was a simplicity of moral outlook and an acceptance of common duty which led men of high intellectual gifts to devote themselves in complete humility to the service of God.

Two types of transgression were mercilessly punished: insubordination and sexual immorality, however slight. In the latter respect Stonyhurst was the prime example of the code that made the Catholic schools, in the words of a contemporary, 'hotbeds of purity'. Fr D'Arcy wrote, 'The whole life of the school in my day was so permeated by religion and moral direction that many who might have succumbed in a more permissive society lived chastely owing to a salutary fear of sin's punishments.'

The Jesuits had the capacity to dedicate themselves entirely to their work in the school, without family or worldly distractions, and all the more single-mindedly since their duties were either wholly academic or wholly extra-curricular. The characteristic feature was the concentration on a particular group of boys. Just as the Prefect had his Playroom, the master had his own class, which he taught for every subject except Mathematics. A master took his class up through the school for several years, and his influence was regarded as decisive in the fostering of vocations. People spoke of such famous figures as Fr Alexander Charnley, who had been Joseph Walton's master, and sixteen of whose pupils from the same class had entered the Jesuit novitiate. Cyril D'Arcy spent four years with Mr Thomas Eastham, a conscientious teacher, 'to whom,' he wrote, 'I owe much for his kindness.'[14] In 1911 Stonyhurst adopted the system of classes general in contemporary public schools and the special personal relation between the master and his class came entirely to an end.

The master was expected to take an interest in his own boys outside the class-room, and among his few non-teaching duties was to take them for class walks in the countryside from time to time. He called boys by their Christian names 'if they deserved it.'[15] A private but famous manual of advice to Jesuit masters circulated in 1900 says, 'A master beginning to teach a class will always do best to use the surname.' (It is notable that in the public schools of the time that would be taken for granted, and not just at the beginning). It continues, 'When you meet one of your boys outside the school-room, do not, if practicable, pass him by unnoticed. A smile, a kind question, an encouraging word – anything to show the boy that you take a personal interest in him, convinces him that you wish not only to be his master but his friend.'[16] We may see these precepts reflected in Vyvyan Holland's words on the Stonyhurst Jesuits: 'They tried to understand the boys and to help them: they had no axes to grind; and they were all our friends, even if at times they were rather severe ones.'[17] Fr Martindale, who came to teach at Stonyhurst in 1905, gave an Old Harrovian's view when he wrote of it as 'a school where the free friendliness between staff and boys seems always the first point on which unaccustomed visitors make their comment'[18]

It was a friendliness which on the master's part must be without self-indulgence. The manual of advice cited above prescribes, 'Do not let the boys know anything of your past history. Be among them as though you had dropped from the clouds.' The reserve as well as the disinterest of the magisterial face presented to the boys contributed to a mystique which led so many of them to see in the life of their masters an ideal to be embraced. Hardly a year passed at this period in which at least one Stonyhurst boy did not enter the Society of Jesus, and often there were four or five. We may see the flowering of the Stonyhurst training in the mature Fr Martin D'Arcy, not only in his keen interest in individuals and concern to get the best out of them but in an essential reserve which went with his genius for friendship – what an American friend spoke of as a *noli me tangere* atmosphere.

It was not only the vocation of its teaching staff that brought the atmosphere of the college closer to that of a religious house than of the ordinary public school. Religious observance permeated its life; the day began with Mass; in every classroom there was a statue of Our Lady, and each lesson began with the Hail Mary; at mid-day the Angelus bell was rung and even cricket matches would come to a halt while the prayer was said. From night prayers to morning prayers complete silence was observed. Saturday nights had almost the character of a small retreat while confessions were heard and the spiritual library was opened, though the custom of silent supper on that evening while the lives of the saints were read had been discontinued in 1880. The feasts of the Church punctuated the school's calendar with a solemnity that has since been lost; Holy Week was celebrated with special devotion, many old pupils returning to make the annual retreat, and the characteristic Stonyhurst singing of Tenebrae was an experience which remained in the mind of every boy. At Corpus Christi the Blessed Sacrament was honoured with all the pomp the college could offer, its rich collection of vestments being brought out for the procession which culminated in Benediction in the garden.

These influences were buttressed by the school's own history and its witness to three centuries of Catholic fidelity. The old house had two priest's holes in which the Shireburns had hidden their Jesuit chaplains. Of the many mission priests that St Omers had produced in the days of persecution, fifteen were numbered among the English martyrs. The families who, like the Shireburns, had sheltered those priests in their country houses were still represented in the school and kept their devotion to the Faith more than an honourable memory; among the contemporaries of the D'Arcy brothers who embraced the Jesuit vocation were Cyril's class-fellow Robert de Trafford, a member of an ancient Lancashire Catholic family, and two companions of Conyers, George and

Walter Weld, descendants of that Thomas Weld, heir of the Shireburns, who had given Stonyhurst to the Jesuits in 1794.

For some forty years past Stonyhurst had enjoyed an acknowledged academic lead among the Catholic schools. The background to it was the Catholic exclusion from Oxford and Cambridge, first because of Anglican statutes and later by the ban of the Catholic hierarchy. Stonyhurst had therefore affiliated itself to London University in 1840, and had been tied to the London curriculum, with its very low classical standards. When Cardinal Vaughan finally lifted the ban in 1895, the Catholic schools faced the task of raising themselves to a much more demanding level. It was a challenge which Stonyhurst showed every sign of meeting, and by 1899 it was sending enough old boys to Oxford to qualify for admission to the Headmasters' Conference, the first Catholic school by seven years to gain that distinction.

The man chiefly responsible for this adaptation was Fr Reginald Colley, Prefect of Studies from 1893 to 1900, a member of the Anglo-Irish family of which another branch produced the Duke of Wellington. Though not an outstanding scholar he was an accomplished, humorous man, who is captured for us in this anecdote of Vyvyan Holland's:

> Father Reginald Colley, the Prefect of Studies, who was always very kind to me and with whom I was on excellent terms, thought I was too conceited about my Latin prose and was always criticizing it. So one day I inserted a passage from a little-read speech of Cicero's into one of my compositions. When I showed it to Father Colley, he said it was verbose and flowery and stilted. Whereupon I triumphantly pointed to the passage I had cribbed. Without a moment's hesitation, Father Colley looked up at me blandly and said: 'Yes, my dear fellow: Cicero can get away with that kind of thing, but you can't'.[19]

Unfortunately at the end of 1900 Fr Colley was transferred to London as Provincial, and his successors proved unable to keep the momentum he had established. By virtue of their Jesuit training the Stonyhurst masters could be relied upon to be proficient Latinists, though usually ignorant of classical niceties, and Stonyhurst boys, while they were probably spared the worst incompetences of public-school and especially preparatory-school teaching, did not enjoy the high scholarship available to the sixth forms of Eton or Winchester. Despite the college's recent efforts to recover its classical tradition, Greek was not a strong subject. While Latin verse composition was thoroughly taught, Greek verse, which was an important discipline at the leading schools, was quite neglected. When D'Arcy went to Oxford he was to envy boys from such schools who could sit down and read a classical text as they might a novel.

As we have seen, Cyril D'Arcy was young for his class, and his companions were not lacking in ability. Besides Vyvyan Holland with his Ciceronian prose, they included Hubert Hull, who rounded off a distinguished legal career with a knighthood in 1959, and Francis Muir, who won a Balliol exhibition in 1905 and was one of the few non-Etonians to gain acceptance by that *jeunesse dorée* which included Ronald Knox, Julian Grenfell and Charles Lister. Moreover Cyril does not seem to have exerted himself, and only in 1901–2 do we find him at the head of his class. He did not emulate his brother by winning a college scholarship.

Conyers D'Arcy finished the school course in 1902 and remained a further two years to study philosophy. He was joined by his cousin Joseph, the youngest of the Walton brothers, whose health had hitherto been too weak to allow his being sent to Stonyhurst; he entered the Jesuit novitiate in 1905 but died while a scholastic at St Mary's Hall five years later. Two other Walton brothers were also Jesuits: Jack, who was a lay brother for a number of years but left in 1905, and Edmund, the second-youngest; he had left Stonyhurst in 1898 and gone to Oxford, where he earned the nickname of Yap through having perpetrated that pronunciation of γαρ (gar) when called upon to translate a piece of Greek. He only stayed a few terms and entered the Society of Jesus in 1900.

Cyril moved up to Higher Line in 1902 and life became less of a struggle for existence. In 1903 he passed into Poetry* and had a new master, Mr Richard Mangan, whose younger brother Francis was a little below him in the school and was to have a closely parallel Jesuit career. Mr Mangan was a good classicist with an enthusiasm for English literature which he was able to impart to his pupils. D'Arcy kept till his death the notebook in which Mr Mangan made his class copy out poems to learn. 'We for the first time began to appreciate the classics,' he wrote in 1969. 'He made us wonder at and enjoy the famous speech of Pericles and the beauty of Virgil. We sang Horace to music.' He also recalled how Mr Mangan, revelling in the beauties of language, would almost sing phrases such as Stevenson's 'phantasmagoric chamber of the brain, with its painted windows and its storied walls.' The seventeenth-century convert poet Richard Crashaw was one of the authors to whom Mr Mangan introduced his class, and it was not mere verbal effect that made his pupil remember all his life the lines:[20]

---

* The Jesuit system retained the seventeenth-century nomenclature of classes, and the two highest were called Rhetoric and Poetry.

That the great angel-blinding light should shrink
His blaze to shine in a poor shepherd's eye,
That the unmeasur'd God so low should sink
As pris'ner in a few poor rags to lie ...
That Glory's self should serve our griefs and fears,
And free Eternity submit to years.

Cyril D'Arcy's life began to blossom out at this stage, and we find him in 1904 in the Poetry Academy – some public exercises given by the class – taking part in a dialogue on the Apology of Socrates and 'maintaining, with much spirit and a fine sense of humour, some paradoxical views on the subject.'[21] He also joined the debating club, where he figured as Member for Killarney.

In other ways life at the top of the school meant a widening of cultural horizons. Boys were taken on visits to the fine library bequeathed by the 10th Lord Arundell of Wardour, a sanctum too precious for their ordinary use. They had tours of the house, which was perhaps, until the opening of Stowe after the first world war, architecturally the most magnificent school in England; and they were instructed in the numerous Italian and other paintings which filled it, the fruit of centuries of collection.

At home Cyril also expanded his aesthetic sense, finding in his father's library an edition of Dante with Doré's engravings. Here he learnt to revere Ruskin as an aesthetic bible, until his more sophisticated contemporaries sneered him out of such Victorian standards.[22] His delight at a Madonna by Fra Angelico in the first volume of Ruskin's *Modern Painters* came back to him thirty years later when the memory enabled him to identify a painting offered him by a dealer.[23]

While in Philosophy Conyers surprised his friends by deciding to become a Jesuit, and this set Cyril's mind in the same direction. Stonyhurst itself was a powerful influence. 'There was such a beauty there,' he recalled in 1971, 'it gave me more and more a sense of vocation. I loved the liturgy, and I loved the music, the Mass.... I was being driven to it by my own sense of perfection.'[24] His first notions, attracted by Giotto as an example, made him think of the Franciscan life. In Poetry he began a friendship with Basil Gurrin, who was moved into the class at this time and who was also destined for the priesthood; it seems that they formed a common devotion to Christ the King to which his mind returned on his deathbed. The D'Arcy motto, *Un Dieu, Un Roi,* made that characteristic devotion of the Society of Jesus all the more congenial to his chivalric ideals, and he preserved a special loyalty to it all his life.

The voicing of his intentions was a cue for various members of the Community to try out some of their religious hobby-horses on him. Mr Mangan confided in him his theory that Our Lord was aware of His divine nature not through omniscience but by revelation – a view that authority would have frowned upon at that time. It was not until 1969 that Fr Martin D'Arcy ventured to publish an article putting forward a similar view. When Pope Pius X's decree on frequent communion came out, Fr Lucas, the eccentrically over-zealous Spiritual Father, almost forced D'Arcy, then in Philosophy, to form a group to petition the Rector for its immediate implementation at Stonyhurst.

An important feature of the school was the Sodality of Our Lady, to which the top three classes were eligible.[25] The Sodalists met every Saturday and Sunday in their own fine chapel to recite the Office of Our Lady; only boys of good character and devoutness were elected, and they were expected to set a good example; they were encouraged to receive Communion not only on High Mass days, as was the general practice, but on the first Sunday of each month. The Sodalist consecrated himself as *Servus Perpetuus* of the Blessed Virgin, and when he left the school received a diploma reproducing a Spanish work of art that depicted Our Lady throned and crowned. Cyril D'Arcy entered the Sodality at the earliest date possible for him, the feast of the Immaculate Conception, 1902, after a short retreat given by the Rector.

No institution was more representative than the Sodality of Stonyhurst's history as a refuge of Recusant piety. The brief of its foundation at St Omers in 1609 hung at the door of the Sodality Chapel. When James Wadsworth published a description of St Omers in 1630 he spoke of the Sodalists' duty of singing 'Vespers and Litanies to our Lady for England's conversion, having written on their church and college doors in great golden letters, "*Jesu, Jesu, converte Angliam, fiat, fiat*".'[26] In 1905 Fr Lucas brought to light the 1629 book of rules of the St Omers Sodality, and no doubt it influenced his direction of the Sodalists of his time. The position of the Sodality was a mark of the high honour that Stonyhurst sought to pay to the Blessed Virgin. The Chapel Landing, where the Lady Altar stood, was the heart of the school, and many boys knelt to pray here on coming out of the chapel or refectory; none passed by without a genuflexion. The opening and closing of May were celebrated here, and here also were hung during that month the May verses written by the boys in honour of Our Lady. When in 1945 Fr Martin D'Arcy published *The Mind and Heart of Love*, the book that enshrined his most deeply-felt reflexions on divine love, he was to dedicate it as *Servus Dominae et Ancillae Domini* – 'A servant to his Lady, the Handmaid of the Lord.'

In 1904 Conyers left the college, after covering himself with glory by taking five wickets against the MCC[27] and thus contributing largely to a famous Stonyhurst victory; he then entered the Jesuit novitiate at Roehampton. Cyril moved into Rhetoric, where his master was Fr

Joseph Keating, an excellent scholar who was later to be for twenty-seven years an exceptionally successful editor of the Jesuit periodical *The Month*. Fr Keating combined an ardent Irish nationalism with an exquisite English accent, and was one of a crop of remarkable Irish Jesuits who arrived at Stonyhurst at this time and with whom D'Arcy formed a life-long friendship. Another was Fr William Bodkin, soon afterwards an outstanding Rector of Stonyhurst and later Provincial. The third was Fr Frank Woodlock, who became a famous preacher at Farm Street.*

On finishing Rhetoric in 1905, Cyril wanted to follow in his brother's footsteps by going into Philosophy. This institution, which was abolished during the first world war, had originated in 1774 when lay students were allowed to stay on after the school course and study philosophy with the Jesuit seminarians.[28] It preserved the nomenclature of the Jesuit seminaries, the students being termed Philosophers and enjoying the title of Mr, a sign of the adult rank to which they had progressed. The Philosophers, who numbered some twenty-five young men in Cyril D'Arcy's year, formed a body completely distinct from the school, occupying the Elizabethan mansion of Stonyhurst, which with its quadrangle and turreted gate-house bore a similarity to an Oxford or Cambridge college. The same model, blended with the ideas of a country house and a London club, inspired the regime they lived under. They had their own private rooms, besides smoking, billiard, dining and drawing-rooms, and had the run of the college's estate, with its fishing and shooting and the opportunity of keeping horses and hunting with the local harriers. The fees, at 120 guineas, were twice those of the boys, and it was a more exclusive milieu than the school. In fact both Conyers and Cyril won the Arundell Philosophy scholarship of £60, so that their father was spared an undue drain on his pocket; but the fact that they became Philosophers at all demonstrates Mr D'Arcy's determination that his sons should enjoy the gentlemanly education for which he had had to struggle. Philosophy was distinguished by a sprinkling of foreign noblemen like the Vicomte Obert de Thieusies, whom D'Arcy was to come across again as Belgian Ambassador in London after the second world war. Former students included the Earl of Kenmare who failed to recognise Mrs D'Arcy; but the characteristic members of the body were scions of the old Catholic families, young men like Robert de Trafford, who exemplified what his class-fellow was to call the spirit of 'the English Catholic squires with their tenacious grasp of principle and their open-air contentment.'[29] It

* The impression might emerge, and not wholly without grounds, that it was Irishmen who largely upheld the reputation of the English Province; but a misleading idea of its character would be given if one did not add that most of them were products of the Society's English boarding schools. Their influence did not save the English Jesuits from being regarded in Ireland as beings from another world.

was a tradition for which D'Arcy never disguised his preference.

Since the middle of the nineteenth century the lay Philosophers' course had been separate from that of the Jesuit students, who now occupied their own seminary, St Mary's Hall, a few hundred yards from the college. In 1885 a new philosophy course had been introduced to implement Pope Leo XIII's call for the revival of Thomist learning. Within its limits, which were to instill the scholastic principles, the course had considerable strengths, and D'Arcy's professor, Mr V. Moncel, was an able exponent of it.[30] The matter of the first term in 1905 included Natural Theology, and Cyril D'Arcy was proficient enough in the subject by December to figure in an Academy, demonstrating a mastery of the scholastic proofs of the existence and nature of God – a line of reasoning which commanded his intellectual loyalty throughout his life.

After the higher department had been abolished at Stonyhurst, Martin D'Arcy wrote, with deliberate overstatement, 'The life of the Philosophers was the nearest approach to ideal education in England,'[31] and he presented a high intellectual scene in which, towards the end of smoking-concerts, the Philosophers would toss challenges to each other such as explaining *entia non sunt multiplicanda sine necessitate* or translating *propter quod unumquodque tale et illud magis*.[32] There were certainly a number of able students in the course, like Obert de Thieusies, who won the Philosophy Gold Medal that year, or Henry Avery, who became a distinguished Jesuit in his native America; but one suspects that the majority of the Philosophers would be more likely to have been heard comparing their golf scores. In fact, if one had to wait to one's last years to get the best out of the school, it was only in Philosophy that one experienced Stonyhurst's *douceur de vivre*. The Philosophers were young men of means, and over the years they had at their own expense laid out a golf course, stocked the ponds that lay before the college's main front, levelled tennis courts and provided other amenities which were accordingly reserved to their exclusive enjoyment. The favourite sport at this time was golf, and Cyril D'Arcy followed the fashion, often with Robert de Trafford as his companion. In the summer the Philosophers played tennis on their courts at the west front or lazed in boats on the ponds under the eagle-topped towers.

Before leaving this charmed existence for the Jesuit novitiate, Cyril wanted to stay on in Philosophy for the full two-year course, as Conyers had done and as his own companions Robert de Trafford and Henry Mather were doing; but his father found this too much of an extravagance.[33] After July 31st 1906, the feast of St Ignatius, he accordingly left Stonyhurst for a two-month holiday before making his way to Roehampton to don the Jesuit habit. His character had developed much from the puny, bookwormish, bullied little boy who had found his first years at Stonyhurst so hard; it was one which was already to make him stand out as exceptional among his fellow novices. He was still small and very slightly built, with black hair and piercing eyes which betrayed how much more he lived in the realm of the intellect than of the body. He had led a sheltered life, and looking back on it forty years on he spoke of himself as having experienced 'too happy a lot' in youth;[34] its result was a certain unworldly naivety underneath the intellectual sophistication. The eccentricities in his immediate family past were reflected in a mercurial, sometimes emotional temperament, but despite them and the hardships of his boyhood he had attained a surprising psychological balance and a great gift for personal relations. From Stonyhurst he took away a critical attitude to the strain of insensitivity which had made his early sufferings possible, as well as to the narrowness of some of the methods and religious attitudes that had been handed down. The college left him nevertheless with a deep love and loyalty, and the sense of a society which was a microcosm of the Kingdom of Christ. His historical sense was nourished on the heroic tale of English Catholicism which Stonyhurst represented, and his ideals of scholarship on its classical teaching. He had relished especially his year in Philosophy and made his own its professed ideal of high intellectual enquiry placed by Catholic gentlemen at the service of their Faith. Next to his philosophical passion was his aesthetic sensibility, bred in his father's library and expanded among the graces of Stonyhurst. For eight years Jesuit discipline and spirituality had been his everyday life; he had now to learn to perfect those lessons with an adult's understanding.

Chapter Two

Jesuit Training

The Society of Jesus which Martin Cyril D'Arcy entered in September 1906 was a body of some 15,000 men gathered in twenty-five national Provinces, themselves grouped into five Assistancies. It was just in the process of holding a General Congregation to elect its 25th General, the German Fr Wernz, who held office for life and governed from Rome. All other offices were held at the will of the General, though the five Assistants, who advised him on the affairs of their respective groupings, were also elected by the General Congregation and replaced by the General as need arose. Provinces were governed by a Provincial, who like most Rectors normally continued in office for six years.

Obedience was the Society's most renowned virtue, but it was also in an important respect a very egalitarian order. All priests, whatever their office, bore the title of Father, and unlike Benedictine monks, for example, who might become abbots for life, they returned to the ranks once their term in authority was ended. Nor were Jesuits normally supposed to accept ecclesiastical dignities, though a few rose to the cardinal's purple. A number of English Jesuits became bishops in the Province's overseas missions (and when they retired went back to the ordinary Jesuit discipline), but a Jesuit bishop in England has never been contemplated.

The strength of the Society of Jesus in England was rooted in penal times, when it had supplied fully one third of the Catholic missionaries working in the country.[1] The general suppression of 1773 had in practice been evaded in England, with the ex-Jesuits continuing to work as secular priests, but it had inevitably proved a set-back to growth; when the Province was officially restored in 1829 it numbered only 109 men. By the eighteen-forties however the Jesuits were once again unmistakably the most vigorous religious order in the country, and they received the lion's share of converts from the Oxford Movement. These in turn increased the Province's intellectual standing, and expansion had been rapid. By 1906 The English Province numbered just under 700 men, divided into 368 priests, 207 scholastics and 118 lay brothers;[2] it could lay claim to a special character, for which its continuous and native tradition was a major reason. There had never been a doctrinaire reimposition of unfamiliar rules, and the English Jesuits had followed their own insular traditions. Such foreign zeal as had irrupted among them had come from Oxford converts. Fr Edward Purbrick, who was Provincial from 1880 to 1888, had had a scheme to put all his subjects into Roman habits. When he left, the stocks of black crape he had ordered for the purpose were much valued at Stonyhurst as material for the Community's bedroom slippers.

Until the middle of the nineteenth century, the English Province revolved around Stonyhurst, its sole college and the centre of all its training, from which men were sent out to a network of mainly rural missions. The headquarters of the Province were not set up in London till 1845, the Theologate was moved to Wales three years later, and the novitiate transferred to near London in 1854. The founding of other colleges also began in those years, but Stonyhurst remained a major source of recruitment, and the Province continued to be governed by Stonyhurst men for many years. All the Provincials from 1888 to 1915 came from that college, and it was not till afterwards that the pattern began to change.

The main work of the Province, as of the whole Order, was educational; it ran three boarding schools, Stonyhurst, Beaumont and Mount St Mary's, and six urban day colleges; their standard was acknowledged as high, and Stonyhurst and Beaumont could justly claim in 1906 to be the two leading Catholic schools in the country, since they were the only ones which had so far gained admittance to the Headmasters' Conference. The Province's headquarters were at Farm Street in Mayfair, where there also worked a busy community of writers, mainly historians, who at the turn of the century produced fully half the Catholic books being published in England. They also brought out *The Month*, a journal of historical and religious scholarship. The nineteenth-century convert influx had given Farm Street a good proportion of its leading scholars, and the church had a reputation for its preaching and spiritual direction which in 1906 was being boosted by Fr Bernard Vaughan with his sermons on the Sins of Society. The second important strand of the Jesuit tradition, its missionary work, was represented by small but enterprising missions founded by the Province in southern Africa, where Fr Augustus Law had a generation ago conducted a heroic apostolate, and British Guiana, where an equally epic work was now being carried on by Fr Cuthbert Cary-Elwes.

Signs were just beginning to appear of a challenge to the Jesuit ascendancy from the Benedictines of Downside, who were not only raising their school itself to the front rank but produced in the *Downside Review* a journal on similar lines to *The Month*, and in Cardinal Gasquet one of the most distinguished Catholic scholars of the period. Nevertheless, as the Benedictines were divided into small autonomous abbeys and had no London church or house like Farm Street, they might be said to suffer a competitive disadvantage against the solid phalanx of the Jesuits. Other orders such as the Dominicans had far smaller numbers. A young man who entered the English Jesuit Province in 1906 could feel himself to be joining a crack force.

He could also look forward to a much longer training than that of any other clergy. It began with two years' novitiate at Roehampton, in south-west London, at the end of which the novice took his simple vows and became a scholastic. He then spent two years as a Junior in the same house, following general studies designed to bring him to a good university entrance standard. Next came three years' Philosophy at Stonyhurst. The scholastic then spent a period as a master or prefect in one of the colleges; this 'Regency', to use the traditional term, took him to the age of thirty, and was typically about five years. Four years' Theology followed at St Beuno's in North Wales, and only at the end of the third of these would he be ordained; that contrasted with a normal age of twenty-four for ordination to the secular priesthood, and there was a rueful joke that for a Jesuit the priesthood was a reward for a well-spent life. Finally there came a third year of novitiate, called the Tertianship, to resharpen the spiritual edge that might have been blunted through this long haul, so that the priest was not fully fledged till he reached his mid-thirties. He then waited a few months longer before repairing to Stonyhurst to take his final vows on the Feast of the Purification, the solemn profession qualifying men to hold the major superiorships. The chief variation on this programme was that between Philosophy and their teaching years the ablest men had in the past taken London external degrees at Stonyhurst, and since 1896 had been going to Campion Hall at Oxford.

Martin D'Arcy entered the novitiate on September 7th 1906. The following day, the feast of the Nativity of Our Lady, was the traditional day when the finished novices took their vows, so that the first experience of the neophytes was to witness that important event which marked the end of the step they were initiating; for Martin D'Arcy the ceremony had the special significance that his brother was among those taking their vows, having begun his novitiate two years earlier. Conyers however was considered sufficiently accomplished to be excused his Juniorate altogether, and he was immediately sent off to Stonyhurst to begin his Philosophy.

With Martin D'Arcy there entered the novitiate two other Stonyhurst boys, who came in from Rhetoric and Poetry. There were five second-year novices from Stonyhurst, including his own cousin, Joseph Walton, who had come in after three years in Philosophy, and Basil Gurrin, who entered from Rhetoric. The novitiate had twenty-six scholastic novices, destined to the priesthood, and nine lay-brother novices, who would share their training until they took their simple vows. In 1907–8 the proportion of old Stonyhurst boys among the scholastic novices rose from eight out of twenty-six to ten out of twenty-eight, a good example of the contribution that, despite the growth of the other colleges, Stonyhurst still made to the English Province.

The novices' life of these years is described to us by Denis Meadows, who came to Roehampton in November 1907, and became a good friend of Martin D'Arcy; after leaving the Society he wrote an account of his Jesuit years. The novitiate was housed in a beautiful Palladian house built by the Earl of Bessborough in the 1760s and renamed Manresa House since its purchase by the Society in 1861. It stood in ample grounds which almost merged into Richmond Park, and enjoyed a pastoral seclusion of which its built-over state of today gives little hint. The Rector and Master of Novices since 1894 was Fr Daniel Considine, who is remembered as one of the greatest novice-masters the English Province ever produced. He was a saintly but austere figure, celebrated for his penances, his abstemiousness and his superiority to common human weakness. Both Denis Meadows and Fr D'Arcy tell the story of a summer day in the Refectory when a wasp settled on Fr Considine's face and he remained apparently unconscious of it as it crawled about for several minutes before the fascinated eyes of the novices; Meadows suggested that it was meant as a deliberate lesson to the novices in the self-control in which they were being trained.

The novices wore an old Jesuit gown (only when they took their vows would they receive a new one of their own), a confection peculiar to the English Province and apparently modelled on a Monsignor's mantellone. It was a loose black garment fastened with three buttons down the front, and without sleeves; or more precisely the sleeves were stylised into two broad strips hanging from the back of the shoulders. Under the gown, lay dress was worn, with the collar and tie and the sleeves of the jacket showing, as if symbolising the intermediate state of the wearer. The novices slept in cubicles like those they had known if they were old boys of the Jesuit boarding-schools. They rose early and spent an hour in meditation before Mass, a practice they would follow throughout their Jesuit career. Breakfast and other meals were eaten in silence, but the food was good and plentiful; undernourishment was not a proper grounding for the life of laborious household chores which the novitiate training entailed. The young men laid the tables, washed up the dishes, kept the house clean, worked in the wood-yard and generally did work which at that time would have been considered the sphere of servants. There was a 'brothers' experiment', when for a week the novice would work in the kitchen, have his recreation with the lay brothers, and answer to the cook as his religious superior. At all times Latin was spoken except in recreation.

Martin D'Arcy found this life of humble usefulness no burden, less so perhaps than the rudimentary Latin that was all the majority of his fellow novices could manage, and decidedly less so (he confessed in later life) than the table manners of some of his companions. With two or three exceptions like Joseph Walton, most of the novices came from middle-class or humbler families, but the Jesuits undertook to burnish their savoir faire a little as well as their haloes. In fact the direction of the noviti-tiate at this time had fortuitously a rather aristocratic character. Fr Considine himself came from the Irish gentry; his Socius for a few months was Fr Herman Walmesley, who was of an old Lancashire Catholic family. In the summer of 1907 he was raised to the post of English Assistant in Rome and was succeeded as Socius by Fr Wilmot, the son of a Papal Count, of whom his obituarist wrote that the example of his polished manners was one of the advantages that novices enjoyed in his time at Manresa. Denis Meadows however described him as 'impressed by old Catholic families and members of the nobility. There were subtle differences in his attitude toward novices from Stonyhurst and Beaumont, and those from less patrician schools.'[3]

In some ways the vocation of poverty, chastity and obedience into which the young novices were being inducted was not very different from the conventions of plain living, decency and service instilled by the public-school ethos; but the temptation to assimilate the Jesuit training to that of contemporary English gentlemen was sternly resisted. Our own age claims to be less overawed by social pressures, but concessions to the spirit of the time have proved more tempting than they were in the age of the Forsytes. There were regular penances like the studded thong which the novices had to strap round a leg, with the metal next the flesh, and which made it impossible for the wearer to walk without limping; another was the whip of several cords which novices had to apply to their bare backs in the seclusion of their cubicles. Martin D'Arcy hated these as much as, one imagines, the rest of his companions did. It would have been easy to do away with such things as relics of a benighted age, or to treat them as purely symbolic gestures to asceticism; but, alongside the modest comfort of diet, dress and lodging, they were retained as signs that the vocation that was being followed was one of real sacrifice, not just a cultured imitation of it.

The essence of the novitiate regime, however, was in the spiritual training; at the heart of this were the Spiritual Exercises of St Ignatius, the origin from which the Society of Jesus itself took its being. In their full form these constituted the thirty-day Long Retreat, which a Jesuit normally underwent only twice in his life. As the foundation of the

Order's spirituality, the Long Retreat was placed as early as possible in the novice's career, and was given in October and November. It consisted in four weeks of silence and daily instructions by the Novice Master, in which he guided the novices in a series of specific meditations; Sundays served as much-needed rest-days from the intensive soul-searching involved.

A pupil of Martin D'Arcy's, Fr Christopher Devlin was later to write of the Spiritual Exercises as intended 'to soak the memory and the senses of the soul in the physical reality of Christ's words and actions, and then to let there be distilled, as it were, in the intellect a word of God, a confused apprehension of His divinity, to which the will 'with a blind and naked stirring' can adhere.'4 The vividness and immediacy of the meditations is a key to their impact and the reason for their demanding nature. The first of the four weeks, whose theme is sin and punishment, is particularly harrowing and forms a low point from which the soul climbs towards its goal, which is the love of God.

At the beginning of the Exercises, the retreatant is taught to reflect on the relation between the infinite Creator and his creature, and then to meditate on sin and the judgment and penalties due to it. In this judgment, the only intercession that will avail is that of Christ. The retreatant makes an examination of his conscience and a general confession to the retreat-giver of the sins of his whole life. He then involves his five senses in an imaginative contemplation of the fires of hell.

The second week begins on a very different note with the meditation on the Kingship of Christ, and with St Ignatius's famous image of the Two Standards – those of Christ and Lucifer, of the Heavenly City and the world. Every soul must make an ineluctable choice between these two, to serve one or the other, and the choice is one which informs every action of his life. To some the image of Christ as King seems a distant, perhaps even an alien one, but to St Ignatius as a nobleman and soldier who had been wounded in the service of Charles V it was one which spoke of the dearest sentiments of loyalty and honour; so it was too to Martin D'Arcy, who had made the devotion to Christ the King part of the chivalric enthusiasm of his boyhood. This noble element in the spirituality of his Order was one which he always felt as intimately his own.

The third week of the Spiritual Exercises has as its theme the Passion of Christ, and leads on to the consideration of the divine love which that sacrifice supremely exemplifies. The fourth passes to the Resurrection, and ends with the 'Contemplation for obtaining Divine Love', pointing to the ultimate attainment of the soul, the reaching of the intuitive knowledge of God.

The Long Retreat, in the words of one of the great Farm Street priests of this time, Fr John Hungerford Pollen, 'is really the chief test of a vocation and for that matter of the entire life of a Jesuit. On these exercises the Constitutions, the life, and activity of the Society are based, so that they are really the chief factor in forming the character of a Jesuit. In accordance with the ideals set forth in these exercises, of disinterested conformity with God's will, and of personal love of Jesus Christ, the novice is trained diligently in a meditative study of the truths of religion, in the habit of self-knowledge, in a constant scrutiny of his motives and of the acts inspired by them, in the correction of every form of self-deceit, illusion, plausible pretext, and in the education of his will, particularly in making choice of what seems best after careful deliberation and without self-seeking. Deeds, not words, are insisted upon as proof of genuine service, and a mechanical, emotional, or fanciful piety is not tolerated.'[5]

If the aim of the Spiritual Exercises was the attainment of the love of God, it was one which could not be allowed to remain on the plane of sentiment or aspiration, but must channel its energy into the work of a day and of a lifetime. It was this practical sense, powered by so intense a spiritual drive, that generated the vast historic achievement of the Society. The task of the novitiate was to build up the habits that would make the work of the future Jesuits effective. Every evening the Master gave the novices 'points' on methods of prayer, which served as the basis for their meditation the following morning. Regular 'Examens' throughout the day served for an examination of conscience, when they judged how well or ill the struggle had gone to win the soul back from Lucifer. Every Saturday night the novices made their confession to the Master, and to each one was assigned an admonitor among his companions to warn him of faults of character; this was an institution which went all the way up the Society of Jesus, the General and Provincials having their admonitors to keep their spiritual eyes open amid the snares of authority. Once a week too the novices were assembled for 'rings', when each one in turn knelt before the Master, and their companions pointed out faults they had observed; on such occasions Fr Considine could rebuke the novice so mercilessly as to reduce him to tears.[6]

It may be thought that this sort of pressure made the novitiate very much a forcing-house of sanctity, and certainly it was a much more intense regime than any the Jesuits were to be submitted to later in their training. In the novitiate the young men were still painfully learning the lessons of self-knowledge and self-discipline that would form the finished Jesuit character. Denis Meadows wrote: 'Most of us were a bit stuffy at that point. I can recall only one of my fellow novices who was not – but then he was an exceptional young man, who has since' (Meadows was writing in 1954) 'become a great English Jesuit.'[7]

This grounding was what in the end made the Jesuits specialists in the spiritual life, in the knowledge of the self and of the labyrinth of conscience. An experience that made men probe so deep into themselves was not calculated to efface personal individuality or the respect for it. The Jesuit training could not, any more than others, guarantee against mediocrity, but its best products were described by John Rothenstein when, from a quite different background, he came upon the Jesuit Community in Oxford: 'They conformed to no stereotype, and I have in fact never encountered any other body of such robust individualists; on any occasion at Campion Hall I would hear expressed the widest diversity of view and I could look forward to some of the opinions being extremely original and entirely unexpected. About one thing they were in agreement: they shared a deep and sensitive concern for individual liberty that is not often encountered, in quite so genuine a form, in other walks of life.'[8]

The austere spiritual genius of Fr Daniel Considine made this training one of special impact. One of his novices wrote: 'What did we learn from him in the Noviceship? It seems to me the most precious thing we could learn – the way to develop a very real, strong and simple attachment to our Blessed Lord and to base all our spiritual life upon that personal union ... Every word he uttered, and sometimes his emotion, betrayed the deep personal love in his own heart.'[9]

In September 1907 the novices began a new year, and Brother D'Arcy welcomed from Stonyhurst Robert de Trafford and the charming Henry Mather, both of whom had been with him all the way up the school and had just enjoyed their second year in Philosophy. Directly from the school came Francis Mangan, the younger brother of D'Arcy's old Poetry master, and Richard Worsley; they were both to go to Campion Hall with Martin D'Arcy and became respectively Provincial and Rector of Stonyhurst.

During that second year Martin D'Arcy came close to death when he contracted blood poisoning from a scratch on his thumb while working in the garden. He developed a high fever of which the doctors could not make out the cause, and after a few days he was told he was going to die that night. He was saved by an old country doctor who came in and immediately diagnosed the trouble; a specialist was called and performed the necessary operation. It was an early visitation of the ill health which shadowed Martin D'Arcy through his extraordinarily active life; but he also remembered it for an experience which influenced his psychological thinking. When the doctors told him that his case was hopeless he felt his nature saying, 'No, I'm not going to die.' The novitiate training had been directed towards mortifying and denying the self, and in such a situation the text-book Christian response might have been a submission to the will of God; yet in this extremity, he recalled, 'I had this extraordinary feeling of self coming on' and his nature refused to give up the struggle.[10]

By chance Martin D'Arcy kept some letters which his brother wrote to him from Stonyhurst in the summer of 1908. Interspersed with news of Yap Walton, who was then at the college as a Prefect, and of the lay Philosophers (which he was bidden to pass on to Robert de Trafford and Henry Mather) there were answers to questions he had received on the subject of beauty, which was then occupying Martin's mind, and to which he evidently expected Conyers to bring from his current studies a mature philosophical view.[11] Another element in that interest came from some writings which had been intriguing him for two years. The private Jesuit magazine *Letters and Notices* had begun in 1906 publishing extracts from the Journals of Gerard Manley Hopkins. A volume of these was in the possession of one of the priests at Manresa and another had been sent from Ireland. The extracts printed were merely Hopkins's observations of nature, but Martin D'Arcy was fascinated by the genius shown in the descriptions. He began enquiring about this unknown figure; Hopkins's poems themselves were not to be published for another dozen years, but D'Arcy formed an interest in his personality which was shared by his fellow novice Denis Meadows.

The culmination of two years of spiritual training came on the morning of September 8th 1908, when in the middle of the Mass the novices made their simple vows to Fr Considine and received Communion from his hands. The brothers were now transformed into Jesuit scholastics; they received their new gown and put on clerical dress, a black frock coat buttoned to the throat, with the Roman collar above. Martin D'Arcy was destined for Campion Hall, but it was decided that, unlike Conyers, he required a further year's study to reach the proper standard.* He moved into the Juniorate, which was then under the Prefectship of the saintly Fr Alban Goodier, later Archbishop of Bombay, a man of great sensitivity and nobility of character, with whom Martin D'Arcy formed a life-long friendship. As far as his studies were concerned, he was not thought in need of the ordinary Juniorate course; he was told to read privately and to put himself under the tuition of Mr Cyril Martindale, with whom he now made his first direct contact.

Cyril Martindale had come to D'Arcy's notice in 1905–6, when he came to Stonyhurst as Master of Poetry. He had become a Catholic at the age of eighteen, at the end of his career at Harrow, and immediately entered the Society of Jesus.[12] In 1905 he had just finished four years at Campion Hall, where he had not only taken a Double First in Classics

---

* There seems also to have been a deliberate policy of keeping the two brothers apart. The only year in their whole life in the Society when they were together in the same house was 1912–13 at Campion Hall.

but won eight university prizes – an Oxford record said to have been beaten only by Gilbert Murray. One might say that he had established the reputation of the fledgling Jesuit house of studies at a stroke, and he was pointed out at Stonyhurst with understandable awe; as a lay Philosopher D'Arcy had admired him from afar. From Stonyhurst Martindale was sent to teach in the Juniorate, and when D'Arcy came to him as his pupil it was one of the formative experiences of his life. 'My commonplace standards in scholarship and criticism were shown up,' he wrote, 'and I was drawn by him to delight in beautiful things and to seek the almost unattainably high.'[13]

He told elsewhere how he began practising his Latin verse for Mr Martindale: 'I'd take a piece of Tennyson or Wordsworth, put him into Latin verse and send it off; then I'd discover from the verses Martindale would send back just what Wordsworth or Tennyson was talking about.' These versions would have been scribbled in the Refectory and would come with a note: 'I can't stand the food we're having at dinner today, so I'm writing this during the meal. I'm sorry, because the cabbage will spoil some of the effects.'[14]

After a year of these stimulating diversions, D'Arcy was sent in 1909 to St Mary's Hall to do his Philosophy. Conyers had just finished that course, which was considered a prerequisite before entering the free-thinking world of Oxford, and moved on to Campion Hall. The Seminary, as St Mary's Hall was usually called, was a barrack-like building of some eighty uniform rooms in rather drab contrast to its neighbour, Stonyhurst College. The regime was austere and enclosed, and provided for a long round of lectures given in Latin. The first year, characterised by Denis Meadows as rather desultory, gave an introduction to logic; the second year included psychology and the third cosmology and natural theology.

The Superior of the house was the outstanding psychologist Fr Michael Maher, and its other luminary was Fr John Rickaby, who had written an excellent volume on *First Principles of Knowledge* for the Stonyhurst Philosophical Series. He was one of two sons of a former butler of the 10th Lord Herries, who had sent the boys to Stonyhurst alongside his own sons; they had repaid his bountiful gesture by becoming Jesuits and ornaments of the English Province. Fr Rickaby had the task of delivering the introductory speech when the scholastics arrived on October 1st, an event known as the *Quamquam* because tradition prescribed that as the opening word. Denis Meadows gives this impression of Fr Rickaby when he came in before the assembled students:

He gave us a quick, surprised glance as though he had not expected so much deference when we stood up for his entrance. He was rather short, had untidy grey hair, steel-rimmed spectacles, and a half-smile playing about his lips as though he was enjoying a little private joke of his own. Perhaps he was, for he was a man with an abiding sense of fun ... He sat down at the table, put on his biretta, changed his mind and took it off again, and then took a quick, quizzical look at us as we sat in a respectful silence.'

Beginning with the obligatory quamquam, he then launched into a dazzling extempore Latin speech 'enriched with the most amazing vocabulary. He slipped in a few topical allusions, made jokes, and even perpetrated a couple of puns.' This performance was greeted with loud applause and the year's course was under way.[15]

The philosophy taught at St Mary's Hall had been officially Thomist since the 1880s, when the seminary had been ordered to adapt its essentially Suarezian and in practice rather hand-to-mouth tradition in response to Leo XIII's initiative urging the study of St Thomas. Fr Rickaby belonged to an older generation and his commitment to the new system was qualified. That was apparently not the case with another of the professors, Fr Stewart; Meadows tells a story of when he was reading St Thomas with his class and an Australian scholastic, whose Latin was too sketchy for the task, thinking he discerned a joke in the text, made his appreciation audible. There was a shocked pause, and Fr Stewart read on; within a few lines the Australian thought he saw the joke followed up, and laughed again. Fr Stewart fixed him with a murderous glare and, without thinking of lapsing into the vernacular, pronounced, *Qui riderent has res, quae sunt e profundissimis in Divo Thoma, haberent animas porcorum.** So saying, he stalked out of the room, his biretta quivering with indignation.[16]

The method of teaching was the one Martin D'Arcy was already familiar with from his days as a lay Philosopher at the college. It consisted purely of lectures, though practice was given in the management of the scholastic technique by the custom of 'circles', in which one student had to explain and defend various theses while a group was commissioned to ply him with objections, the whole argument being conducted in strict syllogistic form.

In a house which (with the brief and ill-starred exception of George Tyrrell) had never had a real Thomist scholar on its staff, the penetration of that system was limited. The innovative work of contemporary French Thomists like Pierre Rousselot had not received much attention, although the library contained what Denis Meadows called 'a fascinating book', Rousselot's *L'Intellectualisme de Saint-Thomas*. Martin D'Arcy said that the book 'inspired many of us',[17] but by itself it was perhaps not for

---

*Those who would laugh at these things, which are among the most profound in St Thomas, must have the souls of pigs.

the moment sufficient foundation for the unreserved enthusiasm he later developed for Rousselot and his neo-Thomist school. He found the scholasticism of the St Mary's Hall lectures so unexciting and so scrappy 'that for a short while I played with the idea of working on a Christian form of Hegelianism.... My holiday with Hegel, however, came to an end when an admired scientific friend of mine said to me with some scorn that a philosophy should not be a toy to play with or tickle the mind but a system to be lived.'*[18] The choice of Hegel in the face of the strict Realism of the scholastic tradition indeed shows how signally he failed to be impressed by the teaching around him.

Among the mentors of his youth whom he recalled with praise, neither Fr Maher nor Fr Rickaby was ever included; he had reached the stage where only really outstanding minds like Martindale's had a penetrating influence on him. His return to Stonyhurst brought him, though, to the world of Hopkins, who had thrilled to the beauty of its countryside. He discovered in the Arundell library the scanty collection of Hopkins's poems that had been published in 1893, with a biographical introduction by Robert Bridges;[20] he began to question people who had known Hopkins, but found that he was remembered only as an eccentric. Fr Maher recalled going to his room and finding him lying on the floor writing poetry in the dark. But Martin D'Arcy was well acquainted from his boyhood with the countryside which Hopkins had described – 'Earth, sweet Earth, sweet landscape,' where 'thy lovely dale down thus and thus bids reel thy river'[21] – and when Denis Meadows arrived in 1911, with the same keen admiration, D'Arcy took him on his first day on a walk by the Hodder, to visit those beloved scenes.

The Catholic intellectual landscape at this time was overshadowed by Pope Pius X's drive against Modernism, a storm at whose centre the English Jesuits had been placed through the writings of Fr George Tyrrell. Tyrrell had been among the most brilliant of the many able converts who joined the Jesuits during the Victorian period, and in the late eighteen-nineties his writings were earning him the admiration of some of the ablest members of the Province, from older men like Fr Herbert Thurston to young recruits such as Martindale. His veering to Modernism began under the influence of Baron von Hügel, and after 1900 he came under suspicion for his attack on the doctrine of eternal punishment. In 1906 he was dismissed from the Society and he was

---

* This is presumably the man who told Fr D'Arcy that he had once been so lonely that he contemplated suicide, until, on reading in the Bible of the God 'who seeth in secret', he realised he was not alone and thenceforth lived his life trembling with an overpowering sense of duty.[19] Fr D'Arcy never disclosed his name, but he was evidently an Oxford friend, and the rebuke described is presumably to be placed during D'Arcy's first or second year there.

excommunicated the following year after protesting against the Encyclical *Pascendi*, by which Pius X condemned the Modernist system.

The regard that Tyrrell had earned among his brethren did not entail any inclination to his philosophical vagaries, or sympathy with his diatribes against such an exemplary Provincial as Fr Reginald Colley. But the Church was falling into an increasingly extreme reaction which was only brought to an end by the death of Pius X. Within the Society there was a ferocious party which was accusing the General himself and his chief advisers of semi-Modernism. The English Province however was not a place for fanatics, its only specimen of that class being Tyrrell himself, as much in his Thomist as in his Modernist phase. Poor Fr Joseph Browne, who was Provincial from 1910 to 1915, was completely out of his depth and tried to play safe by postponing the ordination of men who showed undue signs of original thought. He attempted to do this with Cyril Martindale in 1912, appealing to a legal triviality; but that was foiled by the French Jesuits with whom Martindale was studying. Fr Francis Devas, who was to become one of the most famous of Farm Street priests, had earlier had his ordination postponed by several years, admittedly in exceptional circumstances.★

It was characteristic of Martin D'Arcy's penchant to fix on the philo-sophical aspect of Modernism; the person and writings of George Tyrrell interested him keenly. Modernism was the most purely intellectual movement evident in the Catholic Church at this time (that may largely account for its lack of impact in the English Catholic world), and D'Arcy found it absorbing, even if only as an example of 'wonderful talents squandered'[22] on a completely misconceived objective. His attitude showed his life-long ability to take a dispassionate view of an individual and a philosophy even while they were being subjected to violent oppro-brium. In writings from the twenties to the fifties, long after the Modernist controversy had been buried, Martin D'Arcy was to produce considered criticisms of that system, whose root he traced to the contem-porary fashion for Pragmatism in philosophy. We may assume that in the years before 1914, with Thomism and Hegelianism competing for his sympathies, Pragmatism was a trend for which he had little time. As to his view on the Church's handling of the problem, he held that Tyrrell had been treated by his superiors with extraordinary kindness, though other

★ Fr D'Arcy's attribution of that misfortune to Fr Francis Woodlock in *Laughter and the Love of Friends* (p.62) is evidently a confusion between those two friends of his. He is also wrong in saying (ib., p.93) that Fr Martindale was sent to Stonyhurst in 1913 under suspicion of Modernism, having been denounced by an American priest. This is a confu-sion with what happened, a little understandably, half a dozen years later, after a printer accidentally omitted the word 'not' in a statement of his, 'There is no reason to believe that St John was not the author of the Fourth Gospel.'

agents of the Church's policy might be less to be admired. Nevertheless he repudiated the demonisation of Cardinal Merry del Val, whom he knew personally in Rome in the twenties after making friends with two nephews of his at Stonyhurst.

In 1912 Martin D'Arcy was sent to Oxford, where Conyers was in his fourth year. Like his brother and like the majority of the Campion Hall scholastics, he was sent to read Classics. This course begins with five terms of mainly linguistic study known as Honour Moderations, followed by a further seven terms of Literae Humaniores (colloquially Greats), which contain an important element of ancient and modern philosophy. To read Greats at Oxford was widely considered – in those less utilitarian days – the finest mental training available anywhere in the world, and to Martin D'Arcy, who spoke of this as a time when 'I discovered my life in terms of thought',[23] it was the greatest challenge his career had offered.

Campion Hall was named in honour of the Society's most famous Oxford man, the Blessed Edmund Campion (canonised in 1970). As a fellow of St John's College, Campion had been one of the university's most admired scholars and had presented its welcome to Queen Elizabeth on her visit to Oxford in 1566; but he was intellectually unable to accept the Anglican settlement and, leaving England, he entered the Society of Jesus. He returned with Robert Persons in 1580, marking the beginning of the Jesuit mission to England, but for him it ended within two years in martyrdom. His challenge to the Anglican divines to meet him in disputation symbolised the Society's confidence in the power of intellect to convert men to Catholic truth; the return of his name to Oxford after three centuries was the token of a hope that his vision could at last be accomplished.

The Hall had been founded in 1896, as soon as the English bishops gave permission for Catholics to go to Oxford and Cambridge. Its first Master was Fr R.F. Clarke, a former Fellow of St John's College and the last member of the university to have been obliged to resign his fellowship on becoming a Catholic. It was conceived as a house which would not only give young Jesuits the benefit of an Oxford training but establish the Society's prestige in the university; one of the first two scholastics to be admitted justified his superiors' hopes by winning a Double First in Classics. At that point however Fr Clarke suddenly died. The status of the house was that of a Private Hall, owing its recognition merely to its Master, whose name it officially bore, and on whose death it ceased to exist. Moreover the Master had to be an Oxford M.A., and the English Jesuits only had three other holders of that qualification, all of them converts, as possible replacements. Through the willingness of the Vice-Chancellor to bend the rules – he did not want to lose a house which had already shown such promise – they were allowed to appoint Fr John O'Fallon Pope as Master, and the Hall continued. It was known officially as Pope's Hall; not until 1918 was the house given the new status of a Permanent Private Hall independent of its Masters, and the name Campion Hall recognised by the university.

Fr O'Fallon Pope, selected from such a small field, was not ideally the man the Jesuits would have chosen to uphold their fame. Born of a prominent St Louis family, he was an American gentleman of Jamesian correctness, and had been sent as a young man to Christ Church, where he lived splendidly, giving champagne breakfasts and including a grand tour of Europe in his educational programme. He then became successively a Catholic, a priest and a Jesuit. Martin D'Arcy was taken by his perfect manners and considerateness towards his subordinates. He would never allow people to do anything cheaply but would insist on its being done in the best style. Propriety and punctuality were sacrosanct for him; it was said that he would exclude a scholastic who arrived one minute late for dinner but would give him ten shillings to go and dine at the Randolph, the best hotel in Oxford, so that he should not disgrace the Society by being seen in an inferior establishment. He once took the unpolished Cyril Martindale to the bathroom to give him a personal demonstration of how a gentleman should get into and out of his bath.

The other priest in the house was Fr Joseph Rickaby (the elder brother of John) and he was cast in a very different mould. His table manners evinced his Yorkshire roots more than his father's calling as a nobleman's butler, and Fr O'Fallon Pope found them very painful. Though he had won London University's highest philosophical prizes, Martin D'Arcy came to revoke his schoolboy awe of those achievements when he discovered what a limited field they had been won in and measured them against his personal experience of Fr Rickaby as a thinker.[24] In fact his real strength was as a preacher and spiritual director, and in that respect Campion Hall could not have been more fortunate. He was also a twinkling figure, full of humour, as free from convention as Fr O'Fallon Pope was bound by it, a representative of an old rural England and of a Stonyhurst that he recalled down to his boots, which were those that the boys had worn in the playground in his boyhood.

Campion Hall occupied a modest three-storey building in St Giles formerly known as Middleton Hall. The house had been rendered a little more impressive by Fr O'Fallon Pope's mother, who paid to have it faced it with grey stone and bought some good furniture, but it was not large enough to hold the two priests and ten undergraduates who formed the Community; the overflow was lodged at No.13 St Giles, on the other side of the adjoining pub, the Lamb and Flag. The regime that Fr O'Fallon Pope ran was a very conscientious and very enclosed one. The experiment of dropping Jesuit scholastics in the midst of a secular, non-Catholic university was still new, and there was nervousness about the effect on their religious commitment. They were there to gain high classes in Schools, and were expected to study, not to get mixed up in the social life of the university. In any case they were some half-dozen years older than the average undergraduate, so that even men from their own schools were strangers to them. For Martin D'Arcy there were possible contacts from St Mary's Hall, where he would have had a chance to know lay Philosophers at the college who were going on to Oxford; one such was the brilliant Cuthbert Taunton, who came up to Corpus Christi in 1913 and was killed two years later at the Dardanelles.

The Catholic circle at Oxford in 1912 was not a very interesting one. The Chaplain was an eccentric and tactless man who soon had to be dismissed. His successor, Fr Maturin, was a remarkable preacher but had no time to establish himself before he was drowned in the *Lusitania*. Mgr Barnes, who was appointed in 1915 and was known from his title as the Mugger, was a gentlemanly priest whose influence on his flock was unremarkable. Besides the Jesuit house there was St Benet's Hall on the other side of St Giles, founded by the Benedictines of Ampleforth with similar aims. Until 1909 it had been under the Mastership of Fr David Hunter Blair, a convert baronet who had been at Magdalen with Oscar Wilde and who was celebrated for his unwillingness to let the monastic life interfere with his social engagements. He would have been exposed to the same query as his opposite number at Cambridge, Fr Bede Camm, of whom, when he published a book called *A Day in the Cloister*, one of his monks is said to have enquired, 'Which day was that, Father?' But by 1912 St Benet's was as work-a-day as Campion Hall. The Dominicans had not yet planned their own house of studies in Oxford.

There were two Catholic dons in the university. One was Mr F. de Zulueta, a Fellow at Merton, and later Regius Professor of Civil Law; he belonged to a family well known at Beaumont and Stonyhurst. The other was Francis Urquhart, known as 'Sligger',* then at the height of his fame. He was just down the street from Campion Hall at Balliol, where he had been the first Catholic to win an Oxford scholarship, and then a fellowship, since the Reformation. He was a cultivated man of private means, having inherited part of the fortune, together with the library, of his uncle, the Whig cabinet minister Lord Carlingford. He believed in the Jowett tradition of the university as a place for the liberal education of the governing class, rather than professional study, and he attracted to his

* When Mgr Barnes visited Urquhart in his rooms, which overlooked the Martyrs' Memorial, an attendant undergraduate might have had the satisfaction of seeing Sligger and the Mugger looking out on the Maggers' Memugger. The intellectual acumen required for life in Oxford at this period is readily deducible from these particulars.

rooms an undergraduate circle drawn from all over the univeristy. His courtesy and conversational gifts made him a congenial model for Martin D'Arcy. He too had been educated at Beaumont and at Stonyhurst, and lost no opportunity to be of service to the Jesuits. When Urquhart died Fr D'Arcy made part of the chapel of the new Campion Hall a memor-ial to him with an inscription which testified to the devotion of 'his friends, who will not see such another friend.'

To the university in 1912 might have been applied the description which Evelyn Waugh, not too appropriately, gave of it a decade later: 'Oxford – submerged now and obliterated, irrecoverable as Lyonnesse, so quickly have the waters come flooding in – Oxford, in those days, was still a city of aquatint. In her spacious and quiet streets men walked and spoke as they had done in Newman's day.'[25] The enchantment which has won so many of its pupils worked its magic with Martin D'Arcy, and his university took its place with Stonyhurst – perhaps before it – as an object of affectionate loyalty. This was despite the small part in Oxford life that was permitted to the Jesuit undergraduates. Francis Urquhart was one social channel to the world of the university, but in general contacts were few. When Fr D'Arcy met the brilliant Balliol man R.H. Tawney in curious circumstances thirty years later, he knew him only from tales of his eccentricity which he had received in pre-war days from the Master of Balliol. He also recalled going to tea at New College with a Hindu who said that the supposed mystery of the Trinity was 'clearer than daylight' to him. This sounds like the man Frank Sheed mentions who went to the Vatican claiming to have a mathematical proof of the trinitar-ian doctrine; far from being honoured for his epoch-making discovery, he was refused Catholic baptism.

Other contacts were largely restricted to fellow classicists. We have a glimpse of Martin D'Arcy walking along Turl Street after a lecture one day with Victor Gollancz, who had come up with him in 1912 and had won the Chancellor's Latin Essay Prize in his first year. The conversation must have been just before the Mods examination in March 1914, for D'Arcy asked Gollancz if he was worried at the impending ordeal. Gollancz replied that he did not give much thought to Schools (he in fact got a First), since he was aiming at the university prizes, and added that the night before he had been turning the prophet Malachi into Lucretian hexameters for a diversion. At D'Arcy's sceptical invitation he produced the verses, a tour de force of scholarly ingenuity which he had dashed off at midnight when bored by his prescribed reading.[26]

Martin D'Arcy indeed fell short of such luminaries, and of his own brother's achievement, by just failing to get a First in Moderations. This made him all the more determined to succeed in the Greats course, and he tried his own hand at the university prizes, winning the Charles

Oldham Prize in 1915 for an essay on Lucretius. His consuming interest however was philosophy, and he found in the Oxford dons a much more searching scrutiny of metaphysical problems than he had encountered at St Mary's Hall. This should not be put down to Jesuit mediocrity: Fr Maher and Fr John Rickaby would have been well worthy of philosophy fellowships in an Oxford college, but their task as seminary professors was to equip their students to be Catholic instructors or polemicists. They could not afford the luxury of worrying at propositions as one could in the leisure of an Oxford tutorial. In Martin D'Arcy's day the dominant school in the university was the group known as the Oxford Realists, and he found his lingering allegiance to Hegelianism annihilated by the pitiless logical questioning to which they subjected its metaphysic. Even the devoted Hegelianism of one of his tutors, Harold Joachim, could not recall him to his attachment.[27]

The Realists included H.W.B. Joseph, whom D'Arcy called 'a positive mental magician, with an absolutely needle-sharp mind',[28] H.A. Prichard, who was later Professor of Moral Philosophy, and the Aristotelian J. Cook Wilson, Professor of Logic from 1889 till his death in 1916. It was Cook Wilson who particularly impressed D'Arcy. From the outbreak of the war Oxford was a deserted city, and the lack of undergraduate company probably put him more in that of his tutors. He visited Cook Wilson at his house and got to know him well, admiring him as a man who 'held ordinary beliefs with extraordinary precision.'[29] These most rigorous thinkers delighted D'Arcy's intellectual passion, but they did more. Coming to philosophy with a determination to reach the truth, however unpalatable it might prove, he was relieved to find the certificate of soundness given to principles which allowed him to harmonise his metaphysics with his cherished ideals of art, beauty and love.[30] The saying of Aristotle, 'With truth all things sing together' remained a favourite quotation all his life.

Cook Wilson is an unknown figure today; he published little and, while one who conversed with him is obviously privileged in his judgment, few philosophers would take seriously Fr D'Arcy's estimate of him as 'probably the ablest mind in the whole of the last hundred years in philosophy'.* The complaint against his school (voiced by contemporaries as well as by posterity) is that they were so narrowly critical, and judged by their effect on Martin D'Arcy's thinking the charge seems to hold. No doubt his mind would not have been so honed if his only training had been that of the Jesuit seminary, but he would have written better books if he had not been so influenced in his youth by these

---

*This was said in 1961,[31] but Fr D'Arcy would not have considered that the next thirty years have done anything to throw open the field.

relentless analysts. The notion that philosophy consisted in a close scrutiny of other people's views often stood in the way of his putting across his own ideas as effectively as he might.

In December 1915 Fr O'Fallon Pope's mother died and he was obliged to go to America to settle the family affairs. He was succeeded as Master by Fr Charles Plater, who became one of Martin D'Arcy's dearest friends. A brilliant and admired pupil at Stonyhurst, he was turned by his novitiate under Fr Considine to a heroic self-dedication and in particular an intense concern for the lot of the working man. While still a scholastic he had laid the foundations of the Catholic Social Guild and of the movement for working men's retreats. The inconsequential postings to which this priest of ardent missionary spirit was confined after completing his training in 1912 constitute one of the bad marks against the Provincialship of Fr Joseph Browne.

Martin D'Arcy described the advent of Fr Plater to Campion Hall as one of the formative influences of his life: wrapped up as he then was in philosophy and art, it was Plater who 'showed me by example what love of one's neighbour could achieve.'[32] For Plater his own appointment as Master was one of the many subjects of his ready hilarity, and he threw himself into the work of helping wounded soldiers in the hospitals, or recruits from the colonies who felt rather lost in strange surroundings. Rough khaki figures began to cross the threshold on which Fr O'Fallon Pope had kept such a chaperonish guard. Fr Plater also bent the rules of religious poverty to acquire a bulldog puppy which became a valued member of the Hall. Some verses which the Master wrote in its name begin as follows:[33]

> I'm Jim the bulldog. Candid friends remark
> They wouldn't care to meet me in the dark.
> My face perhaps is ugly. I don't mind it,
> I have the happiness to be behind it.

Plater showed a gift for luring people to his designs reminiscent of Fr Cassidy, of whose regime at Hodder he was an appreciative son. Fr D'Arcy recorded a meeting with some intellectual ladies of North Oxford who had high hopes of enlisting the new Master for their pet schemes and left at the end, utterly charmed, having agreed to all Fr Plater's plans and failed to inveigle him into any of theirs.[34] His charity in word as well as action won the love of his subordinates. The nearest he could bring himself to a criticism of anyone was to regale his listeners with a hilarious account of the person's oddities, ending with the saving coda, 'The dear thing!'

Martin D'Arcy denied that Fr Plater's pastoral ardour detracted, as some alleged, from the academic standards at the Hall. At any rate he himself gained his First in Greats without difficulty in June 1916 – his viva voce was no more than a formality – and he was sent to teach at Stonyhurst. Conyers had been teaching at St Francis Xavier's, Liverpool, and thus close to their parents, but in this year went on to begin his Theology at St Beuno's. In November 1917 their father died, it seems fairly suddenly; Conyers had been summoned to the bedside but Martin was not present. Less than two months previously Mr D'Arcy had composed a letter to *The Times* protesting against the proposal then before Parliament to abolish the office of Revising Barrister without pension or compensation, a measure which threatened to leave him at the age of seventy-two virtually without an income;[35] we may suppose that the worry of this contributed to his death. Mrs D'Arcy moved to Wimbledon for a while to live with her sister and brother-in-law the Eyres, but then seems to have settled in Essex.

When Martin D'Arcy returned to Stonyhurst in September 1916 the college was still under the government of Fr William Bodkin, the last of a line of great Rectors who had maintained Stonyhurst's position since the middle years of the nineteenth century. On taking office in May 1907 he found Stonyhurst in the trough of a brief decline which had begun with the departure of Fr Colley as Prefect of Studies six years earlier. Numbers had fallen by thirty or more since 1902, to under 260;★ in a remarkable recovery, Fr Bodkin had by 1914 raised the total to 395, far higher than Stonyhurst's previous record; and despite the handicaps of the war years, which included the disappearance of the lay Philosophers' department, he reached the figure of 400 before relinquishing office in November 1916. The charm of this 'lovely Irish gentleman', as Martin D'Arcy called him, had contributed to his success, but – although he himself had risen without paper qualifications – he had presided over an improvement of academic standards which crowned Stonyhurst's efforts since 1896 to attain parity with the leading public schools. The excellent Higher Certificate results won in the years 1912–15 were one result of this. Fr Bodkin's successor was the scholarly Fr Edward O'Connor, a Campion Hall graduate and an able mathematician, but a man without the same personal gifts.

Martin D'Arcy was appointed Master of Poetry and Assistant Prefect of Studies – a striking honour for a scholastic who had so far not done a day's teaching, and a sign of the prestige he had earned by his Oxford career; all the same, his task was simply to take some of the burden of work off the Prefect of Studies, not to help in modelling policy. The man he assisted was Fr Ernest Vignaux, who like the new Rector had distin-

★ Reckonings include the Philosophers, college boys and Hodder.

guished himself in mathematics at Campion Hall, of which he later became Master; he was a retiring and cautious person, a good enough Prefect of Studies under an energetic Rector like Fr Bodkin, but incapable of giving his own impulsion to the school under someone of rather similar character to himself. The war years were necessarily a time of disruption, with priests called away to be military chaplains and with boys' horizons filled by the battle-field instead of the university, but the ground lost was never made up, and Stonyhurst's academic record in the first years of peace was abysmal.

Like Mr Mangan when he himself had been in Poetry, Martin D'Arcy sought to convey to his class his own love of the beauties of literature. One of his pupils, Michael de la Bedoyère, was to recall him sitting on the master's rostrum 'crooning lines from Virgil while the boys divided themselves into those who thought it funny and were not impressed and those who thought it funny *and* were impressed. One of these, too bold by half and counting on the appearance that this delightful master did not bother to keep order, was picked up bodily by a wiry pack of taut muscles and deposited under the rostrum. Thus began a lifelong friendship.'[36] The friendship extended through Bedoyère's nine years in the Society of Jesus after he left Stonyhurst and his subsequent distinguished career as editor of *The Catholic Herald*.

His enthusiasm may have been wasted on some members of his class, but Martin D'Arcy's effect on individuals was inspirational. Fr Francis Hannan recalled being sent for private tuition to Mr D'Arcy, who set out to teach him to think for himself: he gave Hannan a succession of essay subjects, 'On Being Yourself', 'Self-Consciousness', 'Tweedledum and Tweedledee' – 'which I took to be intended as an invitation to prove that no-one really has a double ... The fourth step in the series was an essay on the difference between a good photograph and a good portrait. By that time, I think I had got his point.' These were subjects very close to Martin D'Arcy's own psychological interests, but they were not chosen as a chance to ride his hobby-horses. 'He almost never intruded his own opinion,' wrote Fr Hannan, 'but forced us to go to sources and form our own opinions.'[37]

Another disciple was Philip Ingress Bell, then in Rhetoric and Second Head of Higher Line, who came to D'Arcy of his own accord in 1916 asking to be allowed to write essays for him. D'Arcy knew Bell only as a boy whose 'influence in the school was far-reaching, ... he had raised its tone by his hatred of "slackers", and his own high ideal of sportsmanship.'[38] He was not particularly keen at first to welcome this sturdy non-intellectual, but he was finally so impressed by the series of essays that he had them published under the title *Idols and Idylls* in 1918. After serving for the last year of the war, Bell went on to a successful legal career which brought him to the House of Commons and a judgeship.

Other pupils of Martin D'Arcy's who remained his life-long friends included Henry Sire, who was to be his Socius during his term as Provincial, and Michael Trappes-Lomax, later well known in the Order of Malta and as a contributor to Catholic publications. Another was the brilliant Mexican boy Jaime Castiello, who left in 1917 to be a Jesuit in his own country. In May 1918 D'Arcy founded a literary society which has continued an intermittent existence at Stonyhurst ever since. It was called the Popinjay to indicate its liability to the impromptu visit of members of the Jesuit Community, colloquially known as J's or Jays. A whim of its foundation limited it to eleven members, and its method was the reading of a boy's essay followed by a discussion. One of its first meetings was made memorable by Mr D'Arcy's reading an essay by Jaime Castiello in which, says Francis Hannan, 'he had thrown open windows into the mind of Crashaw and also of Francis Thompson.'[39] D'Arcy's own literary ambitions got off to a modest start with the publication in *The Month* for April 1917 of his first article, a review of H.G. Wells's *Mr Britling Sees it Through*. What interested him were the signs that the writer had 'awakened to the notes of God's love' in this unheralded nod of his towards religious belief.[40]

D'Arcy was keeping up his Campion Hall links with regular visits, just as during his undergraduate days he had spent vacations at Stonyhurst. He had been an intermediary between Fr Plater and Cyril Martindale, who until 1916 was on the lay Philosophers' staff, but had not recovered mentally from illness he suffered in his last year of Theology. Fr Plater, who had himself been the professor of Philosophy in 1914–15, felt that Martindale needed wider horizons and, knowing the friendship that linked him to Martin D'Arcy, asked the latter to sound him out on the idea of moving to Campion Hall. D'Arcy passed on this offer during one of his visits from Oxford but, unknown to him, Martindale had taken an instant dislike to Charles Plater when he first met him as a novice and despite constant later companionship had never really thrown it off; he replied that he was not interested, but D'Arcy advised Fr Plater to invite him anyway. When the Philosophers were disbanded in July 1916, on the introduction of military conscription, Martindale consequently moved to Campion Hall.

The sequel was thus told by Fr D'Arcy: 'When he arrived, Charles Plater, who'd been the great noise there at Oxford, stepped aside and passed to Martindale all the most interesting and wonderful persons, keeping for himself the uninteresting ones. Gradually he pushed Martindale into a position of prominence. When I came back to Oxford a year later, Martindale was beginning to expand and grow and get back all his wonderful mental acuity and vitality and zest. In fact, by then he was being talked about in Oxford, and Fr Plater was receding into the background.... And Plater said to me, "Father★, will you just find out if there is anything Fr Martindale wants. If there's anything I can do for him, would you tell me? I don't feel I should ask him myself; but if you find anything he wants, let me know".'[41]

When Plater died, worn out by charity, a few years later, Fr Martindale wrote his life, a worthy enough monument as it seems to the historian, but to those who had known its subject a woeful failure to convey his sanctity and genius. Its ungenerous treatment of one Martin D'Arcy had so loved was a severe blow to the unqualified admiration for Martindale he had felt until then.

One of D'Arcy's visits to Oxford at this time was prompted by more than friendship. In the Michaelmas Term, 1918, he sat for the John Locke Scholarship in Mental Philosophy. He was successful in this, and the prize, worth £180, was the most valuable of the three he won at Oxford; but his week's stay at Campion Hall during the examination was the occasion for his first encounter with Baron Friedrich von Hügel, who was also a guest there. The opportunity of meeting this famous figure was of great interest to D'Arcy. In the context of the Catholic Church in England at the time, he was later to describe Hügel as 'a Triton among minnows',[42] though he also considered him, apart from his great spiritual and mystical strength, a man of insights rather than a systematic thinker. Fr Plater had with him a protégé from a retreat he had given at the American military camp at Didcot, a private called John Bull who asked to be received into the Church, and he took the opportunity to enlist Baron von Hügel and Martin D'Arcy as his sponsors.[43]

A few weeks later D'Arcy wrote to Hügel from Stonyhurst for advice on his future theological studies and was urged to learn German and Italian thoroughly so as to master the best contemporary scholarship. Again when he began his Theology he sought and received advice from Hügel, whom he met a second time in the hospitality of Campion Hall in September 1920.[44] It is to be noted that, according to his obituarist in the *Dictionary of National Biography* Hügel had been saved only by his social position from excommunication at the time of the Modernist crisis, though Fr D'Arcy preferred the view that his books were so impenetrable that the censors never read them; he was also not uncritical of Hügel's role in pushing Fr Tyrrell into a public Modernist stance and leaving him to face reprisals from which he himself remained exempt. Nevertheless it is striking that so soon after the Modernist crisis Fr Plater should have felt free to offer one of its celebrities repeated hospitality in a Jesuit house, and one sees how far the liveliest minds of the English Province remained

★A lapse of memory on Fr D'Arcy's part: by the time he was a priest Fr Plater was dead.

from having their sympathies cramped by the ecclesiastical furore.

1918 was marked by an event of great significance for Martin D'Arcy, the publication by Robert Bridges of the poems of Gerard Manley Hopkins. Until now, it seems, he had known no more of Hopkins's work than the selection published in 1893. The publication of the whole oeuvre showed him how much of a kindred spirit the poet had been in feeling and in thought. The marriage of aesthetic with religious sensibility was one which marked all Martin D'Arcy's philosophy; a passage from one of his books written a few years after this may be taken as an example: 'There are evenings, especially in the autumn season, when a familiar countryside can so change before our eyes that its beauty almost frightens us ... Such is the effect of grace on nature.'[45] And D'Arcy uses this to illustrate his explanation of the difference between natural and supernatural love.

Another resonance was struck by the element of chivalry in Hopkins's thinking and by his devotion to Christ the King, memorably expressed in *The Wreck of the Deutschland*. Hopkins was moved by the report of the German refugees who went down on a stormy December night off the Welsh coast, and of the nun who, as he writes:

> to the black-about air, to the breaker, the thickly
> Falling flakes, to the throng that catches and quails
> Was calling 'O Christ, Christ, come quickly.'

Her cry, says Hopkins, acknowledges the rights of Christ 'royally reclaiming his own.' The end of the poem turns into a prayer to the nun:

> Dame, at our door
> Drowned, and among our shoals,
> Remember us in the roads, the heaven-haven of the reward:
> Our King back, Oh, upon English souls!
> Let him easter in us, be a dayspring to the dimness of us, be a
> crimson-cresseted east,
> More brightening her, rare-dear Britain, as his reign rolls,
> Pride, rose, prince, hero of us, high-priest,
> Our hearts' charity's hearth's fire, our thoughts' chivalry's
> throng's Lord.

The demands of the war, to which the Jesuit Province gave 83 priests as army chaplains, made it necessary to prolong the 'Regency' of scholastics to staff the colleges, and D'Arcy did not therefore begin his Theology till he was thirty-one, a year older than normal circumstances prescribed. In October 1919 he was sent to the Theologate of the Lyons Province at

Ore Place in Hastings. The French Jesuits had been forced into exile by the anti-clerical laws of their country and were not allowed to re-establish their houses in France until the 1920s. Because of its high intellectual status, the seminary at Hastings had for some time been used by the English Jesuits to give their abler men for a year a taste of higher theological scholarship than St Beuno's could offer; Cyril Martindale had been sent there in 1911, when Teilhard de Chardin and Henri de Lubac were among his fellow students. A motive in Martin D'Arcy's case was no doubt again to avoid putting him into the same house as his brother, who was then finishing the course at St Beuno's. Nevertheless (since sending Conyers to Hastings would have achieved the same end), the posting was a response to the reputation he had acquired and his interest in the modern French Catholic thinkers.

The intellectual atmosphere at Hastings was extremely stimulating, and among the professors the one who most profoundly impressed Martin D'Arcy was Fr Maurice de la Taille, who in this very year was appointed to a professorship in the Gregorian University at Rome. He had recently completed his magisterial work on the Mass, *Mysterium Fidei* (published in 1921), whose influence on Martin D'Arcy will be described presently. D'Arcy was enabled to develop his interest in the contemporary French school of Thomism, and to extend his knowledge of Pierre Rousselot, who had been killed during the War. Rousselot was very much a sympathetic figure, not merely a brilliant philosopher but a man of poetic sensibility and the author of a life of the poet Heredia, whose kinsman he was. Another luminary of the French Catholic tradition who gained D'Arcy's allegiance was Bossuet, with his Christian philosophy of history. Following the pointers of Rousselot, he also immersed himself in St Augustine, whose *Confessions* he called 'that matchless classic' and whose view of the place of love in human psychology was to become a central strand of his thinking.

In 1920 he was privileged to collaborate with some of the most distinguished English Catholic writers of the day in a book on *God and the Supernatural*. D'Arcy's contribution, an essay on *The Idea of God*, was only his third piece of work to reach print, after his Wells review and the introduction he wrote to *Idols and Idylls*. It adumbrates some of the ideas that he was to spend his life developing, and exemplifies that taste for the purple passage which is especially visible in his earlier writings. The piece ends with the lines from St Augustine: 'Late have I loved Thee, O beauty so ancient and so new; late have I loved thee. And behold Thou wert within and I abroad, and there I searched for Thee; deformed I, plunging amid those fair forms which Thou hadst made. Thou wert with me, but I was not with Thee.' The splendid rhetoric, at the same time so charged with psychological insight, was a faithful double reflection of Martin

D'Arcy's own mind.

After a year at Hastings D'Arcy moved on to the English Theologate, St Beuno's in north Wales. Conyers had just left, after being ordained, and was sent to teach at Wimbledon, in proximity to the Eyres, though presumably Mrs D'Arcy was no longer living with them. His brother joined a body of some fifty students, in whose company he had a further three years' study ahead of him. An account of St Beuno's, whose wonderful setting had inspired Gerard Manley Hopkins, is given by Fr Martindale in his life of Fr Plater, which appeared in 1922:

> St Beuno's College ... is built half-way up the mountain known as Benarth on the north-east side of the Vale of Clwyd in Flintshire. The scenery is of great beauty. Rhyl and the sea are away to the right; Denbigh, to the left, looms on its crag; the heavy tower of St Asaph's Cathedral lifts itself from among trees some four miles distant; and beyond the hills on the far side of the immense valley, yet other hills float upwards till behind them all you see the crest of Snowdon.
>
> [Behind the college] a terraced garden climbs upward, in summer, all bright flowers and dark pillar-like cypress trees and hedges; at the top is a long walk whence the enormous view can be seen almost in its entirety. Many, when contemplating those wide pastures and roads and farms and villages, and the old town and the spires, must have found no better 'composition of place' for St Ignatius's meditation on the Kingdom of Christ, when he bids you visualise Our Lord going forth through the synagogues, towns and homesteads to convert the land. I have liked to stand there with Charles Plater, and the thought was not far from his mind, and inspired him with noble dreams.[46]

This same ardour and the sense of girding himself for battle was in Martin D'Arcy as he saw in post-war English society a deep need for the Christian vision and, like Hopkins, dreamt of great works to restore the reign of Christ the King over English souls.

Fr Martindale adds of the character of the seminary: 'I doubt whether any house anywhere has a more friendly atmosphere than St Beuno's. There is a warmth of geniality there that makes all the undercurrents of life grow happy: and over it broods the thought, emphasised year by year, of approaching Ordination.' Yet there was a difference between Martindale's and Martin D'Arcy's experience in that the former had gone to Hastings after two years at St Beuno's, whereas D'Arcy had come to the place with the standards of the French seminary to judge it by. Moreover the Rector of St Beuno's appointed at the beginning of 1922 was Fr Henry Davis, whom D'Arcy had already known as Prefect of Studies at Stonyhurst from 1903, and whom the years had not mellowed from the awkward authoritarianism which he had there displayed. There is reason to think that, of Fr D'Arcy's twenty years of Jesuit training, his Philosophy and Theology (with the exception of the year at Hastings) were the least congenial to him, and may have influenced his later attitude to the seminary regime.

As the Theologate was the stage of training in which ordination occurred, the studies were specially directed at preparing for the priesthood. The students had to be taught theology not just as an academic subject; they had to learn how to deal with cases of conscience and apply moral laws to the intricacies of human psychology. Without this training in the guidance of souls Fr D'Arcy would have lacked a great part of his influence, and his philosophy of love would have remained a fine abstraction. The Theologians also had to plumb the mysteries of the divine Sacrifice which they were being prepared to offer. Two circumstances especially helped Martin D'Arcy in this regard. The normal custom was to ordain Theologians after three years, so that they should have a year's exercise of the priesthood in the seminary before being let loose on the world; but as D'Arcy had started his Theology late he was allowed to receive the priesthood at the beginning of his third year, on September 25th 1921. For him the sacrament was pre-eminently, as he wrote privately three years later, 'the call to give myself entirely to God, to rest entirely in his will.' The second circumstance was the publication in this same year of Fr de la Taille's *Mysterium Fidei*, with its new interpretation of the meaning of the Mass.

Fr de la Taille represented the school of French theologians who, in this field as in others, had recently been taking a fresh look at Catholic teaching and stripping away some of the more plodding views imparted in the seminaries. In the case of the Mass, Counter-Reformation theologians had opposed the Protestant view of the Eucharist as the Lord's Supper and the denial of its sacrificial character by arguing that the Last Supper was a sacrifice in itself. This doctrine was supported by some rather lame arguments as to what precisely constituted the immolation at the Last Supper and what corresponded to it as a visible immolation in the Mass. Fr de la Taille broke away from these disputes to present a theory of beautiful simplicity and completeness, whereby the salvific sacrifice was constituted by the whole drama of Our Lord's Passion and Resurrection, beginning with the oblation at the Last Supper, leading to the immolation consummated on Calvary, and completed in the Resurrection, in which God's acceptance of the Sacrifice is made manifest and its efficacy shown in the triumph over sin and death. The unanimity of the four evangelists in treating the Passion and Resurrection as a single narrative and making it the culmination of their Gospels, as the Mass was the culmination of Christian life, made this view traceable to the very origin of the Church. Our Lord's Passion, Death and Resurrection were therefore one Sacrifice of which there were many ritual oblations, and Christ was present in the Mass for all time as the Victim sacrificed but risen and glorious.

It may seem curious that this interpretation was received with violent suspicion by many theologians, who insisted on the supposed need according to Tridentine orthodoxy of defending two separate sacrifices. For Martin D'Arcy however Fr de la Taille's theory was a matchless inspiration to that devotion to the Mass which marked him all his life. His eagerness to broadcast it to the English-speaking world bore immediate fruit in an article for the *Irish Ecclesiastical Record*. In 1925 he again wrote a defence of it as part of a discussion of La Taille's doctrine with two other theologians in *Blackfriars*, and he followed that with *The Mass and the Redemption*, his first complete book, in which he expounded the theory in detail. His allegiance to Fr de la Taille's view is explained in the first of these writings: 'To the present writer, it is the revelation of what may be called the genius hidden in the workings of the Church, which has drawn him back again and again to the pages of this work.' He marvelled at the opportuneness of the doctrine presented at a time when Catholic theology was discovering a new interest in the doctrine of the Mystical Body, and giving expression to the centrality of the Blessed Sacrament in its life through annual Eucharistic Congresses. 'And are we to think it a mere chance that, at such a moment, a view is put forward which harmonizes these tendencies, and lets us see deeper into the beauty of what is our *Mysterium Fidei*?'[47]

To Fr D'Arcy therefore Fr de la Taille's doctrine was one of the most luminous reflexions of the harmony of divine Revelation. He wrote in *The Mass and the Redemption*: 'There is nothing tentative, incomplete, disconnected, or diffuse in the economy of Christ. So profound, indeed, and far-reaching is it, that one can never say that complete apprehension has been reached, and there is danger lest we be dazzled by the beauty of some part and linger on it, forgetting that it is but one arch of the edifice not built by hands. And yet if there be any part of the plan which can be said to form a centre whence our darkened eyes can more easily behold the encompassing splendour, that part surely is the Mass. There are gathered together the virtues of faith and hope and charity; there the waters of grace are seen in their source; there is re-enacted the mystery of love which makes a man-God lay down his life for his friends; there, too, does the Church recognise itself, the royal race, the holy priesthood, the Mystical Body, made up of many members whose head is Christ; there, finally, are consummated the espousals between the bride and the Bridegroom, and a foretaste given of the joys of heaven when we shall be in Christ as Christ is in the Father.'[48]

His experience at Hastings had turned Fr D'Arcy's mind in a more theological direction, but his principal interest was still philosophy, and it is evidence of the reputation he enjoyed in that field that in September 1920 he was allowed to attend a congress of philosophers in Oxford, of which he wrote an account in *The Month*. The gathering included figures such as Arthur Balfour, Bertrand Russell and Friedrich von Hügel, and there was also a delegation of French philosophers, whom D'Arcy dismissed as unimpressive survivals of a démodé anti-clericalism. Their presence however led to a return fixture in Paris in December 1921, to which Fr D'Arcy was also allowed to travel. It was on this occasion that he was taken by an American artist friend, supposedly well up in the latest movements, to see some of the best modern pictures in Paris, which he undertook to explain. The visit ended with Fr D'Arcy explaining the pictures and the artist taking notes.[49]

Shortly before that visit Fr D'Arcy had written again to Baron von Hügel for guidance on the problem of Evil, on which he was writing a *Catholic Truth Society* pamphlet. This was published in 1922, but it cannot be said that the result was remarkable. A more striking success was his winning in 1923 of the Green Moral Philosophy Prize at Oxford for a dissertation on 'The value of the employment of methods similar to those of the physical sciences in the study of human character and conduct' – a reflexion of the psychological bent of his interests which was particularly strong at this period.

The newly ordained Theologians, full of fresh zeal, were much in demand as supply priests in the Province's parishes, and Fr D'Arcy was sent for nearly two months – presumably August and September 1922 – to cover the holiday of the regular priest in the slum parish of Cowcaddens, in Glasgow. Conventional thought might have laughed at the idea of this aristocratic intellectual being assigned to such a duty, but it displays rather the shrewdness of Fr Bodkin, who had been Provincial since 1921, and who made the choice from his personal knowledge and appreciation of Fr D'Arcy. It proved one of the most moving and formative experiences of his life. His first steps were not sure-footed:

> I started off filled with the idea that loving-kindness would be the open sesame to the hearts of my parishioners. They were a fine, rough, independent set of people living in miserable conditions. At one of my first encounters a rather fierce looking woman looked me up and down, and then said disparagingly that the priest whose place I was taking was a real priest, a real man of God. If the people were not on time for church on Sundays, she told me, he would come with his stick, get them up and out, and march them to church.[50]

In a book written soon after this he expressed with feeling the lesson he had learned: 'A priest who, acting on the principle of charity, uses nothing but gentleness, is, *experto crede*, likely to have his mildness interpreted as softness. He will do better on occasions to mix his gentleness with an apparent severity.'[51] It was a lesson he applied all his life, even in more sophisticated circles.

But the lasting imprint of his time in Glasgow was a personal one: 'I fell completely in love with the people there,' he said in old age, 'and it had a great influence on me, because I saw people nakedly: what they really were, and their loves, very deep loves, and an extraordinary family spirit.'[52] Lord Hailsham cited as the legacy of this experience Fr D'Arcy's 'belief in the dignity of the human spirit, acquired, I believe, during his work among the very poor in a slum parish before I ever came to know him, which informed with humanity and grace his uncompromising teaching about what are sometimes the hardest to bear or accept of the ethical restraints imposed by Christian and Roman Catholic ethics.'[53]

On completing his Theology, Fr D'Arcy would have expected to be sent to the Tertianship, but Fr Bodkin had other plans. On a visit to St Beuno's towards the end of the course he asked Fr D'Arcy if he would be prepared to spend another year at Stonyhurst. 'There are three very exceptional and interesting boys there who could profit greatly by studying with you.' Fr D'Arcy was not enthusiastic, but to a Jesuit his superior's whim was law.[54] It was like Fr Bodkin to announce his intentions in that fashion, but the fact was that, with the disruption caused by the war to the long training schedule, priests were being regularly sent to put in an extra year or more of teaching before their Tertianship; Fr Robert de Trafford had been at Stonyhurst in this suspended state for the past two years. And there Fr D'Arcy joined him in September 1923.

Chapter Three

First Disciples

Soon after being told of his posting, Fr D'Arcy began to correspond with one of the boys the Provincial had mentioned, and his letters already seemed to justify Fr Bodkin's words. This was Henry John, the youngest child of Augustus John, whose artistic fame was at its peak in the nineteen-twenties. Through the influence of a Catholic cousin, Edith Nettleship, Henry had been sent to Stonyhurst, and there he himself became a Catholic. The way he embraced the Faith was shown by his response to the Catholic Evidence Guild, which was introduced to Stonyhurst in December 1922. Its aim was to give boys practice in defending Catholic doctrine as soap-box orators, with a view to their putting their skills into practice in London at Speakers' Corner. By the time Fr D'Arcy arrived at Stonyhurst Henry John was turning this training to practical use, with results thus described by his master:

> Here was this boy, handsome, looking like an angel, and with this wondrous power of words, this gift of oratory. The crowds left all the more famous speakers of the Protestant Alliances, the Jews and the Socialists, to gather round this child, to the absolute indignation of the enemies of religion. They'd say, 'That child ought to be in bed!' One evening he spoke on miracles, and right at the end a voice was heard to say, 'Miracles? That bloody boy is a bloody miracle himself!'[1]

But Henry John was not simply an eager product of Jesuit teaching. Under a less dogmatic wand he might have been fetching dew at midnight from the still-vex'd Bermoothes. 'Like an ancient god, the earth could not hold him,' wrote Fr D'Arcy, straining to convey the magic that had captivated him. Henry had not just accepted Catholicism but had seen it as the necessary structure of a world enriched by his own warmth and fantasy. 'His faith was like a campfire round which the young laughed, men sang and worked, and cows jumped over the moon.'[2] Stonyhurst had already had some years to wonder at him, the *Magazine* publishing the astonishing poetry he wrote at the age of thirteen, and memories were fresh of the school production of *The Merchant of Venice* in which, as Portia, he had rendered to the 'quality of mercy' speech the status of a masterpiece.

Christopher Devlin, his Shylock, was the second of the three boys of Fr Bodkin's recommendation. Fr D'Arcy's arrival converted him from the rebellious stance he had taken towards the school authorities, and he was to spend his life in the Society of Jesus, his poetic sensibility being expressed in a biography of the Jesuit poet and martyr St Robert Southwell and an edition of the spiritual writings of Gerard Manley Hopkins. He was, however, less close to Henry John in friendship than the last member of the trio, Tom Burns, who described himself as Dr Watson to Henry's Sherlock Holmes, 'as he was a genius and always the innovator.'[3] The two were united especially by an admiration of Fr Martindale, whose retreat at Stonyhurst they had recently attended.

As Master of Poetry once more, Fr D'Arcy conveyed his enthusiasms as he had done seven years before, but he had now three especially apt pupils. He introduced them to Hopkins, and, in Tom Burns's words, 'He would recite the poetry as if the very spirit of Hopkins had possessed him.'[4] In another place Burns wrote: 'As time went on he would put the intellectual jumps higher by imperceptible degrees, and brought Rousselot and von Hügel into sight. I still have a translation made at his request of Rousselot's essay *Les Yeux de la Foi*. He was fascinated by the paradoxes of the opening: "Love blinds, love gives new eyes for seeing".'[5]

Part of Fr D'Arcy's pedagogical style was to allow himself to be ragged by those closest to him – a liberty he permitted them all his life. After a holiday visit to Paris Henry John sought to shock him by showing him a copy of James Joyce's *Ulysses*, which he had smuggled through Customs. But Burns notes: 'He simply helped one to see the book in a new dimension', and it became the subject of detailed discussion.*

Fr D'Arcy himself, as he reveals in an article of this time, was feeling his way towards an artistic philosophy. He was convinced that an appreciation of art must be based on some conceptual grounding, that 'Art will never render up its mystery or attain its proper grandeur without intercourse with Mind.'[6] Clive Bell, with his doctrine of Significant Form, was the first contemporary who seemed to offer a foothold. But the revelation he looked for came when he read Jacques Maritain's *The Philosophy of Art*, recently translated into English. 'This was the golden book I had long sought for', he wrote, and the role of Thomism in incorporating this world of beauty with those of the reason and the soul thrilled him especially. But this intellectualism was being both attacked in flank and enriched by the human impact of Henry John: 'To one like myself,' he recalled, 'babbling literature and delighting in dialectic, he was a breath of fresh air bidding me not to live at second-hand on books, not to

---

*References in Fr D'Arcy's writings at this period show that he was also familiar with the works of D.H. Lawrence, another writer who was unpopular with H.M. Customs.

read about colours and nature, but to enjoy nature, to enjoy knowledge.'[7]

What this meant in actual incident he described more amusingly in the article just quoted:

> A young friend of mine, whose name will one day, please God, shine across Europe and the New World, showed me a photograph of a Crucifixion by Mestrovic.★ 'Do you like that?' said he. I looked. Now, thought I, fresh from the reading of *The Philosophy of Art*, now shall I speak with the tongue of an angel. 'A form as the splendour of Being fashioned out of a material' – yes, that was it. I looked. I looked a third time. 'A form as the splendour ...' Yes, yes, but what about this Crucifixion? 'Well,' said the youth (he is very persistent). I stared furiously. Where on earth was that form as the splendour of Being? There was a form, it impressed me, but the impression did not set my heart on fire. 'Well,' said the youth, a little impatiently (he is, I have said, most persistent). I began to talk, I spoke of form, the Greek conception of it, Plato, Plotinus, Augustine, the richness ... 'Oh!' said the youth, 'can't you say whether you like it or not?' I spoke severely to him, told him he was unfit to listen to what I had to say, and with a blush I returned sorrowfully to study once more *The Philosophy of Art*.[8]

From this passage we can feel well enough the love and admiration that bound Fr D'Arcy to his pupil. Such feelings posed a problem in the Jesuit discipline of the sentiments, and Fr D'Arcy faced it clear-sightedly. He was too good a psychologist to think that the affection inspired by this 'handsome gypsy' could be assigned to a pure plane of spiritual affinity. Jesuit education was well aware of the dangers of the celibate life of a boarding school, and its discipline was designed to protect the chastity as much of the masters as of the boys. Fr D'Arcy took the case to his confessor, who had the wisdom to see that the relation, however it might come under the warning against 'particular friendships', was beneficial to the boy. Under his advice, Fr D'Arcy made it his study to turn his friendship with Henry John away from self-indulgence and into a mediation of the divine love.

Fr Bodkin's choice of Fr D'Arcy to come and teach this class of Poetry was a tacit admission of the limitations of Stonyhurst education at the time. In 1923 Fr O'Connor was still Rector, but his failure to keep up the impetus given by Fr Bodkin was shown in a decline in numbers of more than forty since the peak of 1917 – and that although it was a period when most public schools were increasing their rolls (Downside jumped from 200 to 330, nearly closing the gap with Stonyhurst).

★ The contemporary Croatian sculptor.

Academic attainments reached a nadir in the early twenties: before the War Stonyhurst had been averaging nearly one Oxford award every year, demonstrating a very creditable adaptation from its long bondage to the London system; but after the War no Oxford or Cambridge open awards were won at all until 1925, and only two between then and 1931. Higher Certificate results also showed a dismal decline. With the consolidation of its position by Downside, Stonyhurst had unmistakably lost its reputation as the leading Catholic school.

Furthermore, it was a decline which no steps were being taken to remedy. Fr Vignaux had been removed as Prefect of Studies in 1920, but his place was taken by Fr L. Bellanti, who, in contrast to his predecessor's Oxford achievements, had no more than a London degree without honours to his name. One would have to go back very many years to find a man of such relative academic insignificance appointed Prefect of Studies at Stonyhurst; and with the Catholic schools now fully geared to Oxford and Cambridge it was not the moment to go back to men trained under the London system.* Fr Bellanti was, however, a more vigorous man than Fr Vignaux, and he promoted a much-needed improvement in Higher Certificate results, though the attainment of really scholarly standards that would have been reflected in university awards was beyond him.

The change that Fr D'Arcy felt most strongly at Stonyhurst was the disappearance of the Philosophers. They had been suspended in the middle of the war, when the senior boys were moved into their rooms, thus relieving the pressure on space caused by Fr Bodkin's expansion; with the arrival of peace it was contended that their quarters could not be spared, and this excuse served against their restoration, even when the fall in numbers robbed it of much of its validity. In two vehement letters written to the *Stonyhurst Magazine* before he came back to the college, Fr D'Arcy urged the restoration of the Philosophers, citing their disappearance as a prime cause of Stonyhurst's loss of both standing and character: 'Their glory has departed,' he wrote, with intentional hyperbole, 'and with it "the secret none can utter" which used to belong to Stonyhurst. It has become a dull repetition of other modern public schools, a place of cranks and pulleys, without the semblance of individuality.'[9] He had, though, a higher reason for wishing to see the course restored. Recognising the limitations of the old studies, he dreamt of a revitalised course that would be Stonyhurst's contribution to the intellectual resur-

* This appointment may be contrasted with that of the old Stonyhurst boy and Double First in Classics at Oxford, Fr Joseph Woodlock, who was an epoch-making Prefect of Studies at St Francis Xavier's, Liverpool, from 1919 to 1937. Such appointments suggest that the Provincial, Fr Wright, who was himself an old boy of St Francis Xavier's, consciously intended to benefit the day colleges at the expense of the public schools.

gence in English Catholicism which he saw developing. It is clear from his second letter on the subject, published in April 1923, that he had conceived in his own mind a detailed scheme of reform, and he urged:

> The time is fast approaching when in England, as elsewhere on the Continent, the reconciliation and revivifying of all things in Christ will become a practical policy, and it will be sad if Stonyhurst loses a golden opportunity of being the first to direct the modern almost conscious craving for the Christian fulfilment, whether in art, philosophy, social ideals, or religion.[10]

How far the Jesuit authorities were from acceding to these lofty policies was shown in the course of Fr D'Arcy's own year on the Stonyhurst staff. Fr O'Connor was replaced as Rector by Fr Walter Weld, who represented in his family Stonyhurst's dearest traditions, but whose intellectual attainments were such that he had great difficulty in saying his daily Mass. He became known for a series of egregious talks to leavers, of which a typical specimen ran as follows: 'You should remember that the reputation of Stonyhurst, and of the whole Catholic body in this country, rests on your shoulders, and you should always be careful that your conduct is worthy of that reputation. For example, if you go to stay at somebody's house, always remember to clean the bath after using it.'

Fr Bodkin's gesture of *pietas* in making such a man Rector of Stonyhurst, and at such a time, was all the more preposterous since Fr Weld's brother George (afterwards bishop and Vicar Apostolic of British Guiana) was a good scholar who would have been perfectly well qualified for the post; and it demonstrates the Provincial's Irish ability to live in a fantasy world in which, as he thought he remembered, Stonyhurst had been governed in unruffled dignity by descendants of the old Catholic families.

The results of the faltering of direction at Stonyhurst were not only in the school's public standing. These were the years when Jesuit education lost its sense of what it was meant to be doing and took to aping the Protestant public schools. In 1921 a 'Committee' was introduced with something of the functions of public-school prefects, and the Head of Higher Line was given the power to beat other boys. An institution called Penance Drill evolved which served as an opportunity for senior boys to exercise their sadistic impulses on the younger.[11] This substitution of a secular and irresponsible source of government for a religious and conscientious one inevitably weakened the moral influence of the Jesuits on their pupils, and added to the loss of personal contact caused by the disappearance of the old class-master system. There was also a surrender to the English cult of games, of which a sign was the substitution of

Rugby for Association Football in 1921, to bring Stonyhurst into line with public-school practice; and the incongruous involvement of the Officers' Training Corps in religious ceremonies at Easter and Corpus Christi reflected the same derivative trend.

It should be added, to lighten the picture, that the twenties at Stonyhurst were an exceptionally fertile period in religious vocations, and if formal academic triumphs were slight it was not through a blink-ered intellectual habit. Not a few boys harmonised a convinced loyalty to the Faith they were taught with a vigorous criticism of established ways, both within and outside the school. The examples include Fr D'Arcy's own pupils as well as older and younger boys, many of whom looked to him as a sympathiser and inspirer. A little further down the school was Bernard Wall, who crowned his school career by winning one of Stonyhurst's rare Oxford scholarships, and whose judgment of the English scene could be well described in the words that Tom Burns applied to himself and Henry John: 'we hated the ruling culture, seeing it as secularist, self-seeking and self-sufficient.' It was a view of life in which Fr D'Arcy's sense of the need to bring Christ into a de-spiritualised society found a ready echo. In Rhetoric there was Quintin Jermy Gwyn, who had just won a place at Balliol and was to rise to the exotic eminence of Grand Chancellor of the Knights of Malta; he valued Fr D'Arcy 'as a kind of sounding board for my adolescent but perhaps not unintelligent ideas and theories' and was quick to seek him out when they were both established in Oxford.

Towards the end of the school year Fr D'Arcy received an invitation from Fr Martindale to join a party he was taking to a *Pax Romana* conference in Budapest. *Pax Romana* had been recently founded as an inter-national organisation for Catholic university students, but Fr Martindale had not been able to get enough applicants of that status, and he suggested that Fr D'Arcy should try to interest some of his boys. Henry John, as a long-standing Martindale enthusiast, leapt at the chance, and Christopher Devlin was also keen to go. Fr D'Arcy thus described what happened when he wrote to Fr Bodkin for permission to travel with them:

It was shortly before he was scheduled to make a visitation at Stonyhurst, and he sent me no answer before his visit. When he arrived, I met him on the staircase and he said to me, 'Oh, by the way, about that going to Budapest. Rome, you know, is very difficult about these journeys now, and I'm afraid I daren't ask because you're sure to be refused.' I went on to my room, and presently Henry John came along. So I said to him, 'Well, Henry, I think you and the others will have to go to Budapest by yourselves, without me. I'm afraid I can't go.' 'Oh, can't you get permis-sion from the Provincial?' I said 'Ssh,' and he said, 'Oh' and walked out of the room. About ten minutes afterwards he came back to me and said, 'The Provincial wants to see you.' So I went upstairs. When I came into the Provincial's room, I found him sitting there really in almost a daze. 'That's an extraordinary boy. That's the most extraordinary boy I've ever met, that Henry John!' Then he said, 'Now, about going to Budapest. I'll tell you what. You just go. You just go.'[12]

When he recovered from the Henry John experience, Fr Bodkin thought of a way of sending Fr D'Arcy on his journey. He allowed the £100 of the Green Moral Philosophy Prize to be applied towards the expenses of the trip, and in fact it paid for Henry John and Christopher Devlin. The party left in August, with Fr Martindale in overall charge but Fr D'Arcy keeping an eye on his two pupils. 'Men have won a martyr's crown for not so much more,' wrote Christopher Devlin. In Budapest Henry defied Fr D'Arcy's prohibition of his plan to swim the Danube and narrowly escaped drowning; and when they went on to Venice he was put in charge of the party's money and lost it. There was more to the trip than mischief, though; we may imagine that Fr D'Arcy shared Christopher Devlin's pleasure in Budapest, where 'We saw the cuirasses glint and heard the halberds clash in the great cathedral, on the Feast of St Stephen the King.'[13]

The testing of Fr D'Arcy's emotional self-discipline in his friendship with Henry John was all the sharper in the close company of the *Pax Romana* trip, and he went to confession every day in the course of it, presumably to Fr Martindale. He could not have found a surer guide than that acute counsellor in his struggle to sublimate earthly love into divine charity. For the next year, while Henry completed his schooling at Stonyhurst, they were necessarily apart, but Henry was as eager as his master to end the separation as soon as possible.

From Venice Fr D'Arcy went straight to begin his Tertianship in Ireland, where his companions included Fathers Robert de Trafford and Basil Gurrin. The English Province at this time had no Tertianship house of its own and had since 1914 been sending its priests to Tullamore in King's County. The most important event of the Tertianship was the repetition of the Long Retreat, which as at Manresa was held in October and November. In the piercing self-scrutiny of the Exercises Fr D'Arcy examined his friendship with Henry John as one of the elements in the endeavour since his ordination to respond to the divine gift of the priesthood which meant so much to him.

The regime of the Tertianship was a slightly less enclosed one than that of the novitiate, since it had to allow the Tertians to exercise their ministry. During Lent they were in demand to help in parish missions. It is not to be supposed that Fr D'Arcy was allowed anything that could be called a social life, but it may have been on this visit to Ireland, or on other unidentified ones which he made in these years, that he began to renew lost contacts with his father's family. He got to know the children and grandchildren of Sir Patrick Coll, who also introduced him to more distant cousins, the 6th Lord ffrench and the 3rd Lord Hemphill. On his mother's side, he had met the children of her brother-in-law Colonel James Creagh of Ballygarrett at the wedding of one of them at the Brompton Oratory three days after his ordination; his brother Conyers officiated, but it seems that Fr Martin D'Arcy was considered too much of a tiro at that point to be trusted with the ceremony. His mother's Carmelite sister in Wells gave him an introduction about the same time to a woman mystic living in the Fulham Road, and his meeting with her made a deep impression on him. She was said to subsist on nothing but the host in Holy Communion and was bed-ridden and in constant pain, having offered herself as a sacrifice for the sins of bad priests.[14]

While Fr D'Arcy was at Tullamore some American Jesuits studying there mentioned to him that they had heard he was to be sent to Rome. The Society liked to keep its members in the dark about their postings and Fr D'Arcy knew nothing of it. 'Yes,' he was assured, 'you're going to be a professor there.' It was not till later that Fr Bodkin wrote to him confirming the destination, but not the object of it. In fact Fr de la Taille had recommended Fr D'Arcy to fill the need for an English-speaking professor at the Gregorian, and in the mean time he was to join the very select band of those who were sent for an extra biennium of studies in Rome after completing the ordinary course. While in London before he left he asked Fr Bodkin what he was to do in Rome, but the Provincial remained Jesuitically clam-like. Fishing for a clue about the rumoured professorship, Fr D'Arcy asked, 'Is it true that I'm not going to come back?' 'Well, I wouldn't be so sure of that,' answered Fr Bodkin, 'looking at me in his very Irish way.'[15]

Despite these last-minute obfuscations Fr D'Arcy and Henry John achieved their aim of getting together again, the latter promptly applying to study at the Gregorian. By now he had entered his father's artistic world, had met and impressed G.K. Chesterton and was shortly to contribute to Wyndham Lewis's avant-garde periodical *The Enemy*. In justifying his removal from that world, Fr D'Arcy claimed that he felt Henry was such an original genius that Oxford would only spoil him. Perhaps he was right, though whether the Gregorian was less trammelling is not so clear; the desire of both of them to be together was paramount in the choice. Henry John had already expressed his wish to become a Jesuit, but the stay in Rome was not, as Michael Holroyd implies in his biography of Augustus John, part of a scheme to groom Henry for the priesthood, and even less was it a plan made at the bidding of Jesuit superiors.

Henry took quarters in the Beda, an institution mainly intended for Anglican converts studying for the Church. Here he met the charming

Alfred Gilbey, who after coming down from Cambridge was preparing for the priesthood. Fr D'Arcy had met him as a boy at Beaumont during the war, when he went to visit Basil Gurrin who was there as a Prefect, and he already knew his elder brothers, who had been Philosophers at Stonyhurst. Gilbey and Henry John became good friends and went off together on holidays which they handled according to their respective penchants: Gilbey, who enjoyed an income from his family's well-known gin business, would check in to the best hotel of whatever place they had reached, while Henry went off into the countryside and made himself comfortable for the night in the crook of a tree.

Fr D'Arcy lived at the Gesù, where the superior was the German biblical scholar Father (later Cardinal) Augustin Bea; when he went to Fr Bea for instructions he was told that he was not to follow the ordinary course of studies and should receive his orders from the English Assistant. Instead Fr D'Arcy went to Fr de la Taille, who told him unofficially that he had been picked as a possible professor of the Gregorian. That still did not enlighten him as to how he should prepare himself. The General told him, 'Just read and spend your time as you see fit.'[16]

This liberal instruction gave Fr D'Arcy the leisure to write his first book, *The Mass and the Redemption*, an English digest of Fr de la Taille's *Mysterium Fidei*. The manuscript was sent to England to be corrected by Fr Basil Gurrin for its publication. Despite the force of the sublime view it interpreted, the book shows signs of having been put together without proper revision, and is a disappointing expression of the central enthusiasm of Fr D'Arcy's spiritual life. By the time he finished it he had made, on the feast of the Purification, 1926, his solemn profession as a Jesuit, taking the four vows that bound him irrevocably to his elected vocation.

Fr D'Arcy's stay in Rome, besides reuniting him with Fr de la Taille, introduced him to some of the most remarkable men of the Society. Foremost of these in every sense was the General, Fr Ledochowski, who is widely regarded as one of the greatest Generals in the order's history, yielding only to St Ignatius Loyola, St Francis Borgia and Fr Claudius Aquaviva. Already in 1906, when he was forty, an age at which most superiors had not attained their first Rectorship, he had been considered a favourite candidate for the vacancy of General, only his weak health causing him to be passed over. After playing an important part in the Society's government under Fr Wernz, he became the latter's successor in 1915 and governed the order through a period of extraordinary increase till his death in 1942. The following description of him by Fr Martindale shows how much he had in common with Martin D'Arcy:

He is a curious man, somewhat hampered by being a Pole, having an enormous ancestry, and having been trained only in court circles, etc.

He is as weak as a feather, with unbelievable energy; minute and mouse-like, until he turns into a sort of eagly-steely-wristed (not taloned: he never scratches) creature; meticulously logical but suddenly expanding into astonishing freedoms – altogether a very extraordinary person.[17]

To visit Rome in the nineteen-twenties was to see the Society of Jesus perhaps at the height of its influence. After half a century of evictions by anti-clericalism and by war, the Curia was solidly reinstalled. Fr Ledochowski was on the best of terms with Pope Pius XI, who could think of no-one better than the Jesuits to entrust new projects to; they had taken over the Vatican Radio on its recent inauguration. The Gregorian University was the centrepiece of their dominance of the Roman academic scene, and the influence of Jesuit spirituality was every-where. An example was given by the English Assistant, Fr Joseph Welsby, an old Stonyhurst boy. He was an indefatigably conscientious man, with a great concern for his subordinates, and so valued as a spiritual director that he was persuaded to take on that service at the Beda and the English, Scots and Irish Colleges on top of his administrative duties. His religious talks, delivered in a staccato voice, had the originality of complete simplicity, and caused one of his retreatants to remark, 'How God must look forward to the Weller's meditation every morning!'

Henry John did not really enjoy Rome, and perhaps Fr D'Arcy was not completely happy, as we may guess from a letter of Henry's to his father suggesting that he come to Rome to 'cheer up D'Arcy and paint the Pope (green) and the town (red).'[18] His admiration for his master was unabated; Fr D'Arcy, he told his father, 'is the *paragon* – he sees every conceivable point of view without being the least bit vague or cocksure, and allows himself to be fought and contradicted perhaps more than is good for me.'[19]

It has been stated that during his time in Rome Fr D'Arcy took advantage of one of his meetings with the General to protest against the suspicions of Rousselot as unorthodox.[20] It is not clear who held such views; there were certainly some fanatical Thomists opposed to any novel interpretation of Aquinas, men like the Dominican Fr Garrigou-Lagrange, who was urging the Pope to depose Ledochowski as a favourer of Modernists. Within the Society, a similar cast of mind was perhaps shown by Cardinal Billot, whose right-wing ardour led to his being stripped of the purple in 1927. Fr Ledochowski was not the man to sympathise with such enthusiasts, by the likes of whom among his brethren he had himself been denounced as a semi-Modernist before 1915. He did, though, form the opinion that Fr D'Arcy's darting genius would not be best employed in a professorial chair at the Gregorian. At the end of his first year in Rome Fr D'Arcy was told that on the grounds of his poor health he would not receive the appointment, and would be returning to England; it was the first official admission he heard that he had been thought of for the lost professorship.[21]

In the summer of 1926 Fr D'Arcy returned to Farm Street. He still had the second year of his biennium to run, but it is not known what form his studies took. Farm Street had some excellent scholars and a great library to instruct him, but one suspects that this posting was a bit of a ruse on Fr Bodkin's part to bring him to Mayfair, where he foresaw that he would shine. Now at the age of thirty-eight he at last entered the fray to win the minds of his time for Christ, and like other Catholic observers he saw himself as part of an advancing army. Recent conversions like those of Ronald Knox and G.K. Chesterton were proofs of the intellectual vitality of the Catholic Church, and with the apostolate of precursors such as Cyril Martindale, they gave a new vigour to Catholic apologetics. Where the tone of the previous generation of converts had perhaps been set by the cosy novels of Maurice Baring and Mgr Benson, the Catholic champions of the 1920s were carrying their arguments into radio and the popular Press. Hilaire Belloc had entrenched his formidable thesis before the yielding front of the Protestant tradition, and imparted a new robustness and confidence to the thought of many of his co-religionists. In a society whose social and religious norms had been shaken by the war, the Catholic vision was offering a conviction which many found nowhere else. Bernard Shaw's prescription of the socialist Superman was brilliantly argued but essentially comfortless. H.G. Wells beguiled the half-educated with the world-view of the suburban amateur scientist. Dean Inge interpreted the civilised but sceptical tradition of Jowett's Anglicanism to the incongruous medium of the popular Press; and the inventor of detection's most analytical brain sought an alternative to the consolations of religion by telling his public that he believed in fairies. This was the setting for a Catholic advance which was already highly visible and which was to advertise itself in a crop of notable intellectual conversions over the next dozen years.

In the matter of elite conversions, nowhere was more experienced than the Jesuit house at Farm Street. Its foundation dated back to 1844, and is a remarkable example of the Order's strategy of going straight to the heart of power. At that time there were yet no Oxford converts and, with the exception of a handful of representatives in the two Houses of Parliament, the Catholic upper class in England consisted of a squirearchy which was not much seen in the confines of Mayfair. The policy of the Jesuit Province, carried through with brilliant success over the next hundred and twenty years, was to found a fine church staffed by able preachers, and a house of writers whose work would likewise serve for the dissemination of the Faith. The strong reputation of the church received a striking boost after 1901, when Fr Bernard Vaughan was posted there and began his series of sermons electrifying London society. The young Duchess of Norfolk, who as Baroness Herries in her own right belonged to a family of long Stonyhurst affiliation, was prompted by his preaching to lead an anti-Smart-Set in support of his protest against Edwardian luxury. The church's extraordinary record is shown in a roll of three thousand converts instructed between 1910 and 1935, the grandest of them being the 9th Duke of Marlborough, received early in 1927.

That is not to say that the Jesuits set themselves to chase titles, and even less were they in Mayfair to indulge in the lotus-eating life. Evelyn Waugh, when he saw their house in 1930, described it as 'superbly ill-furnished. Anglicans can never achieve this ruthless absence of "good taste".'[22] Priests were chosen on the score of their ability and wisdom as preachers, confessors and instructors. There were men in the Society, like Fr D'Arcy's cousin Yap Walton, who were known for the aplomb with which they moved in the best circles, but they were not normally posted to Farm Street. When Cardinal Vaughan was made Archbishop of Westminster in 1892 the Province could have scored an easy success by bringing his brother, who was already gaining a reputation as a preacher, to London; instead he was kept in Manchester, even after he won the favour of the Prince of Wales and other royal personages by his preaching at Cannes, and it was not until after the Prince had succeeded as King Edward VII and interposed his influence that Farm Street acquired its brilliant ornament. Fr Vaughan himself was happier teaching a catechism class of East End urchins than attending the drawing rooms of his Mayfair admirers.

The Superior of Farm Street from 1926 to 1934, Fr Roy Steuart, an elegant, witty descendant of an old Scottish family, might have seemed specially chosen for an apostolate to high society, but he was also a notable writer on the mystical life and a valued director of souls. Fr D'Arcy knew him already from his time in charge of the lay Philosophers at Stonyhurst from 1908 to 1916, and he developed a close friendship with him. The Community at Farm Street boasted some scholars of high reputation, foremost among them Fr Herbert Thurston, who at this time was crossing swords with his Stonyhurst contemporary Conan Doyle over his gullible attitude to Spiritualism. Fr Thurston's life-work of debunking pious legends prompted the story of a dying Provincial who called him to his bedside to plead, 'Father, one last prayer before I die: leave us at least the doctrine of the Trinity.' The intellectual integrity of his work was the counterpart of an austere sense of duty and personal self-discipline.

Fr D'Arcy rejoiced to be back in the saintly company of his Prefect of Juniors, Archbishop Alban Goodier, who had just resigned the see of Bombay. Another priest who was no stranger to him was his old Master of Rhetoric, Fr Keating, a fellow Hopkins enthusiast, and now in full flow as an excellent editor of *The Month*. A third, from the same period of his life, was Fr Frank Woodlock, with whom he developed his closest friendship. Fr Woodlock was a handsome man of charm and of combative instinct which made him a vigorous and winning polemicist. He was not in the same league as Fr Martindale, whose incisive ability to communicate with the contemporary mind had by now won him a national reputation as a writer and an early star of the BBC's religious broadcasting. Among the younger men was the irrepressible Fr Frank Devas, who in thirty years at Farm Street established himself as a much-loved spiritual director. The newly-ordained Fr James Brodrick was the latest accession to the house's roll of talent, and was beginning his life's work of learned but popular biographies of figures such as St Ignatius Loyola and St Robert Bellarmine. By any standards these were vintage years at Farm Street, and in old age Fr D'Arcy looked back to the period with pardonable nostalgia.

The house possessed a good library which besides serving its own scholars was open to the public, and it was no doubt one scene of Fr D'Arcy's studies. He launched himself into a strenuous writing activity; in 1927 he published a booklet, *Catholicism*, which seems intended as a little informative manual like the *Catholic Truth Society* pamphlets, but which is a remarkable contribution to that genre. Though the latter part is less inspired, the first half of the work is one of his most magnificent pieces of writing, setting out in exalted prose his view of the supernatural, of human and divine love, of the redemptive Sacrifice and of the Mystical Body.

Fr D'Arcy joined the London Society for the Study of Religion, a circle in which the name of Baron von Hügel, who had died in 1925, was held in high honour. He also got to know Hügel's niece, Gwen Plunket Greene, who became a Catholic at this time and in 1928 published Hügel's letters to her. She was accepted as a distinguished member of the Catholic intelligentsia, and was the mother of a band of glamorous children who were to be part of Evelyn Waugh's inspiration for the Flytes in *Brideshead Revisited*.

Another body Fr D'Arcy joined was the Aristotelian Society, to whom he delivered his first paper in May 1927; characteristically, he provoked a lively discussion, in which he was able to sit back while his opponents fought out their own differences among them. An article of his had been published in April by the philosophical *Hibbert Journal*; another appeared in the American journal *Thought*; he attacked Bertrand Russell in *The Month* in August 1927, and in September, besides contributing to a correspondence in *The Times* on the nature of the mind, he made his debut in *The Criterion*. This was a journal which T.S. Eliot had founded to promote his traditional and Christian approach in the artistic field, and Fr D'Arcy defended the Thomist philosophy against misrepresentation by John

Middleton Murry. He was introduced to Eliot by Henry John and found that they had been contemporaries at Oxford in 1914–15, when Eliot had Harold Joachim as a tutor.

Henry John had stayed on at the Gregorian for a second year. In the summer of 1926 he made a pilgrimage to Manresa in Spain with Christopher Devlin, who then entered the novitiate at Roehampton. It seems that Fr D'Arcy visited Henry John in Rome in the winter of 1926-7, and Tom Burns, who was his travelling companion, was given a typical glimpse of his priestly passion. He refused to make the journey by train non-stop because that would have meant missing his daily Mass. He insisted on staying overnight in Paris and Milan, and the two sallied out fasting in the cold early mornings to find a church where Fr D'Arcy could say Mass, before resuming their journey. Tom Burns then went on a trek with Henry John to Tripoli and Tunisia, where they blended into the scene by donning Arab dress. In that costume they returned to London and finally succeeded in embarrassing Fr D'Arcy by springing themselves upon him in the decorous setting of Farm Street.[23] Henry joined Christopher Devlin in the novitiate in September 1927, while Tom Burns settled in London and in May of the following year launched a little review called *Order*, in which the young Catholic talents of the day launched gadfly attacks on established opinion.

Farm Street helped to introduce Fr D'Arcy to a cultivated world in which he was soon moving with a growing circle of acquaintance. One of the leading friends of the church was Lady Catherine Ashburnham, who in 1924 had inherited the estate of her father, the sixth and last Earl of Ashburnham; she was still in her thirties at this time, but remained unmarried and was the last of her family. It was the custom for priests from Farm Street to go down to act as chaplains at her great house of Ashburnham Place in Sussex, which had a magnificent collection of paintings. Fr D'Arcy became a frequent visitor and a friend of his patroness, who shared his keen interest in her collection. This friendship was an early step in his increasing immersion in the artistic world, from which he eventually was able to bring leading figures to add to the Ashburnham circle. In the thirties Lady Catherine was delighted one week-end when he brought down with him Sir Edwin Lutyens and Captain Robert Langton-Douglas, the latter an ex-Director of the Dublin National Gallery who was regarded as Bernard Berenson's principal rival and as the leading authority on Sienese art.

Acquaintances from a more Bohemian milieu included Augustus John, whom Henry took him to see in 1927, just before he became a novice; but no real friendship developed at least before 1935. A closer relation was that with Eric Gill, whom Fr D'Arcy could soon claim as something of a disciple; he cited Gill's book *Art Nonsense* in his own *St Thomas*

Aquinas (1930) as an example of the trend back towards form and order in contemporary art. In turn Eric Gill's *The Necessity of Belief* leant on Fr D'Arcy's *The Nature of Belief* (1931). Together with the artist and poet David Jones, who also soon came within the D'Arcy circle, Gill represented a radical movement drawing its inspiration from Catholic doctrine, from Maritain's Thomist analysis of art and from the mediaeval past. Its stricter votaries formed an arts-and-crafts community at Ditchling Common, dressing in smocks and excommunicating the twentieth century.

At the end of his biennium year, in October 1927, Fr D'Arcy was sent to Oxford, but he kept a room at Farm Street for the vacations. He became the first member of Campion Hall to lecture for the Greats syllabus, beginning a course of lectures on Theories of Knowledge in the academic year 1927-8. As Campion Hall was not equipped for public lectures he taught at Balliol, where Francis Urquhart was now Dean and Senior Tutor. Fr D'Arcy continued to lecture on epistemology and ethics and on Aristotle throughout his time in Oxford, and gave special seminars on St Thomas Aquinas.

Campion Hall had expanded somewhat since Fr D'Arcy's absence: its undergraduates remained at the same number of ten, and in 1927 included Michael de la Bedoyère, then finishing the Greats course; in the following year however he left the Society. There were now eight graduate members of the Hall in residence, of whom seven were priests. The Master was Fr D'Arcy's old Prefect of Studies from Stonyhurst, Fr Ernest Vignaux, who was far from thinking himself by merit raised to that bad eminence. After a year in the post he had got over the extreme domestic diffidence with which he began, but he lived in terror of the academic wolves lurking beyond his front door; Fr D'Arcy must have tried him sorely with his policy of opening up the Hall to the university by inviting members of all ranks to taste its hospitality. Fr Vignaux sought to keep himself abreast of modern culture by reading P.G. Wodehouse, and liked to share discovered pearls with his brethren, but he confessed himself baffled when Fr D'Arcy tried to bring Hopkins within his horizon.

The Catholic presence in Oxford was more substantial than a dozen years before, and it had gained particular prestige through the chaplaincy of Mgr Ronald Knox. As the most brilliant undergraduate of his generation and a rising star of the Anglo-Catholic party when Chaplain of Trinity, he had been a notable convert to the Catholic Church, and his appointment as university Chaplain in 1926 was the result of some inspired wire-pulling by Francis Urquhart, who thus handed over his thirty-year leadership in Catholic Oxford; by 1932 he was too ill to teach, and he died in 1934. Mgr Knox was much loved by a generation of undergraduates, to whom he was always 'Ronnie'. For all Fr D'Arcy's superiority in skills more attractive to the young, like comparing the merits of the film stars of the day, nobody ever called him Martin. Knox had a wit which was not reserved to the cut-and-thrust of high-table conversation, as when he exclaimed to an Irish priest who was pouring him a triple whisky, 'Whoa! I'm only a convert.' It is not recorded whether Fr D'Arcy was the intermediary in his meeting with Sir Edwin Lutyens. It was Lutyens's habit on such occasions to make some quite pointless remark and watch the surprise of his interlocutor; on this occasion he came out with: 'Did you know that when you chop vegetables the temperature rises?' 'Yes,' replied Knox without batting an eyelid, 'and when you cut acquaintances there's a coolness.' Ronald Knox remained the product of Balliol and his donnish past, with a very Oxford reticence and shyness about him which sometimes found Fr D'Arcy's more extrovert brilliance rather alarming. One of the forms his self-effacement took was to refuse to instruct would-be converts among his admirers, and priests like Fr D'Arcy to whom they were passed on perhaps gained an inflated reputation as fishers of Oxford men.

A venture emanating from the chaplaincy was the Catholic Evidence Society, which had been begun a year before. Fr D'Arcy quickly took this over and renamed it more stylishly the Cardinal Pole Society. He ran it on something of the same lines as the Popinjay at Stonyhurst, though its aims were more doctrinal. The meetings, which were held at Magdalen, began with a talk on some aspect of Catholic belief given by a member, and Fr D'Arcy would then lead a cross-examination of the speaker, which would develop into general discussion.[24]

From the start however Fr D'Arcy had no thought of limiting himself to his Catholic or his curricular duties. He immediately joined the university Poetry Society, which was then in a period of exceptional brilliance. Among its members were W.H. Auden, who was in his last year reading English at Christ Church, Louis MacNeice, in his second year, and Stephen Spender, who came up in 1927. Cecil Day-Lewis had just gone down but was teaching for a year at Summerfields and still visited his old haunts. Fr D'Arcy's chief contribution was to introduce Oxford to Gerard Manley Hopkins, who until now had received so little attention that Bridges' edition of his poems, though published in 1918, was not sold out till twelve years later. Auden was an immediate devotee, both of Hopkins's poetry and of his religious ideas.

Oxford at this time had a number of striking figures among its younger dons, such as Maurice Bowra, whom his circle regarded as *Stupor Mundi*, or G.A. Kolkhorst, who, fortified with a private income, conducted a rival salon in Beaumont Street; but Louis MacNeice wrote of Fr D'Arcy: 'he alone among Oxford dons seemed to me to have the glamour that medieval students looked for in their masters. Intellect incarnate in a beautiful head, wavy grey hair and delicate features; a hawk's eyes. I suspected his religion, of course, but it at least, I thought, has given him a *savoir faire* which you do not find in these wishy-washy humanists; it was a treat to watch him carving a dish of game.'[25] This admiration of Fr D'Arcy was general among the poets, and he was called upon to review the annual anthology of *Oxford Poetry* which they published. They also discovered that he would put up with a great deal of good-natured teasing. The Poetry Society had close links with the Christ Church Essay Society, into which Fr D'Arcy was also inducted. This led to a friendship with Professor F.A. Lindemann, later Lord Cherwell and Churchill's scientific adviser in the war, who at this time was engaged in his brilliant but controversial work of raising the Clarendon Laboratory into an institute of international reputation. The meeting between them was thus described by Fr D'Arcy:

> I promised a paper to the Essay Society at Christ Church and forgot all about it. A few days before it was due Wystan Auden and some others called to remind me. Wystan told me to my dismay that they had billed me to talk on 'Freedom and Authority in Religion.' I said it was controversial; I could not do it, so then they said laughingly – 'You must because we have invited Canon Rawlinson [the chaplain of Christ Church], Jacob and Prof. Lindemann who is a strong atheist and the rudest man in Oxford. He will keep you in order.' It was an amusing and satisfying evening for me because to my surprise the Prof sided with me throughout and mocked those who attacked me. I said: 'I was told you would be so opposed to my point of view; I want to thank you.' He answered: 'Father, your position is impregnable, granted the major premise of the existence of God. And what are we poor scientists to know about that?'[26]

The Poetry Society used to invite well-known personages to address it, including at this time Edith Sitwell and Eric Gill, though the latter failed to impress. Fr D'Arcy brought along one of his discoveries, Georges Cattaui, a Catholic convert and diplomat at the Egyptian Embassy who was an authority on Proust, a figure whom he greatly resembled. To Fr D'Arcy he owed his introduction to various circles of English literary society. Later, in the thirties, Vita Sackville West was much in contact with the Poetry Society while her two sons were at Balliol; she was at that time keenly interested in Catholicism and became a life-long friend of Fr D'Arcy's.

When he arrived in Oxford, undergraduates up from Stonyhurst formed a natural first point of contact for Fr D'Arcy. Quintin Gwyn, in his last year at Balliol, immediately started coming round to see him. Bernard Wall came up to Brasenose in 1927 and valued him as an exponent of the neo-Thomism which was beginning to dominate his interests; he spent hundreds of hours with Fr D'Arcy in his room at Campion Hall, while he rolled his cigarettes, or over numerous lunches and dinners discussing St Thomas, St Augustine and the Fathers, and talking about art.[27] One of the first things Wall did on arriving at Oxford was to join the Distributist Society, whose principles were those which Belloc and Chesterton were disseminating in the more radical Catholic circles at the time, inspiring the Ditchling Common experiment. The Distributists at Oxford were a sleepy bunch in 1927, and Wall lost no time in becoming their president and transforming the society. His distributism was evidently of the less demotic school, for when he started inviting figures like Chesterton, Dean Inge and Galsworthy to address the club he dined them in white tie and tails, and in fact the Distributists soon lost touch with their original objects. One day Wall came to Fr D'Arcy and begged him to come to the next meeting since his committee had invited Bertrand Russell as the speaker. Russell was then notorious especially for his attacks on Christian marital ethics, and was considered a very dangerous man. Fr D'Arcy blenched at taking on such a foe, but at the meeting was able to reply to Russell's attacks on European treatment of coloured peoples, framed on high moral grounds, by pointing out that by Russell's own philosophy ethical principles were merely an individual's private feelings and he had no right to expect others to share them. This was an inconsistency in Russell's position to which neither then nor at any later time in his impassioned career was he able to provide an answer.[28]

Fr D'Arcy also set himself to enlarge the horizons of the young Jesuits at Campion Hall itself. One of them was Tom Corbishley, a brilliant classicist but imbued from his Lancashire upbringing with a contempt and ignorance of Protestants and public-school boys. To cure him, Fr D'Arcy got the Master to invite two leading specimens of those categories to a meal at the Hall. The guests were two Old Etonians, Quintin Hogg, now Lord Hailsham,* and his friend Richard Best, whose father was a Lord Justice in Ulster and a prominent Orangeman. Lord Hailsham recalls that when he received this invitation in the Trinity term of 1928 he had never heard of Campion Hall; Fr D'Arcy, though, knew him from the Christ Church Essay Society, including the meeting where Prof Lindemann became his ally.

The impression Fr D'Arcy made on Quintin Hogg he described as follows: 'the only adjective which really serves, God save the mark, is Mephistophelean, aquiline, dark, handsome, with a friendly but apparently sinister grin, redeemed, but only at a second glance, by gentleness and compassion.' The outcome of the friendship thus initiated might have justified the wildest diatribes against Jesuit cunning: Richard Best was

*His father had just become Lord Chancellor under that title in March 1928.

received by Fr D'Arcy into the Catholic Church, outraging his family traditions. Quintin Hogg was an agnostic when he crossed the Campion Hall threshold, since, though brought up in an Anglican milieu, he could not take the intellectual basis of Christianity seriously. His conversations with Fr D'Arcy changed that. Not only did he discover the philosophical foundations of Christian belief, but he entered a friendship of subtle and enduring influence, in which the world of the spirit and the love of good were the almost imperceptible background. 'Exactly how Martin D'Arcy manages to convey the lessons he teaches me,' wrote Quintin Hogg years later, 'I have never been able to discover.' He remained a devout Anglican, but he found in Fr D'Arcy, uniquely, a depth of spiritual insight that made him turn to him in the hardest moral trials of his life.[29]

Quintin Hogg's impression of Fr D'Arcy is echoed by Elizabeth Harman (now Lady Longford), who was in her second year at Oxford and came from a strictly Nonconformist and sceptical background. 'My introduction to the Revd Martin d'Arcy, SJ, took place at a Balliol lunch party. His elegant figure, dark wavy hair, aristocratic features, intent eyes and air of subtle sophistication immediately made me think of Mephistopheles – a character who in any case I tended to equate with all but the untidiest priests. But when, at the end of lunch, Father d'Arcy politely offered me my coat back to front so that I could not get into the sleeves, I realized that I had got him wrong.'[30]

Also in her second year was Lady Helen Asquith, grand-daughter of the former prime minister. Her mother, Katharine, the widow of Raymond Asquith, had already become a Catholic and had brought with her into the Church her young son (the inheritor of H.H. Asquith's earldom on his death in 1928). Helen however did not take that step until this year, and on Mgr Ronald Knox's advice began attending Fr D'Arcy's seminars, which like others she found extremely stimulating.* From this meeting developed Fr D'Arcy's close friendship with the Asquith family, and another link with the artistic world. Katharine Asquith's mother, Lady Horner, owned the beautiful Manor House at Mells in Somerset, a property of the Horners since the Reformation. She was herself the grand-daughter of the Glasgow millionaire William Graham, and inherited his notable collection of Italian and Pre-Raphaelite paintings. Her hospitality, in Evelyn Waugh's description, 'was at the same time informal, illustrious and affectionate',[31] and she entertained a wide circle of artists and writers, whose works added to the attractions of Mells; so far, however, she had maintained a resolute ban against Catholics (she showed an unexpectedly Orange resentment at the Asquiths' migration into the

---

* She was a first cousin of Quintin Hogg, but both declare that this had nothing to do with the latter's getting to know Fr D'Arcy.

Church). It was one of the triumphs of Fr D'Arcy's charm, as will be seen, to find the means of penetrating this sanctum.

At Oxford in the twenties and thirties the more aristocratic undergraduates kept up the social habits of the Edwardian era, and freely held lunches and dinners for their friends and for the more lively among the dons. There was some competition to secure interesting guests, and Fr D'Arcy was much in demand. For such young men and women he possessed a unique fascination, in which charm and an unassuming enjoyment of youthful company formed the first bond. He was interested in what they had to say and would thrust his head forward to listen with a piercing gaze under bushy brows, then throw his head back to savour the speech as if locating an elusive vintage. An American journalist once described his mannerism in these words: 'Father D'Arcy has remarkable eyes, which seem to be trying to penetrate an interviewer's thoughts at one moment, and appear to turn inward the next as he weighs the answer to a question.'[32] It was not a show but an expression of his interest in individuals and instinct for drawing the best out of them. Lord Longford has identified a further strand in his fame when he writes: 'The cleverest undergraduates who took Greats (ancient history and Philosophy) were inclined to be intellectually snobbish, if they will forgive the word. They admired sheer intellect, most of all dialectical intellect.'[33] The appearance of this swordsman who could engage in rapier-work with the best adversaries of his day was fashionable news in such circles. And beyond all this was an aura of mystery, a sense that the charm and the brilliance were not just froth, but that beneath there was a religious steel and a spiritual knowledge which would take an enquirer as deep as he wished to plunge.

The years when Ronald Knox and Fr D'Arcy were together at Oxford were a golden age for Catholicism in the university, in which they represented a new phase in the Catholic presence there. Hitherto the Catholic dons, Francis Urquhart and Professor de Zulueta, had kept a scrupulous discretion vis-à-vis the outer world. They both indeed, and Urquhart especially, rendered priceless quiet service to their Church, but they belonged to a generation in which Catholic gentlemen were reticent about their religion and appreciative of the courtesy of the established order in making a place for them. There was a touch of that attitude in Ronald Knox, but he knew the Anglican world from within, and had ridiculed its confusion of mind too keenly not to be a challenge to it even while he deflected would-be converts. In one way Fr D'Arcy was less of a polemicist; he never criticised the Protestant Churches, but his acute mind saw in post-war England a vacuum which only Catholicism could fill. His lunchings-out gave him a web of imperceptible influence, so that when young men and women turned to him he could support them with the firmness they were looking for.

Fr D'Arcy was extending his contacts outside Oxford, and among the earliest was the artist and novelist Percy Wyndham Lewis, one of the most controversial figures of the contemporary intellectual scene. Lewis is virtually forgotten today, though in 1955 T.S. Eliot called him 'the most distinguished living novelist'. His opinions were a violent medley of the ultra-modern and the ultra-reactionary which at first did not earn Fr D'Arcy's respect; but in 1927 he published *Time and Western Man*, attacking among other things the contemporary cult of time, or delusion that the truth of a philosophy was to be judged by its modernity. In a review in *The Month* for December 1927, Fr D'Arcy hailed it as 'one of the most significant books of the age', an example of the reaction against production-line modernity which he himself was preaching. He sent Lewis a copy of the review, saying of the book, 'I do a certain amount of propaganda for it here in Oxford and find people awake or awakening to your point of view.' Lewis wrote back proposing a meeting, and a friendship developed of which Lewis's charcoal portrait of Fr D'Arcy, drawn in 1932, was a product.[34] In the early thirties Lewis discovered the Nazis as an aristocracy of intellect and started contributing to Mosley's Fascist journal. These were leads that drew Fr D'Arcy as little as the Ditchling Common enthusiasts did, but they may be counted among the influences which Henry John suffered to his harm.

Fr D'Arcy also got to know G.K. Chesterton, Hilaire Belloc and Maurice Baring, the literary triumvirate of English Catholicism. From the particular bias of his friendships, in which Baring took first place, it seems that they may have come through Ronald Knox. He and Maurice Baring were long-standing members of the circle of the beautiful Lady Lovat, to whose entourage Fr D'Arcy was soon recruited, becoming a frequent guest at Beaufort Castle in Inverness-shire, where the Lovat estate amounted to a principality. As a Jacobite family the Lovats earned his special approbation, and Lady Lovat and he had breathed the same air in youth; a daughter of the last Lord Ribblesdale, she had been growing up within a few miles of Stonyhurst during the same years that Martin D'Arcy was there. On her marriage to Lord Lovat at the age of eighteen she had adopted her husband's Faith and became the centre of an intellectual and stylish Catholic circle.

Fr D'Arcy used to go down every year for Maurice Baring's bachelor week-ends at Half-Way House in Rottingdean. A bond between them was their devotion to the memory of Mary Queen of Scots, the subject of Baring's *In My End Is My Beginning*, published in 1931, and Baring had some indirect Jesuit connections. Raymond de Trafford, a cousin of Fr Robert de Trafford, and a well-known figure in twenties and thirties society, was a close friend. Maurice's niece Daphne Baring had recently married Arthur Pollen, nephew of the Jesuit scholar John Hungerford

Pollen; she painted Maurice Baring's private chapel at Rottingdean and was later to paint the memorial chapel to Francis Urquhart at the new Campion Hall, the crucifix of the altar being modelled by her husband.

An old diplomatic friend of Maurice Baring's was Sir Esmé Howard, at this time engaged in his outstanding service as British Ambassador in Washington. He belonged to a branch of the family of the Dukes of Norfolk which had become Protestant two generations before, but had been converted by Cardinal Merry del Val. Sir Esmé returned in 1930 as Lord Howard of Penrith, and likewise became a good friend of Fr D'Arcy's, enlisting him in his favourite cause of promoting good relations between English and American Catholics. The Howards were active in the Catholic intellectual scene, and Sir Esmé's sons, went on from Oxford in the twenties to figure in the journalistic circle of Tom Burns and Douglas Woodruff.

Other Catholic friends of Maurice Baring were the Herberts of Pixton, in Somerset. Mary Herbert and her three young daughters were celebrated in his epigram:[35]

> Three Graces – and the Mother were a Grace
> But for profounder meaning in her face.

The eldest daughter, Gabriel, was to earn Fr D'Arcy's approval by driving ambulances for the Nationalists in Spain in the Civil War, and in 1937 he performed the marriage of the youngest, Laura, to his own convert Evelyn Waugh. Their grandmother was Lady de Vesci, who in her youth had been a famous beauty and one of the 'Souls'. When Mary Herbert became a Catholic she was anxious that her mother should follow her, but the atavistic suspicions of the Irish Protestant Ascendancy, which Lady de Vesci inherited, were too strong. When Fr D'Arcy, at Mary Herbert's request, approached the question she drew back, and he dropped it. Some years later Mary Herbert rang Fr D'Arcy up at Farm Street, where he was for the vacation, to tell him that her mother was dying of double pneumonia. He hurried out to Lady de Vesci at Windsor and was greeted with the words, 'Oh, Father, I'm so glad you've come. Will you receive me into the Catholic Church?' In fact she lived several years longer, dying in 1939 well into her eighties.[36] With the Asquiths of Mells, the Herberts gave Fr D'Arcy a footing in the West Country for which, perhaps remembering his unclouded early childhood, he formed a lasting affection, and he made almost yearly visits to Pixton and Mells throughout his life.

Pixton may have been the setting of the anecdote Quintin Hogg told as an example of Fr D'Arcy's gift of delicate rebuke: 'I remember asking him rather brashly at a country house where we were both staying what

God would think of me if I uttered a blasphemy. "Surely He would not," I was arguing, "pay much attention, seeing that I am as small as I am, seeing that He is as great as He is." "I expect," said Fr D'Arcy, "He would think of you exactly as you are".[37] A more rueful memory of an undergraduate stay at Pixton was when, during a shoot, he bagged a pet black and white rabbit which strayed in front of the beaters, a story on which Fr D'Arcy mischievously dined out for years.

Fr D'Arcy was making numerous converts at Oxford among current and recent undergraduates. Among the latter was Robert Speaight, who was in the first years of a remarkable acting career, and who delayed his reception till 1930, largely, he says, out of 'a horror of fashionable conversions.' Anne Jackson, a member of the Poetry Society, was received by Fr D'Arcy before she went down that same year; as Anne Fremantle she became the centre of a largely English literary circle in America and kept in touch with Fr D'Arcy all her life. Other converts, including the Wykehamist classical scholar Douglas Carter and the future novelist Jimmy Oliver, were passed on by Fr D'Arcy to join Tom Burns's work on *Order* and at Sheed and Ward. On a more social level he brought followers like W.H. Auden, Stephen Spender, Robert Speaight and Georges Cattaui to Burns's parties and regular Saturday lunches in London.[38]

The Dominicans appeared in Oxford in 1929 with the opening of Blackfriars, just across the road from Campion Hall. The first Prior, Fr Bernard Delany, an old boy of the Jesuit college of Stamford Hill, was already well known to Fr D'Arcy as the editor of the journal *Blackfriars*, to which he had been contributing for some years, and they got on well. When in 1932 Fr Delany changed places with the illustrious Fr Bede Jarrett as Provincial, one imagines that the new Prior, who had been at Stonyhurst just before Martin D'Arcy, must have been even more welcome, but Fr Jarrett died eighteen months later. Fr D'Arcy continued to have dealings with his fellow Thomists at Blackfriars, such as Gervase Mathew, but Robert Speaight considered that there was a surprising lack of contact between these two centres of Catholic Oxford. He attributed it to the criticism which Fr Vincent MacNabb had made of Fr de la Taille's theory of the Mass in the Dominican journal, an attack which Fr D'Arcy found unforgivable.[39] As far as his view of Fr MacNabb goes that may be true, since the Dominican's articles are less than generous, combining a jejuneness of thought with a peremptory assumption of his own superior competence as a theologian; but they had appeared as early as 1924 (one of them cheek-by-jowl with an article of Fr D'Arcy's), and the latter seems to have been able to contain his resentment of the rival order for a decade or so.

Alan Pryce-Jones tells us of a verse which used to be circulated by the Dominicans:[40]

Are you rich and nobly born?
Is your soul with sorrow torn?
Come, and we shall find a way:
I'm Martin D'Arcy, sir, SJ.

Various other rhymes of the same tenor were in vogue at the time, aided by the facility of rhyming D'Arcy with classy. It is relevant to comment that the Dominicans, having no prominent public school under their management, lacked the opportunities of the Jesuits and Benedictines to gain aristocratic adherents. As it would be out of the question to attribute envy to these devout men, we may suppose that here was a case of distance lending awe to the view of Fr D'Arcy's conquests. Undoubtedly for a Catholic priest Fr D'Arcy's life among the rich and nobly-born was exceptional; one might cite other clerical aristocrats like Abbot Sir David Hunter Blair, but they lacked the brilliance and spiritual power to make their social round look like an apostolate. Most Catholic clergy either were too intimidated or lacked the social inclinations to hobnob with the fashionable. Fr D'Arcy had a lively taste for society without as well as with a capital S; but his preferred style of talk was inevitably more at home among the sophisticated. One can see this style in his books, elevated, well-read, allusive, quick-witted, viewing life from a pinnacle, and escaping all forms of parochialism, including the kind of class parochialism betrayed by the Dominican ditty.

The long Oxford vacations allowed Fr D'Arcy to keep a foot in the Farm Street camp, where his ally was Fr Frank Woodlock. In 1928 they held a series of weekly pulpit dialogues on the subject of Immortality at which by the final day it was impossible to find standing room in the church. Of the converts who came Fr D'Arcy's way through his work at Farm Street the most famous was Evelyn Waugh, who was referred to him in July 1930 by Olivia Plunket Greene, great-niece of Friedrich von Hügel. The wide-eyed, rosebud-mouthed Olivia had succeeded her elder brother Richard in the undergraduate attachment which Waugh had formed for him, and he described himself as having fallen in love with the entire family. On July 2nd 1930 his diary records: 'To tea at Alexander Square with Olivia. I said would she please find a Jesuit to instruct me.'

As this entry suggests, Evelyn Waugh knew exactly what he wanted. The success of *Decline and Fall* and *Vile Bodies* had brought him affluence and made him, at the age of twenty-six, the darling of cocktail-party society; but he was in a state of spiritual disorientation through the break-up of his first marriage. His ruthless mind saw no answer to his plight save in the Catholic Church. 'Blue chin and fine, slippery mind,' was the impression he recorded on July 8th, after his first session with Fr D'Arcy. One biographer has suggested (Waugh himself would hardly have enjoyed the comparison) that his dry, even simplistic approach to Catholic doctrine was the model for Rex Mottram's comical conversion in *Brideshead Revisited*; but the cases are far apart. Waugh was familiar from boyhood with Christian teaching; what he needed was to have a feeble presentation of it given the force and clarity he found lacking; he was not looking for moral uplift. What Fr D'Arcy said of him, 'It was a special pleasure to make contact with so able a brain',[41] was a tribute which he could have reciprocated. On September 29th Fr D'Arcy received him into the Church in a fittingly understated ceremony at Farm Street.

No more than a few words are needed to refute the often-repeated identification of Fr D'Arcy as the original of Father Rothschild in *Vile Bodies*. Simple chronology makes this an impossibility: *Vile Bodies* was published six months before Waugh met Fr D'Arcy, and so far from its being based on any personal knowledge of Jesuits, Waugh seems to have imagined that a Jesuit Rothschild might have the odd family million tucked away. Moreover in 1930 Fr D'Arcy was a decade or more off from the habits that could have made Father Rothschild an apt caricature. Travel in privileged or even ordinary conditions was not yet part of his life; his circle were cultivated people at Oxford or in country houses, and so far from belonging to a family of millionaires he hardly yet knew any.*

To aid his integration into the Church Fr D'Arcy encouraged Waugh's friendship with various Oxonian Catholics such as the old Downside boy Douglas Woodruff, who was becoming known as the wittiest of the sub-editors on *The Times*, and Christopher Hollis, whose conversion had taken place some years before. Hollis was teaching at Stonyhurst, where Waugh began to spend some time, and the experience is said to have stimulated his interest in the Recusant tradition which he expressed in *Edmund Campion* and in his later novels. Waugh for his part gave Fr D'Arcy more of a social whirl than most of his converts were probably good for. His diary records lunching with him and Frank Pakenham at the Savile Club eleven days after his instruction began, with another luncheon party the next day at the St James's Club including Fr D'Arcy, Lord David Cecil (then a young Fellow of Wadham) and Georges Cattaui.

A sequel to Waugh's conversion came in early 1933, after the publication of *Black Mischief*. *The Tablet*, traditionally the leading Catholic

---

* One passage in *Vile Bodies* might seem to point to an Oxford figure, where Father Rothschild reminds Adam Fenwick-Symes: 'We met at Oxford five years ago at luncheon with the Dean of Balliol.' But Evelyn Waugh regarded Urquhart as the archetypal upper-class Catholic influence-monger, and had impersonated him in a farcical film turning on a plot to lure the Prince of Wales into the Church.

periodical in England, had been since 1920 under the editorship of Ernest Oldmeadow, a convert of Nonconformist origins who had been appointed by the paper's proprietor, the uninspired Cardinal Bourne. Under Oldmeadow *The Tablet* rapidly sank to the tone of a parish magazine. He launched a typically foolish attack on Waugh's book, denouncing it as blasphemous and obscene. His assumption that he was his Church's authoritative mouthpiece was not shared by the leading Catholic writers, who had long deserted *The Tablet* and on this occasion found his silliness a final provocation. The editor was astonished to receive a letter in support of Waugh from eight of the most distinguished contemporary figures in the Church, including Fr D'Arcy, Fr Martindale and Fr Steuart.★

Three years later Cardinal Bourne died and his successor sold *The Tablet* to a consortium consisting of George Pollen, Douglas Woodruff and Tom Burns, the last of whom had made his opinion of the old management clear in the pages of *Order*. Oldmeadow was retired, and under the long editorship of Douglas Woodruff *The Tablet* fully recovered its reputation. If it was sweet revenge for Evelyn Waugh, for Catholics at large it was a relief to see their leading organ of opinion once again fit for an educated readership.

The lesson of this incident is not that Fr D'Arcy subordinated decency to artistic freedom. An entry in Waugh's diary for July 12th 1931 shows the limits of his tolerance: 'I took Father d'Arcy to luncheon at the Ritz & there he saw Hamish [St Clair-Erskine] with Susan Carnegie so that shocked him so then Wanda [Baillie-Hamilton] came & kissed me a lot & that shocked him.' What he found shocking in these sights is not explained, but in matters of propriety Fr D'Arcy was essentially the product of the upbringing which he had received at Stonyhurst, and which he shared with all other Catholics of his generation. Quintin Hogg gives us another example from what he called a 'Rabelaisian encounter' between Marie Stopes and the chaplain of Christ Church a few years earlier, in which Fr D'Arcy intervened: 'He said what every young man, Christian and pagan, should understand in connection with sexual matters, that in all things connected with bodily conduct a certain reticence and a certain delicacy and even fastidiousness was indispensable to civilised behaviour.'[42]

Through Evelyn Waugh Fr D'Arcy met his Oxford contemporary Lord Clonmore, the heir of the Earl of Wicklow and thus representative

---

★ In the ensuing controversy Oldmeadow had the crassness to print a letter in his support from Marie Stopes, who was regarded as beyond the pale by all decent-minded folk. Her attitude was due to the fact that she had been irreverently handled by Waugh in *Black Mischief*.

of a great Irish Protestant family. In their undergraduate days Waugh
had already discerned a Christian piety 'hidden behind his stylish eccentricities',[43] and he had since taken Anglican orders. He resigned the
curacy he held in Somers Town in 1930 and was received into the
Catholic Church the following year. Fr D'Arcy also introduced him to
the group of young Catholic journalists around Tom Burns, and
Clonmore took to that water to such duck-like effect that by 1937 he
was editor of the *Dublin Review*.

Evelyn Waugh records in his diary for July 23rd 1936: 'Dinner
Travellers' Club: Billy [Clonmore], Chris [Hollis], D'Arcy; jolly evening.'
Three months later he went to speak to the Catholic undergraduates at
Cambridge, where Alfred Gilbey was in the early years of his very
popular chaplaincy, and (October 18th): 'Found sherry party including
Father D'Arcy at Father Gilbey's.'

The 'slippery mind' that Waugh noted on his first meeting with Fr
D'Arcy was partly a reference to a habit of conversation which darted
from argument to illustration and from parallel to allusion, sometimes to
the bafflement of his hearers; partly perhaps it suggested the mercurial
temper with which Fr D'Arcy ran classical order and romantic brio in
puzzling harness. By 1936 Waugh was using another word for it; he went
to Pixton for Christmas with the Herberts and notes on Christmas Eve:
'Father D'Arcy came, very dotty.' And on December 27th: 'D'Arcy still
here and dottier.' When he married Laura Herbert four months later, his
comment suggests that conducting weddings was not a frequent duty of
members of Campion Hall; at the rehearsal with Fr D'Arcy and the other
celebrant, Fr More O'Ferrall, (April 13th 1937) he found: 'Both sensa-
tionally ignorant of simplest professional duties.' In Fr D'Arcy's
conversation, however, so Patrick O'Donovan tells us, this sabre-toothed
commentator was 'dear, gentle Evelyn'; and he adds that that was probably how Evelyn Waugh showed in Fr D'Arcy's company, so great and
civilised was his natural authority.[44]

To retreat to the early thirties, Fr D'Arcy struck up excellent relations
with Albert Einstein while he was living in Oxford, and he gained new
adherents among the undergraduates as the generations changed. Isaiah
Berlin of Corpus Christi, whom he was to describe as 'that extraordinary
genius',[45] became one of his closest friends after attending his Greats
lectures, and was a frequent visitor at Campion Hall, where his cultural
impact consisted in popularising Russian tiddlywinks among the
Community.[46] Another brilliant undergraduate was A.J. Ayer at Christ
Church. From the basis of a Jewish ancestry and an Etonian education he
had developed a militant atheism, and he chose Fr D'Arcy's afternoon
seminars as a battle-ground for it. The following is his account: 'Among
the very few classes that I attended for pleasure was one given by Father

D'Arcy. I think it was nominally about Thomas Aquinas, but it very soon developed into a running argument between him and me about the possibility of proving the existence of God. I do not remember how the audience reacted, though it must have been vexatious for those who wanted to learn something about Aquinas. If it was vexatious for Father D'Arcy he did not show it, and we remained on friendly terms ever since. Many years later I heard that he had described me to his convert Evelyn Waugh as the most dangerous man in Oxford, but if he really held this view he never allowed it to affect our personal relations.'[47] Equally, Fr D'Arcy never allowed friendship to soften his sense of the moral harm done by clever atheists like Ayer and Bertrand Russell.

Henry John became an undergraduate at Campion Hall in 1931, and a new phase in his friendship with Fr D'Arcy began. His life in the Society had already proved a strain, a growing conflict developing between the gypsy side of his nature and the severity of the religious life. The background of Augustus John's household, where troops of legitimate and illegitimate children roamed about naked, was a far cry from Jesuit discipline, and especially from the prim novitiate, where Fr Peers Smith sought to emulate Fr Considine's austerity without his spiritual genius. Henry John suffered great sexual turmoil, which Fr D'Arcy was not well qualified to help him over. By the time Henry went on to the Philosophate in 1929 his psychological balance was far from that of the exuberant schoolboy Fr D'Arcy had first known. It was intended that he and Christopher Devlin should come to Campion Hall together, but they quarrelled violently and the decision was taken to separate them.

Henry thus came to Campion Hall alone to read Philosophy, Politics and Economics, and here was another cause of contention. Fr D'Arcy had advised him against that School; he had not altered his belief that Oxford philosophy, especially when deprived of the saving grace of classical culture, would be bad for Henry John, and in the thirties he was growing increasingly critical of the direction of the university's philosophy as exemplified by Ayer and his Christ Church tutor Gilbert Ryle. Other influences on Henry John were perhaps more pernicious, for example that of Wyndham Lewis, who exemplified the 'passionate intensity' that was taking over the younger generation all over Europe. Fr Martindale wrote: 'Henry, I consider, spoilt himself by his idea that you could do nothing save by *violence*. Frankly I thought Henry John was becoming so neurotic that his sanity was in danger. This is not impressionism – I had reasons.'[48]

Fr D'Arcy was the recipient of letters which give colour to such fears: 'I cannot *stand* the idea of myself as introspective and hesitating when there are things to be done, souls to be saved.' This tortured attitude was not the spirit of chivalrous dedication with which the youthful Martin D'Arcy had faced his mission a few years earlier, and it was alien to his creed of order and harmony. He wrote back to Henry, worried over 'your periods of heats ... the temperature you rise to, the complications.'[49]

Chapter Four

Campion Hall

Campion Hall was rented from St John's College on a forty-year lease which was about to expire in 1936, and the college had given notice that it required the property for its own use. It was therefore decided to build a new Hall on the site owned by the Society on the other side of the Lamb and Flag. Fr Vignaux's approach to the problem of finding an architect was to enquire in Catholic clerical circles, where he was told of a Birmingham architect called Norris who had done work for Catholic houses. He was engaged to draw up plans, which were ready by the end of 1932 and provoked general dissatisfaction in the Senior Common Room.

In January 1933 Fr D'Arcy became Rector and Master of Campion Hall. It was an unusual time of the year to change superiors, but whether the appointment had anything to do with Fr Vignaux's uninspired rebuilding plans is not known.* At any rate Fr D'Arcy determined that the Society of Jesus should not bear the opprobrium of inflicting this piece of mediocrity on Oxford. He spoke to the director of Claridge's, Mr Gelardi, whose son he had known a few years before at Stonyhurst, and who condemned the plans on the grounds of practicality.[1] Fr D'Arcy next took the question to Katharine Asquith's mother, Lady Horner; his own account was that as an experienced hostess she could give an informed opinion on domestic matters. One is inclined to suspect that it was part of a plan to break down the suspicion she had so far shown towards him. 'I was the first priest she had ever allowed in her very beautiful house,' he observed with triumph. Lady Horner proved delighted to be consulted on such a matter, and Fr D'Arcy's charm carried all before it. His hostess got on the telephone to Sir Edwin Lutyens, who had done work for her at Mells a quarter of a century before and was on the best of terms with her, and it was arranged that Fr D'Arcy should go to see him.

Lutyens was hailed at this time as the greatest English architect since Wren (mainly, perhaps, by those who knew no other architect's name),

*Fr D'Arcy always used to give 1932 as the date of his taking office. Perhaps he had been notified in advance, but no reason is known for a delay in making the appointment effective.

77

and basked in the prestige of having designed the new imperial capital at Delhi. The aplomb with which Fr D'Arcy went to him for advice about an insignificant building was wholly characteristic. Lutyens also condemned the plans (he described them to the Architectural Association as 'Queen Anne in front, Mary Ann behind'). Fr D'Arcy invited him to Campion Hall for a night, and thought of a ruse whereby Lutyens would 'revise' Norris's plans and the latter would enjoy the glory of having designed a building in partnership with England's premier architect. But Norris would have none of it, holding that his existing drawings were beyond improvement. Fr D'Arcy left things as they were for the moment; he evidently decided that the only solution was to start afresh on a new site, which would give an excuse to discard Norris's plans. It may be that he was beginning to prefer the idea of a much more prominent building to that of an annexe at the back of the St Giles property. This large-minded approach was fully supported by the Provincial, Fr Henry Keane, himself a previous Master of Campion Hall (1921–6), and one of the ablest holders of that office.

Fr D'Arcy was fortunate in the men he had under him at Campion Hall. Academically the most brilliant was the Egyptologist Fr Eric Burrows, who had accompanied the Oxford and Chicago universities' expedition to Kish in 1924 and was the official cuneiformist for Sir Leonard Wooley's expedition to Ur in 1926. Fr D'Arcy had been a year behind him in the novitiate, and the affection he had for him suffered a harsh blow when Fr Burrows was killed in a car crash near Oxford in 1938. The Minister of the Hall (the Rector's deputy and household manager) was Fr Leslie Walker, who besides being an able philosopher was an extremely capable man of affairs and fully competent to take care of administrative details. As these were not among Fr D'Arcy's skills he was lucky, with a large building project looming, to be so well supported.

Immediately Fr D'Arcy introduced a new regime at the Hall. He recognised as absurd the policy of sending men to Oxford and segregating them from all except its academic life. He encouraged the scholastics to make friends with other undergraduates and to join university societies. Entertainment of their tutors by the Master changed from a routine courtesy to an intellectual treat for those invited. One of Fr D'Arcy's scholastics wrote: 'He was a superb. and a devoted superior, aware of everything going on in his community but by reasoned policy non-interventionist or at any rate as little interventionist as possible. His courtesy was the first quality that impressed us scholastics – we had never been treated like princelings before – and one came to understand that it was fundamental. For it was an expression of his profound respect for human beings and for the dignity of being human. He gave everybody breathing space; he encouraged their initiatives and trusted them through thick and thin; if one made a choice he disagreed with, he respected this too and left one to discover the consequences for oneself. If on some rare occasion he had to come to one's room for a book, for instance, he was full of the most profuse apologies for intrusion, for personal privacy was another of the attributes of being human that was beyond price. He treasured every spark of individuality.'[2]

One who was at Campion Hall under Fr D'Arcy for many years told Robert Speaight: 'He was at his best, I believe, as a spiritual guide, if ever one went to him in difficulties or in a jam or in perplexity. He was just marvellous: immediately aware of the intellectual point, if any, intuitively and by a sympathetic penetration and empathy aware also (and this isn't as common as one might think) of the range of emotions involved; very honest; perceptive and totally understanding; wise; and, of course, pretty tough. The framework of religious life he took as read; within the framework, he would discuss anything at all, and he was immensely liberal. But tough, as I said. 'Agonizing reappraisals' or existential decisions whether or not, for example, to go to Mass would have been, quite simply, out.'[3]

His gifts were exhausted in the case of Henry John, whose character had changed much from the joy and freedom of his boyhood. The highly intellectualised passion for his adopted Faith, in which a militant Thomism dominated, had turned him into a neurotically artificial personality. He was struggling in particular against a strength of sexual temptation which may have been the decisive factor in making the Jesuit life too hard for him. It is hard to avoid blaming Fr D'Arcy for mismatching him to such a walk of life; but it was admiration, not pressure, that had led Henry John there. Nothing was further from Fr D'Arcy's genius than to force dispositions, let alone to foster obsessiveness or repression, but Henry John was unable to emulate the self-disciplined ardour with which Fr D'Arcy himself had taken to the Jesuit life. The happy fantasy of ten years ago had run out of hand and acquired monstrous overtones. It may have been the very strength of his affection that disabled Fr D'Arcy from giving the guidance in which he was so rich to others. In 1934, after completing his course at Campion Hall, Henry John left the Society, his relations with Fr D'Arcy wretchedly impaired.

Released from obligations of celibacy, Henry John began running after a series of girls, and by the summer of 1935 he had fallen in love with Olivia Plunket Greene. He planned to spend part of June with her in a bungalow in Cornwall. Olivia had, in Fr D'Arcy's words, 'a peculiar and inimitable cast of faith of her own',[4] and used to assert that the Virgin Mary appeared to her urging her to a life of chastity. She wrote to Henry explaining that she could not enter into an immoral relationship with him. Shortly after this letter, on June 22nd, Henry left the bungalow to go for a swim, and leaving his clothes at the top of a cliff climbed down to the sea. Either he fell or he drowned while swimming; his body was carried away and was not found till after two weeks of searching. On June 28th, when hopes of finding him alive had vanished, Fr D'Arcy wrote to Augustus John looking back on the unhappy friendship and the hopes he had formed at the outset of it: 'I thought that the world lay at his feet. He changed much & I did not for a while see eye to eye with him. But only at Whitsuntide he came to see me, & it looked as if he were beginning to recover that spontaneous & happy character with all its brilliance, which he himself had seemed at one time to choke.'[5] When Henry's body was found his funeral was held in Cornwall, and at his father's request Fr D'Arcy said the requiem, at which, in Tom Burns's words, 'neither Augustus nor anyone there could quench their grief.'[6] Fr D'Arcy dedicated his next book *The Pain of this World and the Providence of God*, to the memory of Henry John, *tam cari capitis*.★

As a memorial to his son, Augustus John painted Fr D'Arcy's portrait in 1939. With elongated forms that recall El Greco, it seems some way removed from a likeness, and yet it conveys the elegance and quickness of mind that photographs fail to capture. Stanley Parker made another portrait three years later, and his description shows the fascination artists found in Fr D'Arcy's emaciated features: 'A wonderful face, wasted to the bone by the rarest and most exquisite emotions, seared with the imprint of the deepest thought, consumed, almost, by the inner fire which blazed and smouldered in his eyes.'[7] His portrait fails entirely in reflecting these qualities; Augustus John had to throw representation to the winds to achieve it. The portrait was intended as a gift for Campion Hall, but Augustus John kept it in his studio until John Rothenstein, fearing the artist's itch for revision, cut short his doubts by picking it up and taking it to the Hall in 1941, while Fr D'Arcy was away in America.[8]

During 1933 various sites were looked at for the new Hall, and again Fr D'Arcy asked Lutyens up to Oxford. Of three possibilities he was shown, Lutyens unhesitatingly chose one in Brewer Street, where a garage had just gone out of business. It was possible to purchase this property and the house next door, Micklem Hall, an ancient and rather ramshackle building with a deep garden behind, along which the façade of the new Hall might show to advantage. Fr D'Arcy next asked Lutyens if he could recommend some young and interesting architect who could be commissioned for the work. 'Why not ask me?' said Lutyens. 'But, Ned,' said Fr D'Arcy, 'you have the reputation of being most appallingly expensive.' Lutyens was keen to work in Oxford, where there was yet no building of his, and offered to do the work for a minimum price.[9]

★ 'That head so dear.' Horace, Odes I, 24, line 2.

The sequel to this was that Mr Norris cited Sir Edwin Lutyens before the Architectural Association for unprofessional conduct, and claimed from the Hall a fee of £1,600, which was 7.5% of the cost of the projected work. The Association cleared Lutyens, but the Hall, in spite of its claim that Norris's plans were only preliminary and therefore entitled him to no more than 1.5%, decided to pay him £1,200 to avoid public brawling.

While this storm loomed, Fr D'Arcy went off on a Hellenic Tour in the Mediterranean. These tours were an idea of Sir Henry Lunn whereby prominent people were encouraged to go on a ship-board holiday by the lure of superior culture, and well-known scholars like Fr D'Arcy were engaged to give lectures, in exchange for which they had their passage free. Fr D'Arcy was invited by Sir Henry Lunn's son, Arnold, who had just become a Catholic and received his First Communion from him.* This particular trip, in the Long Vacation of 1933, took in Venice, Greece, Constantinople and the Holy Land. The company included Evelyn Waugh, Alfred Duggan (afterwards well known as a historical novelist, but at this time struggling with alcoholism), Christopher Hollis, Lady Lovat, Katharine Asquith, her children Lady Helen and Julian (the 2nd Earl of Oxford and Asquith, who came up to Oxford a year later), and the Herbert sisters Gabriel and Laura. All of these were already well known to Fr D'Arcy; a new acquaintance was the young Infanta Beatrix of Spain, whom he described as very beautiful and Evelyn Waugh as highly intelligent, and whom he promptly added to his roll of friendship.

The tour was remembered by Fr D'Arcy as 'probably the most enjoyable three weeks, from the human point of view, I've ever spent in my life';[10] it is captured for us by the manic pen of Evelyn Waugh in letters to Lady Diana Cooper. Princess Marie Louise, a grand-daughter of Queen Victoria and a lady of the most rigid propriety, in Waugh's account 'is the centre of the rowdy set and can be seen any evening standing rounds of champagne cocktails to rows of tarts in highly coloured cache-sexes and brassieres.' A rather tiresome clergyman called Canon Wigram appears as 'A man of unexampled excellence. Roused wild jealousy in Father d'Arcy.... Father d'Arcy suspected him of leading Protestant landslide among Catholic converts but was discovered to have no religious beliefs.'

He also writes with more approximation to fact: 'Poor Father d'Arcy is very ill and worried but he has a good argument now and then with

---

* The year before he had conducted a controversy with his Oxford contemporary Ronald Knox, and was converted by his own arguments against Catholicism, of which he was henceforth one of the leading apologists. When he was knighted in 1952, he asked Fr D'Arcy to give him Communion on the morning of his dubbing.

Chris [Hollis] and me and that cheers him up.'[11] Katharine Asquith described the habits of what was styled the 'Catholic Underworld' (Waugh, Hollis and Duggan were viewed as distinctly below social par), who met in the bar after dinner and passed the evening in intense discussion of religious issues, under Fr D'Arcy's lambent leadership.

On the way back Gabriel and Laura Herbert stopped off at Altachiara, their family's magnificently sited house on the Ligurian coast, named in translation of Highclere, the Herbert house in England. Ronald Knox was staying there at the time with their mother Mary Herbert, who in later years had Fr D'Arcy too as a guest there, though whether this was the occasion of his first visit does not appear.

In the summer of 1934 the Brewer Street site was ready and an appeal was launched for £30,000 to build the new Campion Hall. Fr D'Arcy was hoping that the Duke of Marlborough would pay for the chapel,[12] but the Duke died in June, leaving a non-Catholic heir. The most notable response to the Hall's need came from Evelyn Waugh, who wrote his excellent biography of St Edmund Campion (1935) and donated all his royalties from it to the Hall. In September 1935 Fr D'Arcy's mother died, aged eighty, leaving him £1,000, which was presumably applied to the building fund. She had been living in a nursing home in Sussex, evidently incapacitated, since Conyers had been paying her bills for the previous three years.[13]

On November 24th 1934 the building of the new Campion Hall began with a ceremony in which the foundation stone was laid by Archbishop Goodier and Lord Oxford and Asquith, who had just come up to Balliol. Lutyens's arrangements for the design of the Hall were made wholly with Fr Walker;[14] Fr D'Arcy made no attempt to interfere, satisfied that having enlisted the leading architect of his age he was giving Oxford a building worthy of the university he loved. The site Lutyens had to deal with consisted of a stretch along Brewer Street and a long narrow plot behind. It was decided to preserve Micklem Hall, which had been a set of fashionable undergraduate lodgings, traditionally occupied by Christ Church men; its dining room on the ground floor was earmarked as the senior common room. The new building, appended to its east side, was an L-shaped design with the shorter range on Brewer Street and the longer running southward from it alongside the Micklem garden. In Brewer Street the Hall had its nose hard against the cliff-like wall of Pembroke College chapel, and like other university buildings in narrow streets had to content itself with an understated façade. The normal approach was from the direction of Christ Church, and at that corner the space left by the adjoining choir school, slightly set back from the street, afforded an opening for a little show; but Lutyens severely refused the opportunity and presents the visitor with the blank, semi-octagonal end of the chapel, whose geometric charms are appreciated by few except professional architects.

Lutyens had entered a phase in his life when he held that art should consist in the avoidance of any striving for effect, and the limitations of the site and his budget gave the opportunity to make Campion Hall a paradigm of that approach. The main range can only be viewed in sharp perspective from the narrow spaces in which it is set, and is accordingly lofty and with steep pitched roofs. Its principal façade is that on the garden and is in what may be called Lutyens's cottage style. Classicism is represented by the central doorway framed by pilasters and an entablature.

The two most notable rooms are the chapel and the library. The former, which rises the height of the two upper floors, its windows lit from Brewer Street, is small but lofty, with a barrel vault and an apsidal end. The apse is almost filled with a wooden baldachino projecting from the wall and supported in front by two large columns. Into the design of the chapel, baroque in allusion but very plain in detail, Lutyens incorporated Sir Frank Brangwyn's striking monochrome Stations of the Cross, which had been made for Bruges cathedral. He also took trouble to design all the details of the chapel's fittings, among which mention is due to the cartouche-shaped lights over the screen separating the entrance-lobby from the body of the chapel.

The library is a well-lit space given character by Lutyens's careful design of the furnishings; it has an excellent central fireplace, well-varied partitions to the book-cases, and some quirky details like a set of wooden steps with split treads so that one foot is always at a different level from the other. Lutyens's country-house experience is one of the first notes recalled by the house, and was supported by Fr D'Arcy's own habits of management. Evelyn Waugh mentioned his custom of leaving tactfully-selected books at his guests' bedside, and commented: 'It was remarkable that the only house designed for religious in the University should appear less monastic than the secular colleges.'[15] Lutyens told John Rothenstein that he considered this strictly functional house his best building.[16] The remark, like the design itself, looks like an example of the minimalist passion which overtakes many twentieth-century artists in their old age.

At the beginning of October 1935 enough of the Hall was built for the student body to move in, though the library was not ready for another month and the refectory had to be partitioned to provide a common room. The chapel was first used in January 1936, and in May a lunch was given to clergy and Catholic members of the University to celebrate the consecration of the altars. On June 26th the hall was officially opened by the Duke of Alba in the presence of 250 visitors. Edwin

Lutyens was there, together with the leading patrons of the project, including Evelyn Waugh, Lady Horner, Katharine Asquith and Mary Herbert.[17] Fr D'Arcy also had a coat of arms designed for the Hall and chose its motto: *veritatem facientes in caritate*.

The opening of the new Hall entailed virtually no enlargement of its Jesuit intake. From eleven in 1934-5 the number of undergraduates rose to thirteen and no further. There were many rooms to spare, and Fr D'Arcy began the policy of opening the Hall to Jesuits from abroad, members of other religious congregations and some secular clergy. Though their number remained select, he was highly satisfied with the experiment. He also used the rooms of the old Micklem Hall as lodgings for an assortment of lay residents (a Norwegian and a Dutchman figure in the early years); of these one of the most assorted was his cousin Jack Walton, the former Jesuit lay brother, whose eccentric manner of serving Mass was a leading element in the impression he made on visitors.

A succession of brilliant undergraduates added to the prestige of the Hall. Bernard Basset won the Lothian Prize in 1939 for an essay on Voltaire; Vincent Turner won the Gaisford Prize for Greek Prose and in 1938 was awarded the best First of the year in Honour Moderations, with alphas on all fourteen papers, an achievement which he followed up with an equally outstanding First in Greats in 1940. In 1939 Robert Wingfield-Digby won the Stanhope Prize for an essay on Pope John XXII.

Evelyn Waugh's diary for November 8th 1936 records: 'Went to Campion Hall and saw D'Arcy's latest *bric-à-brac*. A fine Murillo, probably genuine, fine vestments, a lot of trash including watercolours by undergraduates and reproductions cut from books, bits of china. A statue of 'a queen' which D'Arcy chooses to regard as a Madonna. A bogus Lely of Nell Gwyn. Dined at Campion. Painful scene between Father Walker and D'Arcy with regard to a cigar.'

What Waugh calls a bogus Lely of Nell Gwyn must be the picture which Fr D'Arcy insisted was Mary of Modena; Fr Walker always annoyed him by referring to it as Nell Gwyn.★ This and a portrait of James II were hung in the senior common room fashioned in the old Micklem Hall. Its inspiration was the elegant guests' dining room at Stonyhurst which was likewise lined with old panelling, hung with Stuart portraits and filled with fine silver, and in commemoration of his own college Fr D'Arcy gave this room the same name, the Stuart Parlour. Here was the scene of Campion Hall's renowned after-dinner conversation.

★ Waugh inadvertently called it Nell Gwyn in his honeyed description of 'The Hospitality of Campion Hall' which he wrote for *The Tablet* in 1946. The slip must have made the article for Fr D'Arcy a resounding example of the Lucretian tag:

medio de fonte leporum
surgit amari aliquid quod in ipsis floribus angat.

Its Master, as Robert Speaight wrote, 'thought of Campion Hall as a shrine of Christian civilisation – something that Oxford once had been and was no longer.' He wished also to vindicate the Jesuits from the charge of bad taste often raised against them. To have brought the vision of a great architect to his university was an achievement he was proud of. And yet Lutyens's severe building did not really reflect Fr D'Arcy's courtly taste, which was seen rather in the famous *objets d'Arcy* with which he embellished it. The first accessions were ornaments for the chapel, and Fr D'Arcy began his matchless collection of vestments. 'I came across a set of 17th century flowered white vestments,' he wrote, 'and managed to secure them easily. Soon I was looking everywhere for chasubles and copes. An Italian refugee from the Fascists had brought with him mediaeval chasubles. I bought one of the 14th century, with its orphreys and Renaissance background.'[18] This search brought him into the world of art-dealers. From an Armenian Jew in London he got some chalices and a chasuble with 13th-century work on one side. Cultural barriers were thrown down in the hunt for beauty. 'Walking down the High I saw a gorgeous Chinese robe of cloth of gold with dragons and birds worked on it. With the help of a nun sempstress, it proved easy to transform it into a chasuble. All one had to do was slit the armpits and add a small gold cross on the back. Some Spanish nuns, who did work occasionally for the Cunard Line, made a red gothic chasuble in honour of the English Martyrs – and a Spanish frontal of the 17th century in honour of Our Lady was made into a handsome, if heavy, gothic chasuble for BVM. A golden silk Persian towel served as a tabernacle covering, and period beflowered frontals were used for festive occasions.'

Fr D'Arcy's chief find came just after the end of the second world war. A dealer friend in South Audley Street, C.John, rang him up and alerted him to a lot that was part of a Christie's auction. Going there the next day with an American woman friend with whom he had been lunching, he found that the catalogue description of the lot was mainly of two fine oak frames, which were lying against a dim wall; but inside the frames he saw the two pieces of a superb mediaeval chasuble. His friend offered to buy the lot for him, and as only one dealer had penetrated the catalogue's oversight, but had told him 'I won't bid against you' (Fr D'Arcy describes him as 'notorious' but a good friend of his), she was able to acquire it easily. It was then realised that one of the finest chasubles of the middle ages – a Burgundian piece of about 1480 – had come onto the market, and dealers vainly offered Fr D'Arcy large sums for it.

The magnificent collection thus built up was, by Fr D'Arcy's insistence, kept in regular liturgical use. He would give instructions to the sacristan every evening on which vestments he would wear the next morning, and so far as possible he wore them all in sequence. These splendid habiliments were an affirmation of his belief that one of the functions of the Mass was to pay royal honours to the King of Kings.

The decoration of the rest of the house was marked by equally extraordinary finds. One of the first came just before Fr D'Arcy left for America on a fund-raising tour in February 1935. He was lunching with Sir Edwin Lutyens in London before catching the boat train to Southampton, and Lutyens pulled out a photograph of a very large wood carving belonging to a friend of his. The subject was obviously religious and the owner wanted to give it to a Catholic church. Lutyens wondered if the projected Catholic cathedral of Liverpool, for which he was then making his superb plans, would be a suitable place. Fr D'Arcy looked at the photograph and immediately saw that the carving depicted St Ignatius and his early companions, who were clearly recognisable. He told Lutyens that the obvious place for it was Campion Hall. The carving was a seventeenth-century Spanish work, nearly life-size, and Lutyens incorporated into his plans for the Hall a place where it could be fitted into the wall at the foot of the main stairs.

A piece that faces it on the stairs themselves has another tale attached to it. Eric Gill offered to make a stone carving of Fr D'Arcy's patron saint, St Martin of Tours, with the beggar to whom he gave half his cloak. Fr D'Arcy was very pleased to agree to this commission, in which he himself was to be the model for St Martin. What he did not realise was that he was expected to pay for it, and when Gill discovered that Fr D'Arcy thought of it as a gift he turned him into the beggar instead.

Early works of art given to the Hall include a Madonna and Child, given by Hilaire Belloc early in 1936, with a verse of his own at the bottom of the frame. The Duke of Alba presented a two-volume Bible of the House of Alba. Laurence Whistler (the brother of Rex) engraved a little poem on a pane of the door giving onto the garden. A book given by Merton College in 1936 was of exceptional value intrinsically and for its associations: it was a Venetian incunable containing two works on Aristotle, and had been the property at Oxford of St Edmund Campion, whose name appeared three times inscribed in it. A friend of Fr D'Arcy's, Bertram Bisgood, gave many presents, including a large Murillo of St Augustine with the Divine Child. Two of his sisters gave a Madonna and Child said to be by Morales, which, after experts such as Tancred Borenius had pronounced it a fine example of the artist's work, was worked on by the Austrian restorer Sebastian Isepp during the War (he was among many distinguished refugees who gravitated to Campion Hall) and found to be half covered in over-painting with the real Morales revealed underneath.

Isepp was responsible for the discovery of other masterpieces. He identified as of the school of Veronese a painting Fr D'Arcy had bought for

£3 in an old shop in Wallingford. Another picture was offered to Fr D'Arcy by a dealer he met at a party in Hampstead. Invited to the man's shop, he saw a very large picture which he was told came from a Yorkshire inn. He thought he saw quality beneath the dirt, but having no money to spend refused to be interested. The dealer rang him up persistently and finally said, 'Make any offer.' Fr D'Arcy named £5 or £10, which was accepted. The painting was brought to the Hall and some time later, in 1943, Isepp got to work on it and attributed it with confidence to Giulio Romano, the friend of Raphael.

While the Hall was being built Lutyens was approached by Jose-Maria Sert, the most outstanding Spanish mural artist of this century, who offered to paint the apse of the chapel for nothing if Lutyens would secure him the commission to paint Liverpool cathedral. Lutyens was unable to promise this, for the good reason that his design was never built, and the opportunity to make a notable contemporary contribution to the Hall was lost. The painting of the adjoining Lady Chapel exemplifies a hitch in Fr D'Arcy's usual wizard's touch in artistic matters. The commission was given, on John Rothenstein's recommendation, to an agnostic artist whom Fr D'Arcy engaged under the misapprehension that he was a Catholic, and the result hardly renders the expression Fr D'Arcy would have liked to give to his devotion to the Blessed Virgin.

Among the benefactors of the Hall was Paddy Shannon, a small man with what Fr D'Arcy called 'one of those old aristocratic Irish faces', whom he met about 1932 at a gathering in Oxford. He introduced himself to Fr D'Arcy as a distant connexion of his, and said that he was planning to write a history of the D'Arcy family. Like many of his declared intentions this one proved barren, but he was a mine of genealogical information, and was able to enlighten Fr D'Arcy about a history on which his father had provided scanty details. Paddy Shannon had a house in Oxford and entertained lavishly among the undergraduates – it seems that he figured technically as tutor, but as he disappeared unaccountably for long periods this does not seem to have been too serious. He was an authority on old silver, and once dined Monsignors Knox and Elwes in Scotland on a complete set of D'Arcy family plate. He had an expansive Irish generosity which made it difficult for Fr D'Arcy to stop and eye something with interest in a shop window without Paddy's immediately offering to buy it. Besides the portrait of Mary Queen of Scots which graced the Stuart Parlour, he gave a number of smaller gifts and later bought for Fr D'Arcy an antique chasuble, once the property of the Weld family, which he donated to Stonyhurst.

The Duke of Alba was a major artistic conquest of Fr D'Arcy's, and it was to suit his convenience that the date of the opening had been postponed, falling a few days after the end of the university term. Some biographical details will explain Fr D'Arcy's interest. Jacobo (Jimmy) Fitzjames Stuart was, as 10th Duke of Berwick, the descendant of James II through his illegitimate son, the great Marshal Berwick, and as 17th Duke of Alba was the head of the premier family of the Spanish nobility. He was a keen connoisseur of his family's magnificent bibliographic and artistic collections, on which he published books; he had been on the board of the Prado, president of the Spanish Academy of History, and a member of other bodies such as the British Academy and the Rockefeller Foundation. As a liberal monarchist he had kept out of his country's politics during the military government of Primo de Rivera; on the General's fall he served as Minister first of Education and then of State (foreign affairs). He resigned on the fall of the monarchy in 1931 and went into exile, his estates being confiscated by the Republican regime. Fr D'Arcy may have got to know him through Professor de Zulueta, who had been educted at Beaumont with the Duke and like him belonged to a Spanish noble family of strong monarchist traditions.

When the Spanish Civil War broke out in July 1936 the Duke of Alba quickly offered the Nationalist side his services as its representative in England. To have Spain's premier Duke and a former foreign minister in that role was a great coup for Franco's cause; when his regime was recognised by the British Government the Duke was accredited as Ambassador. The Duke of Alba saw the Nationalist revolt as an opportunity for the restoration of the monarchy, and unlike Franco was not put off by the expression of left-wing opinions by which Don Juan sought to gain support. Throughout the second world war the Duke played a key role in saving Anglo-Spanish relations, but when it became obvious that Franco had no intention of restoring Don Juan to the throne, and in obedience to the wishes of the man he acknowledged as his rightful sovereign, he resigned in 1945 and ended his days in disgrace with the regime.

Fr D'Arcy's friendship with the Duke of Alba was one cause of the very strong line he took on the Spanish Civil War. Another was the visit he had paid to a Catholic convention in San Sebastian in August 1935. He was impressed by the reaction that the anti-clerical regime was provoking among Spanish Catholics and by their efforts to recover their country's tradition and a Christian philosophy of history. His attitude to the Spanish Republic had been critical from the beginning,[19] and when the Civil War broke out he immediately saw it as an opportunity to restore the Christian polity, declaring that the Nationalists were fighting 'to keep the name of Christ alive in their country and on their children's lips.'[20]

One or two English Catholics, like Hilaire Belloc, had expressed approval of Mussolini, but support for the Spanish Nationalists was more general among his co-religionists, no doubt because their movement was a response to a real anti-clerical danger. The Jesuits, who were well informed about the massacres of their brethren and other clergy, were particularly immune from the rosy views of the Republican regime favoured by posterity, and Fr Woodlock distinguished himself as a public partisan of the Nationalists. Republican sympathies were largely confined to the circle of Eric Gill, whose opinions became more conventionally left-wing as his style of living became more conventionally bourgeois, and who openly declared for communism. For this Fr D'Arcy attacked him in the *Catholic Herald* in 1937, speaking of 'mental strain' and finding in Gill 'a loss of power in judging his ideas.'[21]

Because of the criticism being heaped on the Catholic Church as the ally of dictators, Fr D'Arcy was asked by Cardinal Hinsley to go on a second Hellenic Cruise in February and March 1938. The trip, which began at Toulon and took in most of the Mediterranean, was designed as a forum of discussion among various Christian leaders, including several Anglican bishops, and Fr D'Arcy, who was asked to sum up the discussions, found himself facing a chorus of condemnation. Towards Fascism he was cool, pronouncing a measured criticism of the Italian invasion of Abyssinia, but in the matter of Spain he defended his views with his usual vigour, describing as 'benighted' those Catholics who refused their blessing to the Nationalist cause.[22]

Fr D'Arcy's contemporary political outlook had been expressed in a book of 1932, in which he remarked that 'Time has not so far justified' the expectations that Italian Fascism 'would be entirely in harmony with the Church's ideals.' On the right-wing movements of the Continent he wrote: 'With much, too, in the philosophy of the right the Church has sympathy, with its insistence, for example, on legal and social traditions, on the need of discipline, obedience and authority; but nevertheless with the extremes, such as the Nazis have advocated, it can have nothing to do.'[23] That was written before Hitler came to power; Fr D'Arcy made no further public pronouncement on Nazism until his wartime broadcasts.

In domestic affairs he upheld a theoretical Toryism, though of a vintage that had little to do with contemporary party politics. What he looked for in a statesman were his own qualities: style, courage, nobility, and a grand historical vision. He was accordingly a strong admirer of Winston Churchill even while he was out of office. 'All during that period of the thirties,' he said in 1961, 'I swore by Winston Churchill ... I felt he was *the* man.'[24] He also welcomed the glamour that the Prince of Wales seemed to be bringing back to the stolid House of Windsor, though whether his dynastic sense permitted him to sympathise with

Churchill's defence of the marriage with Mrs Simpson is a different question. Churchill's sister-in-law, the vivacious Lady Gwendolyn Churchill, herself the daughter of a convert family, was a great friend of Fr D'Arcy's, and fanned his interest by telling him in 1934 that she thought Churchill might become a Catholic. Fr D'Arcy might have used his friendship with Lady Gwendolyn and other relations of Churchill's, such as the Duke of Marlborough, to engineer a meeting with the great man, but he let the opportunity slip.

Catholic monarchism and its associations automatically had Fr D'Arcy's sympathies, but Churchill is an example of the robust exponents of Protestant Toryism whom he also enjoyed. Others were Dr Johnson and the Duke of Wellington; but Robert Speaight blundered when he thought to please him with the gift of a first edition of Bolingbroke's *The Idea of a Patriot King*. A pseudo-Anglican opportunist Jacobite had no attraction for him.

Against liberalism as a philosophy Fr D'Arcy's convictions were firm. Robert Speaight tells us that Lord Acton was one of his few intellectual dislikes. In *The Decline of Authority in the Nineteenth Century* Fr D'Arcy wrote in 1937: 'The Catholic Church has steadily turned its back on the principles of liberalism and free thought. At the time the intransigence of the Church caused much heartburning and indignation, but the years have vindicated its decisions.' John Rothenstein, who first came to Campion Hall about 1937, writes: 'I was conscious that my inherited liberalism could show itself in an anticlericalism that provoked his ridicule and even his antipathy.'[25] Yet there was an element of mischief in such conflicts; in conversation Fr D'Arcy's style was to provoke, and Michael de la Bedoyère wrote of 'the entertainment, the paradoxes, the impish insistence on making the worse the better cause as he leads the lively conversation among his guests in his common room, the dilettantism in art, the unconventional political views.'[26] A consequence was that his guests were sometimes misled. 'I have heard his indignation,' writes Rothenstein, 'when his Jesuit confrères have put it to him that this doctrine [of Divine Right] was a Tudor aberration particularly well dealt with by their Jesuit predecessor, Cardinal Bellarmine.' We can check this recollection against Fr D'Arcy's piece on *The Decline of Authority* just quoted, where he cites the doctrine of Divine Right as an example of post-Reformation usurping of spiritual authority by secular rulers.[27]

Fr Vincent Turner got to the heart of Fr D'Arcy's thought when he wrote: 'Behind his talk and underlying much of his playfulness was a vision of an ordered universe in which everything had its place and was aware of its limits, of a hierarchized world. Yet, within this world, and made possible only (he thought) by strict measure, his preference was for the widest diversity and variety, for the exuberant and even the eccentric. He treasured and fostered their strong individuality. Uniformity he abhorred; group consensus spelt mediocrity.'[28]

From his liberal and middle-class viewpoint, Rothenstein describes Fr D'Arcy as inclined 'to attach more importance than circumstances seemed to warrant to the higher aristocracy, even to Hapsburgs and other members of former royal houses.' He was one of many who were content to smile at the foible of such unrealistic views in a man of such intellect. Quintin Hogg, not the most naive of observers, noted rather 'the candid, but sometimes cryptic utterance, betraying often that he knew more of the world than one did oneself.'[29] Fr D'Arcy, seeing human history under its eternal species, inhabited imaginatively other periods as well as his own, and above all he cherished the Christian epoch which venerated earthly monarchy as the reflexion of the divine. To those for whom the contemporary world and its fantasies are the only reality his refusal to accord it that pre-eminence seemed a retreat into illusion.

At a personal level, Fr D'Arcy's sympathies were broad. With men like Lindemann, Bowra and Ayer included in his friendship, it is hard to think of any criterion that would have excluded a person from it, and Fr D'Arcy himself did not help anyone to find out. Tom Burns writes: 'One would pull his leg now and then about some boor or bore, and try to trap him into making some damning judgment. But the trick always failed: "A dear soul, a dear soul," he would reply with the knowledge that he had outwitted the questioner with an unchallengeable statement.'[30] One catches the echoes of Fr Plater. The conversation Fr D'Arcy fostered rejoiced in the splendours of language and in poetry caught from unsuspected sources, such as the description by an Irishwoman of her drunken husband 'wandering over the roads of the world and returning home like Ulysses after his travels', or an Oxford woman's admiration of a Jesuit friend: 'a tall candle burning bright for the Lord, a pillar of fire shining into the night.'[31]

Several writers have described the guest nights at Campion Hall which were the chief setting for such verbal and ideological revels; two of them, Evelyn Waugh and Sir John Rothenstein, devoted separate essays to the subject. Waugh, shortly after Fr D'Arcy's Mastership had ended, wrote a piece on *The Hospitality of Campion Hall* to commemorate that unique period:[32]

In the near future when books of reminiscence appear which cover the 1930s, and, opening them at the end, we search the index, as we used, for an indication of their character, how often and in what diverse company – between Caldey and Catholic Truth Society, perhaps, or Cabinet meeting and Camrose, or Café de Paris and

Castlerosse, according to the tastes of the writer⋆ – we shall find the entry: 'Campion Hall, delightful evening at'.

We came from all quarters as guests of the house; fellows and under-graduates, gowned, from the neighbouring colleges, refugees from foreign tyranny, editors of Catholic papers from London, Under-Secretaries of State visiting the Chatham or the Canning, the President of the Royal Academy, the Spanish Ambassador, and men marked by no notoriety but distinguished by the high privilege of the Master's friendship. You never knew whom you would meet at Campion Hall but one thing was certain, that for a single evening at any rate they would all fit harmoniously into the social structure which the Master, without apparent effort, ingeniously contrived. Men you knew only by repute and, perhaps, had distrusted from afar, here revealed unsuspected points of sympathy; men you had seen at a disadvantage in other company shone here in the reflected light of the house's welcome; old friends seemed mysteriously to recover the engaging qualities which had attracted you in youth. And you yourself, growing daily in the outside world, it used to seem, narrower and duller, did you, too, not feel at Campion Hall an ease and receptiveness that you thought lost?

The evening had its own invariable and memorable rhythm. You dressed, if you were a Catholic, in time to slip into the back of the chapel for Benediction; then after an exchange of introductions in the ante-room, you were led to Hall. The entertainment began, as all good entertainment should, with some formality. Grace was expected but many an experienced diner-out, accustomed to open a light conversation as he unfolded his napkin, was taken unawares by the recital of the Martyrology. After a false start conversation began when the Master signed his thanks to the reader. Guests sat at High Table with the senior members; below them were the scholastics under the plaster flower in the ceiling, set there, Sir Edwin Lutyens used to explain, so that they might talk *sub rosa*. Their turn came when the party adjourned to dessert in the library. Here we divided into groups and the scholastics were picked and distributed at the several small tables. They had an eagerness for discussion, born of long hours of silent study, that was exhilarating after the feebler talk of London; each had a topic he required to air. 'This is Mr So-and-so, who is reading Modern History. He is reading your last book and wants to ask you …', '… Mr So-and-so, who is much concerned by what you said in the House

⋆Caldey Island was the seat of a religious community, Lord Camrose was a leading news-paper baron, Lord Castlerosse (son of the 5th Earl of Kenmare) was a gossip columnist of the inter-war years.

of Commons about secondary education ...', '... Mr So-and-so, who is writing a thesis on Egyptian cenobites and wants to know ...' Thus they were led up to the guests and for half an hour subjected them to polite but penetrating cross-examination. Then they returned to their books and the nucleus of the party again adjourned, now to Micklem Hall, down the steps into the rosy light of the Senior Common Room.

The half circle of chairs in the Stuart Parlour was the setting for the culmination of the evening's hospitality. More often than not we were joined here by newcomers; Mgr Knox, perhaps, between whose lodging in the Old Palace and Campion Hall the lane was worn smooth by the feet of scholastic emissaries carrying telephone messages; or Lord David Cecil lured from the domestic fireside; or Mr Pakenham tousled from some unseasonable agitation in the purlieus of the Morris motor-works. Here in the single semicircle, while the Father Minister passed between us with the decanter and cigar-box, the conversation was wide and free. I never knew anyone be a bore there; no one held forth; no one was ever intimidated by superior celebrity. Father D'Arcy has among his many gifts the supreme art of conducting a conversation. Sometimes he could be drawn into the defence of some romantic, anachronistic thesis; more often he was content to catch the ball and pass it, swift and spinning, to another hand. The topics are infinitely various; Mr Christopher Hollis maintaining that Roosevelt was recovering a lost province to Christendom; Mr Rothenstein attempting a Thomist version of the art-jargon of the Paris studios; Mr Scrymgeour-Wedderburn★ displaying immense scriptural knowledge on a point of exegesis; Sir Edwin Lutyens riveting the attention with a series of Rabelaisian puns and pencilled diagrams. I hope someone has made notes of some of the conversations; they were the best I ever heard.

The use to which Fr D'Arcy put his guest nights for his scholastics' education was extended to his own purposes. When writing a book, and especially during the war years when he was gestating *The Mind and Heart of Love*, he would direct conversation to the subject he was working on, and his principle of provocation elicited lively expressions of opinion which stimulated his own thought. He then retired to his room to put down his impressions in writing, an evening's coruscating talk being often the induction to hard work into the small hours of the morning.

John Rothenstein first knew the Hall shortly before 1938, when he

★A convert and former President of the Oxford Union; later a minister under Macmillan as 11th Earl of Dundee.

was appointed Director of the Tate Gallery at the age of thirty-six. He devotes a chapter to Campion Hall in the second volume of his autobiography:[33]

> Were it rumoured that someone of outstanding interest was visiting Oxford, it was likely that he would be found to be dining at the high table of Campion Hall.* He would be induced to talk about the subject about which his fellow guests would particularly wish to hear, but at any moment the flashing eyes of Father D'Arcy would invite the participation of some obscure person, who, because the moment was so appropriate, was in a position to shine to his best advantage. I have listened to better talkers than Father D'Arcy, but never known anyone able to orchestrate so brilliantly the talk of his companions. I had the good fortune to be invited to dine at Campion Hall on many occasions and have heard at the high table and in common room afterwards good talkers dazzle, the tongues of the tongue-tied loosed and, more remarkable still, the garrulous muted. During the ensuing years I was in the company there of Ronald Knox, David Cecil, Evelyn Waugh, Graham Greene, Isaiah Berlin, Donald MacKinnon, Frank Pakenham, Maurice Bowra, Christopher Hollis, C.S. Lewis, Douglas Woodruff, Robert Speaight, David Jones and many others whom it was a delight to listen to. I recall, for instance, a lively description by Louis MacNeice of how he had once been with Yeats when he was crystal-gazing and how Yeats announced in portentous tones, 'I see a lady in a red dress ...' and how somebody pointed out that she was a reflection of a poster on the opposite side of the street.

Besides the names Rothenstein mentions, habitual guests from Catholic circles included Joseph Thorp, an old Stonyhurst boy and one-time Jesuit who was for many years dramatic critic of *Punch*, Michael de la Bedoyère and Sir Shane Leslie. Sir Edwin Lutyens had naturally a special place in the Hall's honour; he was familiar for his rather schoolboy humour, of which he had left solid symbols about the house, like the ceiling rose in the Refectory which Evelyn Waugh mentions. He specialised in risqué jokes, such as one inspired by an anti-Catholic warrior called Longbottom who had been making himself objectionable; when Mr Longbottom died Lutyens made a little drawing for Fr D'Arcy showing a gravestone with the inscription *Ars no longer*.[34]

An effect of Campion Hall's move to Brewer Street was to make Mgr Knox an immediate neighbour at the Old Palace, where he remained

---

*Rothenstein may have been remembering ex-Chancellor Brüning of Germany, who dined at the Hall in 1938.

Catholic chaplain to the university till 1939. As he refused to install a telephone, Campion Hall became a convenient recipient of messages for him. Both Mgr Knox and Fr D'Arcy were careful to avoid living in each other's laps. Knox's reserve and shunning of the histrionic bred a certain wariness and even a touch of satire which Isaiah Berlin detected in his attitude to Fr D'Arcy's reputation.[35] But when a friend, concerned at his moroseness, asked him what would make him happier, Knox replied, after due consideration, 'If I could go for a walk every afternoon with Fr D'Arcy.'[36] When he was writing Mgr Knox's biography Evelyn Waugh unearthed this remark and relayed it to Fr D'Arcy, to whom it was news. He replied: 'I had an affection for him & a great admiration for his gifts, but I never realised, while he was living, that the affection was mutual. That made me rather slow in inviting myself to, for instance, the Old Palace.'[37] But when Mgr Knox was offered a bishopric in 1939 he went for advice to Fr D'Arcy, 'who I think knows me better than any other priest in Oxford',[38] and followed his advice and his own inclination in refusing.

Sir Isaiah Berlin testifies that the prestige Fr D'Arcy enjoyed as a thinker in Catholic circles was not reflected among his university colleagues. He was regarded as a competent lecturer on Aristotle, but his special interests struck no chord in the philosophical Faculty. Christopher Hollis has remarked of this period: 'The Greats Dons made strangely little attempt to consider the metaphysical claims of the Christian religion. They jumped straight from Aristotle to Descartes with no passing mention of Aquinas or any other scholastic in between.'[39] They were even less interested in neo-Thomism and the question of the place of love in human cognition which was Fr D'Arcy's particular passion. There may have been an element of the resentment against those dons who made a name for themselves in journalism and wireless − the sort of dislike of the 'television don' that later made A.J.P. Taylor unpopular.* Fr D'Arcy is remembered as having opened up Campion Hall to the university and raised its reputation therein, but it would be mistaken to think of him as conscientiously running about to make donnish contacts. He achieved what he did by following his own social bent, and that did not lead him much to other colleges' high tables; the society he enjoyed was that of undergraduates, and there his success was extraordinary. In 1934 a vote of the Oxford Union[40] elected him to its Standing Committee, as a sort of deputy, it seems, of the Senior Librarian. It was a choice which undergraduates of a few years before would have thought

---

*Fr D'Arcy inherited Fr Martindale's position as a popular radio exponent of Catholic doctrine, making his first BBC broadcast in May 1932. In 1936 he became the Catholic representative on the BBC's religious broadcasting committee, a seat he held till 1945.

incredible, since no other member of Campion Hall had impinged on their consciousness, let alone attained the necessary popularity.

Fr D'Arcy took part in his first debate in November 1934, when he spoke after Ronald Knox on the motion, 'This House considers that debunking in modern biography has been carried too far.' He did justice to the social fame that had preceded him, but was eclipsed by Ronald Knox with his whimsies on debunking versions of well-known tributes, such as Tennyson's to the Duke of Wellington:

> Bury the great duke
> With an empire's disapprobation.
> Bury the great duke
> Somewhere in the neighbourhood of Waterloo Station.

A more unpleasant occasion came a year later, when a debate on birth control was held. It is difficult to appreciate today not simply the opposition but the spontaneous disgust that contraception then inspired in Catholics and other conservative moralists, and the choice of subject was a deliberate violation of the Union's rule against debating subjects of religious controversy. The gesture was made by the President, Brian Farrell, a radical atheist, who in Fr D'Arcy's estimation 'had done an awful lot of damage just in the two or three years he had been there.'[41] He had further weighted the scales for the contraception side by choosing as speakers Max Beloff, who was that term's Treasurer, Elizabeth Pakenham and Bertrand Russell, opposed only by a little-known undergraduate and by Dr W.J. O'Donovan, a Catholic medical doctor who had recently been a Member of Parliament.* The Oxford Union was unfamiliar to him, however, and he was not up to the occasion. Mgr Knox spoke next against the motion; his name was not on the paper, and he was there reluctantly under obedience to his bishop, who insisted on a stand for Catholic doctrine; after speaking briefly he left the hall. Fr D'Arcy had only come to give him support, but he was so angered at the way the debate had been slanted that he rose to speak, and devoted himself mainly to an attack on Bertrand Russell. The motion was carried by a large majority.[42]

The thirties were a time when a number of Fr D'Arcy's younger followers were beginning to make a name for themselves. Michael de la Bedoyère took over the editorship of the *Catholic Herald* in 1934 and in his thirty years in charge converted it from a small north-western paper into one with a circulation of over 100,000, expressing a distinctively liberal brand of Catholicism. Bernard Wall in the same year founded his

---

*His son Patrick had just come up to Oxford from Ampleforth; he later became a well-known journalist and was a life-long friend of Fr D'Arcy's.

own review of literature and ideas, *The Colosseum*, to whose early numbers Berdyaev, Maritain, Mauriac, Eric Gill and Fr D'Arcy himself were contributors. Lord Clonmore was editor of *The Dublin Review* from 1937 to 1939. With Douglas Woodruff (a good friend and intellectual sympathiser if not actually a disciple) at *The Tablet* from 1936, Fr D'Arcy could be sure of a good press.

1936 was something of a literary climacteric for English Catholicism: Chesterton died in that year; Baring was beginning to suffer from the *paralysis agitans* which not long after forced him to retire to Lady Lovat's solicitous care in Scotland; and Belloc was by now doing little but repeat his old themes. The new generation thus came all the more into its own in the later thirties. Its leaders were a roll-call of Fr D'Arcy's friends: Ronald Knox, Fr Martindale, Arnold Lunn, Christopher Dawson, and a little less intimately perhaps Frank Sheed and his wife Maisie Ward, who in 1926 had started the publishing firm of Sheed and Ward. Fr Adrian Hastings has written of this time: 'There developed the very strong sense of a Catholic intellectual community, self-confidently speaking of 'the Catholic Revival', sunning itself in country houses or at Campion Hall, publishing its books with the young Frank Sheed, its articles in the revivified *Tablet* of Douglas Woodruff or the *Catholic Herald* of Michael de la Bedoyère, drawing in new members from the worlds of letters, art and even academia.'

Fr Hastings adds: 'D'Arcy was by far the most influential clerical intelligence of the decade. It is likely that since Newman no other priest has exercised so deep and prolonged a personal influence upon the English Catholic intelligentsia, and behind the glittering eye of the living Jesuit was the still more pervasive influence of the dead Jesuit. The 1930s were the decade of the belated triumph of Gerard Manley Hopkins... Listening to Martin D'Arcy reading *The Wreck of the Deutschland* could be a spiritual experience not easily forgotten.'[43]

Fr Hastings identifies a further distinction: Fr D'Arcy had one foot in the camp of the 'gentlemen apologists who were so much in their zenith in those years', but he was also a portent of a new generation in the English clergy. Mgr Knox and Fr Martindale, for all their public appeal, were not theologians. Fr D'Arcy, with his keen interest in the theological developments of the time, was a pointer to the much greater intellectual professionalism which was to be developed by Thomists like Fr Gervase Mathew and by the Benedictines of the *Downside Review*.

Of Fr D'Arcy's conquests from academia the leading example is Frank Pakenham (Lord Longford), who became a Student of Christ Church in 1934*. They had been friends for a few years, having probably been introduced by Evelyn Waugh, whose lunch with them *à trois* in 1930 has been

---

* The title of Student at Christ Church corresponds to that of Fellow at other colleges.

mentioned. Lord Longford records having read *The Nature of Belief* when it came out in 1931, and a later glimpse is given by Lady Dorothy Lygon, who described an impromptu visit she and Evelyn Waugh paid to Frank Pakenham and his wife Elizabeth about 1933 at their house in Stone, near Aylesbury. They arrived to find Fr D'Arcy already in residence, and the evening was spent by the men immersed in 'high-level Roman Catholic topics' while Lady Dorothy was left to darn Evelyn Waugh's socks. The following day Waugh took them all to lunch at the Spread Eagle in Thame, then under the management of the famous hotelier John Fothergill.[44]

Frank Pakenham preserved a link with Oxford in the early thirties through a part-time lectureship, and he joined with the other young men of the place who made much of Fr D'Arcy socially. He took him to the neighbouring Charlton, where his contemporary the second Earl of Birkenhead (son of F.E. Smith, who had died in 1930) ran a lively and youthful circle. Lord Birkenhead and Fr D'Arcy were soon fast friends. The house had Catholic contacts: Vyvyan Holland was one of the company, and Lord Birkenhead's sister, Eleanor Smith, who became well known as a novelist before her early death, was received into the Church about this time.

In 1934 Pakenham moved to Oxford on gaining his Studentship. He was then still a pillar of Conservatism, but his wife professed the staunch Socialist faith which she has since displayed in her well-known series of reverent royal biographies. Her influence was leading Frank Pakenham to the Labour Party, and he resigned from the Carlton Club a year later. By 1937 he was in the position of chairing a Labour meeting addressed by Harry Pollitt, the General Secretary of the British Communist Party, in the Oxford Town Hall, and his party's supping with this devil pricked his Christian conscience. By chance as he left the Hall he saw Fr D'Arcy, who turned and looked at him briefly as he walked down the street towards Campion Hall. It made him feel like St Peter in the court of the High Priest.[45]

It was some months more before the cock crew. In the spring of 1938 his spiritual bereavement reached a crisis. Christ Church was governed by the canons of the cathedral, Gamaliels of their Church at whose feet an Anglican might most naturally have gone to sit; but Frank Pakenham did not think of them. Fr D'Arcy, he writes, 'stood out in my mind as the one man capable both of understanding my personal problems and of providing an objective answer to the dominant agnosticism of the time.'[46] He headed 'like a homing pigeon' the short distance down Brewer Street from Christ Church, and luckily he found Fr D'Arcy in. 'Within half an hour he knew all, and no doubt more than all than I thought worth telling him about myself.' Over the next eighteen months he read many books at Fr D'Arcy's prompting, including the admired St Augustine, and if this sounds over-intellectual we should balance it with Lord Longford's words: 'Never can I express what I owe to Father D'Arcy for what he did

*Fr Martin D'Arcy's arms as a Conventual Chaplain ad honorem of the
Sovereign Military Order of Malta.*

Martin Valentine D'Arcy, 1897 (father)

Madoline Mary D'Arcy (mother)

The new Jesuit: M C D'Arcy just after taking his vows, 2nd October 1908

The class of Rhetoric (Stonyhurst) 1904–5,
Far right: M.C. Darcy, 3rd from right: Henry Mather and leaning on aim, Robert de Trafford.
The master is Fr Joseph Keating and behind him (3rd from left), Basil Gurrin.

Group at Campion Hall, 1916.
Seated from right: M.C. D'Arcy, Fr. C. Plater with Jim, Fr Joseph Rickaby.
Back row, 2nd from left: E. Helsham (Provincial 1950–52), 3rd: R. Worsley
(Rector of Stonyhurst 1929–32), 4th: F. Mangan (Provincial 1939–45).

Henry John, aged about 16

Rev. M. C. D'Arcy, S.J.

Wyndham Lewis's portrait of Fr D'Arcy, 1932
'Intellect incarnate in a beautiful head, wavy grey hair and delicate features; a hawk's eyes'. (Louis MacNeice)

The opening of Campion Hall, June 1936
(the Micklem Hall garden and West front of Lutyens's building).

Group at the opening of Campion Hall

Back row from left: Evelyn Waugh, Lady Horner, Katharine Asquith, Hon. Mary Herbert.
Front row from left: Sir Edwin Lutyens, Fr D'Arcy, the Duke of Alba, A. D. Lindsay
(Vice-Chancellor of Oxford University), Mgr Ronald Knox.

A picnic with the Asquiths at Stour Head, August 1938

Standing, L to R: John Sparrow(?), Clarissa Churchill (who married Anthony Eden, 1952), Venetia Stanley (Asquith's grand passion 1912–15). Sitting: Lord Acton, Katharine Asquith, Fr. D'Arcy. With back to camera: Julian Asquith, Earl of Oxford and Asquith.

Portrait of Father Martin D'Arcy by Augustus John, 1939

*Cartoon by Fr Sam Dolan of Fr D'Arcy with Fr Basil Gurrin as a little dog,
c. 1942*

Frederick Shrady's head of Fr D'Arcy, 1954
(replica at Campion Hall of the original in the Metropolitan Museum of Art).

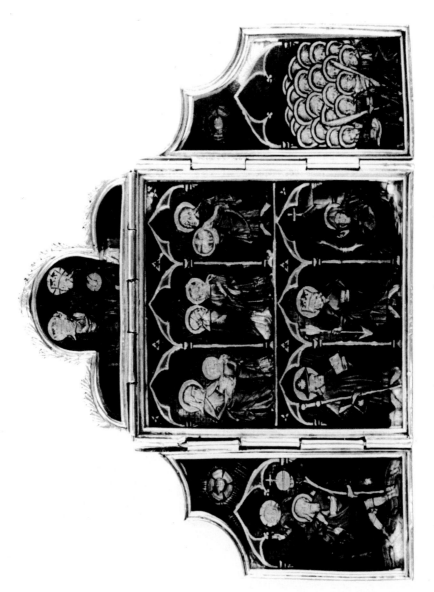

The Mary Queen of Scots triptych

The Chapel at Wardour Castle

Fr D'Arcy sets the ton *at Santa Monica, 1960s, with Mrs (Pat) Anderson*

*Fr D'Arcy's eightieth birthday party at 21 (New York). From left: Evelyn
Johnson, Fr D'Arcy, Jane Engelhard, the Duke of Windsor, Maria Shrady,
Viscount Margesson, Mrs Edmund Wilson, Senator Mansfield;
(in front) Phyllis McGinley and Dan McKeon.*

for me then and later.' As a maker of converts however Fr D'Arcy lacked the killer instinct; he made the Catholic Church seem so wonderful that his neophytes hesitated to barge their way into it. When the war broke out in September 1939, with Fr D'Arcy away in America, Pakenham was still an Anglican. It took the more ruthless hand of Evelyn Waugh, who appreciated the state of mind of an officer about to go on active service, to give him the final push with a well-timed letter. Elizabeth Pakenham, so lately Fr D'Arcy's opponent at the Oxford Union, trod the same path six years later, and Fr D'Arcy's friendship with her husband widened to embrace her. When in 1969 their daughter Catherine was killed in a road accident they invited Fr D'Arcy to stay with them and, in Lord Longford's words, 'he provided her with inexpressible comfort.'[47]

Fr Hastings's judgment on Fr D'Arcy is interestingly echoed by Lord Longford's: 'He was a unique figure in the Oxford I knew as an undergraduate and a don. I would submit that no individual had so great an influence on such a wide circle of intellectuals and others ... no-one, I feel sure, went so deep with so many as Martin D'Arcy.'[48] Of the counsel he himself received from him, the injunction 'Keep close to the poor' was the one that most influenced his political outlook, for Fr D'Arcy was alive to the unreality of many who, from an aristocratic or public-school background, embraced the socialist doctrine.

The chapter of Fr D'Arcy's triumphs in the wider world must end with a word about difficulties within his own Order. When the plans for Campion Hall were being prepared the Provincial, Fr Keane, gave full support to Fr D'Arcy's ambitious views; but by the time the building began in 1934 he had been succeded by Fr Joseph Bolland, who was a very different type of man. Fr Bolland was himself an alumnus of Campion Hall and had won a Double First in Classics. His ability can be gathered from the fact that in 1927, while still only Prefect of Studies at Heythrop, he was appointed a Consultor of the Province, one of the four advisers to the Provincial, a post usually reserved for major superiors. He was a Glaswegian, an odd-looking man with disproportionately short legs almost to the point of deformity. Fr Caraman wrote: 'His diminutive stature (I think) made him rather afraid of people'[49] and he compensated for this by a waspish use of his intellectual sharpness, which only served to increase his isolation.* As Provincial he went out of his way to put men into uncongenial postings and to confound expectations. Fr D'Arcy could find it in his heart to love almost anyone, but if there was one class of person that pained him it was the insensitive and inconsiderate, nor

---

*Fr Bolland had a nice line in caustic wit. When Instructor of Tertians he noticed that his young priests were getting slack in coming down for their meditation in chapel early in the morning, and he addressed them as follows: 'Attendance at morning oblation is very bad. And if you don't believe me, go and see for yourselves.'[50]

was Fr Bolland a man to respond to perceptive efforts to penetrate his armour.

When the Hall was being built, Fr Bolland ordered Fr Walker that the rooms of the Community should contain no wardrobes, no desks and only two chairs. He relented on the wardrobes when Fr Walker showed him that chests of drawers would be more expensive, and the ban on desks was palliated by using tables with as much drawer space as possible. In spite of this ruling, Fr Walker considered that the Provincial did not interfere with the material side of the construction.[51] Whether Fr D'Arcy found the same on the academic side is more doubtful. Fr Bolland had no sympathy whatever with Fr D'Arcy's high humanistic views, and saw Campion Hall as a factory to turn out men with the right qualifications. He would have been an incongruous presence at the opening of the Hall in 1936, but he had luckily been sent away on a visitation of the New Orleans Province, which brought his subjects a respite of more than twelve months. On returning he entertained himself by choosing to overrule the custom which left the choice of undergraduates for Campion Hall in the hands of the Master, and in 1938 he sent Fr D'Arcy a man to read Geography, a thing that had not been thought of since the foundation of the Hall.

Fr Bolland represented a school of thought within the Society which disapproved of Fr D'Arcy's liberalisation of the Campion Hall regime. The young men sent there had always been a privileged elite, and if on top of this they were to enjoy three or four years' partial exemption from the Order's austere way of life many felt that an altogether too casual attitude was being promoted. During the thirties a number of scholastics left the Society from Campion Hall, though whether more frequently than at other stages of the training would require exhaustive research to determine. In 1938 one of the Hall's ablest undergraduates decamped without getting dispensation from his vows, a conduct which the Society viewed with less patience; there was obviously a special danger when young men were shown the value that the wider world set upon their talents. Such defections crystallised a concern for which an uneasiness about creeping laxity was perhaps an underlying motive. Lay opinion tends to take the liberal side, but the proper judges of the religious life can only be those who live it. Certainly no-one was more imbued than Fr D'Arcy with the Ignatian ideal, and he believed in leading by example. For those who shared his high standards his rule was an inspiration; whether it failed with the less devoted may remain a matter of opinion.

There are indications that the Roman authorities had second thoughts about Fr Bolland's appointment, for, apart from his unusual American interlude, he was relieved of office after only five years and reduced to being a professor at Heythrop.* The next Provincial was Fr Francis Mangan, with whom Fr D'Arcy's relations had long been as friendly as could be wished for.

Fr D'Arcy was the object of accusations that he used his Mastership as a power base for a career of merely worldly exploits. The milieu of the Catholic clergy was a far more limited one than that of the Church of England, where Oxford and the intellectual and social high spots were taken for granted, and such criticisms came from men in the Society for whom Fr D'Arcy's feats hinted at worlds outside their grasp. The building of an Oxford house designed by the leading architect of the day was, for example, a unique achievement for an English religious order. To take the aptest point of comparison, one can cite the failure of Lutyens's project for the Catholic cathedral in Liverpool and its supersession by an ill-constructed wigwam. For all the brilliance of its leading lights, the Society of Jesus was not unfortunately exempt from the type of mind that measures all by its own standards, and such attitudes could be justified by reproving comments against worldly elitism. Fr D'Arcy was an elitist in the sense that he wanted to see the Society at the top, and effortlessly at home there, in intellectual achievement, in its social relations, in cultural sensibility, in its public influence (one should add, in its theology and spirituality); certainly not in the sense that he intended contempt towards those who felt intimidated by any of those standards. What he did not realise was that some of the obscure might begrudge his glittering triumphs. The problem was that Campion Hall represented too small a section in the Province; his own standards would one day be swamped by those of a smaller-minded school.

---

*Since 1900 the only other English Provincials whose term of office has been ended before six years have been Fr Browne (1910–15) and Fr Helsham (1950–2), who developed cancer, Fr Bodkin (1921–6), who was required to head the new Heythrop College, and Fr D'Arcy, who was removed in the circumstances described in Chapter 7.

Chapter Five

The Pursuit of Love

Fr D'Arcy wrote a score of books in the course of his life and something like three hundred contributions to newspapers, wireless or books of multiple authorship; this reckoning excludes lectures, seminars and religious talks that were never published. In the nineteen-thirties his production was at its peak, often with seven or eight such published items a year.

Those who knew him judged that he was not at his best in writing; cold print failed to capture the magic of his conversation or his spiritual talks. His prose runs on fluently, allusively and with erudition, but it lacks the vital element given by the interplay of general talk, as one feels in the over-long paragraphs when the philosophical going gets tough. Fr D'Arcy himself lamented in later life that he had been a failure as a writer. That may be thought relatively true in comparison with his personal influence, but his writings can nevertheless claim some unique achievements in the context of contemporary Catholic writing; they presented a sublime and noble view of Christian history and they introduced the English-speaking world to a dynamic and inspiring strand in neo-Thomist thought which retains its interest today.

If Fr D'Arcy failed to do himself justice, neither did he betray himself as a writer. His works reflect his cultivation, large view and unfailing courtesy; his often-repeated parenthesis, 'if my analysis be correct', is a disclaimer of an ambition to impose his way of thinking; contemporaries are scrupulously given their due titles: Lord Russell and Père Huby, for example. Fr D'Arcy was not a polemicist, and was at his worst dealing with *ludicra* like Bertrand Russell's *Why I am not a Christian*; the obtrusive worthlessness of such offerings served as a prod to his irritation rather than a handle wherewith to wipe the floor with their authors. One of the things he did best was a purely impartial presentation of a question, and his article on the Catholic Church for the Chambers Encyclopaedia was singled out by the *Times Literary Supplement* as a model of what an encyclopaedia article should be because of its objectivity.

Fr D'Arcy was regarded as a particularly cerebral figure, and many found his philosophical flights too soaring to follow. This was at any rate not due to his taking himself too seriously, any more in writing than in social life; when he was told of an overheard snatch of talk on a London bus, 'Don't take on, dearie. Be a philosopher and don't think about it', he relished it to the extent of putting it at the front of one of his books.[1] More earnestly but with equal humility, his view of what he was about in his writings was declared at the beginning of an early work: 'Life is more than philosophy, and the welfare of human souls comes first when one has to think and behave as a man amongst fellow men.'[2] He frequently quoted St Augustine's dictum, *Nulla est homini causa philosophandi nisi ut beatus sit*: the only motive for a man to involve himself in philosophy is to achieve sanctity. This view governed his whole *oeuvre*, and he wasted no time on questions which had no value for a soul climbing to God. Those who measure the standing of philosophers by their weightiness in the construction of original systems have inevitably found him wanting. That was not an aim he ever set himself, since he regarded the Thomist view, judiciously expanded, as the firmest possible framework for philosophical enquiry; his contributions to that system were valuable and stimulating, but he did not seek to take philosophy back to the drawing board. The very balance of his work between independent books and contributions to joint productions reflects his social character as a thinker, no less than as a personality.

Almost the first philosophical task Fr D'Arcy set himself was that of explaining the rationality of religious knowledge itself. His book *The Nature of Belief*, published in 1931, is one of his most substantial, and from the philosophical point of view the most rigorous and systematic. In it he sets out psychological views which will be touched on in more detail presently, and taking as a starting point Newman's *Essay in Aid of a Grammar of Assent* he develops and modifies Newman's theory. His thesis is that belief of any kind is not the mere inspection of a chain of argument but an entry into a three-dimensional world in which facts converge, support each other and form a structure whose completeness and solidity provides a firm basis for conviction.

Where Newman had been brought up on the eighteenth-century Anglican philosophers, the lodestar of Fr D'Arcy's thinking was the philosophy of St Thomas Aquinas. As we have seen, this was not a foregone conclusion: for a time his allegiance to the whole tradition of Realism was in question. If the influence of his Oxford tutors, and especially Cook Wilson, recaptured him for Aristotelianism, it did not specifically point him back towards St Thomas. His enthusiasm for Gerard Manley Hopkins might well have led him to share Hopkins's fascination with Scotism, as it did Christopher Devlin at the instance of Fr D'Arcy's own teaching. It was a system well calculated to appeal to his warm and mobile intellect, but he could not dispense with rigour and solidity in philosophy, and these were qualities which, while he appreciated the insights Scotus brought to Christian truth, he found only in Thomism.

In 1930 he published his *St Thomas Aquinas*, a biographical as well as philosophical study aimed at a general readership. Within that framework he took the exposition of St Thomas's thought to the limits of the practicable. When G.K. Chesterton produced a book on St Thomas Aquinas shortly afterwards, Fr D'Arcy had the impression that his own was the only book on the subject Chesterton had consulted. That must be judged quite probable, but if so Chesterton could be said to have succumbed to a subtle Jesuit wile. With the Thomist revival of the late nineteenth century, two schools of interpretation had developed. One may be called the Dominican school, wedded to a faithful rendering of the Angelic Doctor's teaching and, in more extreme cases – those whom one Catholic writer classified as the man-eating Thomists – inclined to denounce attempts to improve on it as proof of radical doctrinal corruption. Another viewed the text of St Thomas in an altogether more dynamic way, not necessarily because it wished to disagree with him but because it saw in his teaching pointers to truths which were open to highly fruitful development. Many of this latter school were Jesuits, and they were the influences, one may say, that turned Fr D'Arcy decisively to the Thomist system; he viewed it not as an immutable corpus but as a philosophy whose function was 'to reduce to order all that is good in human thought, no matter to what age it belongs, and to grow as a living system reconciling the present with the past, succouring the tiny fresh truths which are ever springing from the soil and adapting them to its own life.'[3] In his *St Thomas Aquinas* he therefore freely used the works of his contemporary Jesuit mentors to interpret the significance of St Thomas's thought, and did his utmost to bring out the dynamic element hidden in the serene and even dry tenor of the Thomist canon.

What especially caught Fr D'Arcy's interest in the approach of the neo-Thomists was the effort to complement the abstractness and objectivity of St Thomas's thought with an exploration of the subjective basis of belief, in other words of the human psyche and the springs of its cognition. Among the Jesuit thinkers who had struck out in that direction, the first in time was Fr Pierre Scheuer, who taught philosophy in Belgium in the early years of the century. He was followed by Fr Pierre Rousselot in France, who was killed in 1915, and by his fellow Belgian Joseph Maréchal, who produced in the 1920s a monumental series of highly original volumes, *Le Point de Départ de la Métaphysique*; amongst other aims in his ambitious scheme he exposed the failings of Kant and demonstrated how his notions could be corrected and completed in the context of the Thomist system. Maréchal and especially Rousselot became Fr D'Arcy's particular guides. His sense of the need to produce a Catholic and Thomist view of the personality led him at about this time, he tells us, to contemplate writing a book on psychology. This never took shape, but the whole trend of his writings on the subject of love is a witness to his absorption in this psychological search.

The roots of this neo-Thomist school were traceable to a revolution in the French intellectual scene which took place towards the end of the nineteenth century, a sudden counter-attack on the dominant scientific Positivism which thought of itself as having won a final victory over outmoded metaphysics. The Voltaire of this rebellion was not a Catholic apologist but a Jew, Henri Bergson, who in 1888 wrote his *Essai sur les données immédiates de la conscience*. He championed the claims of intuition against a purely deductive or inductive view of knowledge, and set up the primacy of human vitality and action against scientific materialism. His characteristic gift to his disciples was the concept of an *élan vital* which defied any materialistic attempt to define it. Amongst other lines of influence, he became an inspirer of the Modernists in their urge to subjectivise religion, and he later inspired evolutionists like Teilhard de Chardin.

Bergson's philosophy required some adaptation before it could be made to serve Catholic orthodoxy, and the first mediator appeared in the person of his disciple Maurice Blondel. As a young professor at Lille Blondel published his book *L'Action* in 1893, rejecting as forcibly as Bergson did the aridities of Positivism. He propounded a type of Hegelian dialectic deduced from the very nature of human action. Man must by nature act and take up some position, he argued; however inconsequential, the logic of that action will force him to go further, so that the drive of his aspirations must lead him higher and higher and in time to what, as a mere man, he finds himself unable to rise to: the end of his efforts must be either *vouloir indéfiniment* or *vouloir l'infini*. If he is consistent with himself, he must be led to religious faith, and to beg God to complete his life.

This thesis made a great impression on the Jesuit neo-Thomists who have been named, but the task they saw was to refine the buccaneering impressionism of Bergson and Blondel and incorporate their insights into a solid and cogent philosophy. Rousselot wanted to get away from the anti-rational element in Bergson's thought and restated Bergson's dichotomy of concept and intuition in terms of St Thomas's *ratio* and *intellectus*, the reasoning process and the understanding. The relation between them was one not of opposition but of incompleteness and completeness. Reason, hampered by its mediate type of knowledge, strove to overleap itself into intuition, the most perfect type of knowledge. Intuition is used here not in its colloquial sense but in the scholastic sense of that unmediated knowledge of things possessed by God and the angels.

In developing this theme, Rousselot appealed to the Thomist and

Aristotelian principle of potency and act: every creature has an indefinite degree of potency, arising from its imperfection and the possibility of attaining a more perfect state, and to the extent that it attains that state it passes from potency to act. Thus God alone is pure act, without any element of potency. Applying this to human nature, Rousselot saw man as striving to attain his own full identity from a basis of incompleteness and imperfection: 'to actuate himself, to realize himself and pass from potency to act, will be for him to tend to this conquest, to this adequation. So it is therefore, on the one hand, that the sense of operation characteristic of humanity, which is its intellection, ought to be taken from the innate desire which the human subject has of equalizing itself, of winning its own nature.'[4] In intellection, which he regarded as the characteristic and essential form of human action, the passage from reasoning to immediate intuition corresponded to this process of self realisation.

As an example of the inherent human desire to attain the perfect act Fr D'Arcy quoted the story of how Michelangelo, standing before his completed statue of Moses, struck it saying, 'Speak!'.[5] Following Rousselot, he argued that in the attainment of that ultimate perfection the conflict between the incompleteness of a person as a mundane being and his essential integrity is resolved, and that 'the culminating act of a spirit is to be itself in an undivided act of self-to-itself, an act of self-realisation or self-expression, in which all that one is is actualised in the very form of thought.' St Paul's image that we now see in a glass darkly is given an application to the whole of human cognition: 'The form in which we think (which is the past content of experience absorbed into the self) is therefore a prelude or foretaste of a diviner state in which there will be no latent dispositions but instead full noonday consciousness.'[6]

The passage from potency to act thus implies a change in our manner of knowing. Just as by that passage human nature reaches an identity with its true self, so it reaches a sort of identity with what it knows. A mind which had fully attained this state of act would no longer rely on mediate perception but would have direct intuition of things, and more of persons, through perfect empathy with them. We can see a foreshadowing of this doctrine in a passage of St Thomas's: 'There is one special mode belonging to the rational nature wherein God is said to be present as the known is in the knower and the beloved in the lover. And since the rational creature by its own operation of knowledge and love attains to God Himself, according to this special manner, God is said to exist in the rational creature, but also to dwell therein as in his own temple.'[7]

This philosophy places the self and its intrinsic nature at the heart of the question of what it is to attain truth. So far, however, it provides no account of the motive power which impels the soul thus to realise itself. For the answer to that question Rousselot was drawn to St Augustine, whose thought he wove into a synthesis with Thomism which is his characteristic contribution. In his effort to explain his own Odyssey towards God, St Augustine gives us the first psychological treatise to be found in ancient literature, the first search into the inner working of the spirit. He found the motive force of the intellect in love, a love which, from his neo-Platonist grounding, he understood as an attraction for and assimilation to the highest. The Platonic doctrine of harmonies taught that like was known by like, and the soul recognised the resonance of truth and goodness within itself, judging that resonance by absolute and perfect norms. In his youthful searchings for truth, therefore, Augustine described himself as unconsciously hungering after the perfection which he ultimately knew as the God of Christian revelation. 'I loved not yet, yet I loved to love ... I sought what I might love, in love with loving, and safety I hated, and a way without snares. For within me was a famine of that inward food, Thyself, my God.'[8]

For Augustine this yearning, this refusal to be content with a comfortable inactivity, in other words this impulse of love, was integral to thought and to the attainment of truth; the love of God reached at the end of it was the entire fulfilment of that impulse. 'For if the poet have leave to say: *trahit sua quemque voluptas*,* speaking not of compulsion but of love, not of obligation but of pleasure, how much more ought we to say that every man who is gladdened by truth, gladdened by goodness, gladdened by justice, gladdened by everlasting life, is drawn to Christ, who is all these things.'[9]

Rousselot thus follows St Augustine in constructing a philosophy in which desire or love is the motive power driving us towards truth. Fr D'Arcy sketches the interconnexion between thought and desire when he points out that we are cross when stuck and grow merry when the end comes in sight,[10] that we love the people and places that we are familiar with and, for example in scholarship, we seek to know better what we love. The fuller working out of this connexion he found in Maréchal: 'Within the cold clarity of truth he discovers a buried warmth of desire. Truth and goodness are one finally, and judgment and love belong to the same movement towards them. P. Maréchal therefore gets, so to speak, inside thought and gives us a kind of metaphysical psychology. In doing so, if he be right, he has supplied modern Thomism with what it needed, namely, an analysis of love and desire and personality.'[11]

The identity of knower and known in the perfect act can thus be assimilated to the identity of lover and beloved in perfect love. This was a

*Each man is drawn by his own pleasure (Virgil, Eclogues 2, line 65).

concept which Fr D'Arcy liked to illustrate by a favourite parable: 'In the well-known Persian story the lover comes to the house of the beloved and knocks. When asked who is there, he answers: 'It is I.' The beloved replies: 'There is no room for you and me.' He tries vainly again and again. Finally when asked the same question he answers: 'It is Thou', and the door opens.'[12]

To say that knowledge and love are one is not, however, to make truth a subjective thing. Other appetites have in themselves no criterion beyond their own satisfaction (though they may be controlled by reason); but the search for truth is not like this. We cannot believe something because we like it; only what we perceive to be the objective truth has the power to satisfy the appetite of the intellect. In Fr D'Arcy's words: 'The desire which fires our nature and is immanent in thought has a character distinct from all others. It is obedient to something greater and higher than itself; it cannot reach its end unless it foregoes any possible private satisfaction for the sake of learning what external reality forces it to think and by conforming itself to a moral good which is its law and not its own manufacture.'[13]

The reason for this, firstly, is that absolute truth is God himself; but secondly, if we look at the psychological implications of that fact, it brings us to the question of the innate longing for God which the Christian philosophers have progressively discovered in human nature. Aristotle himself gave the doctrine that God moves all things as the Prime Mover of the cosmos by being the object of their love (and this is the notion behind Dante's famous closing line of the *Paradiso*, *l'amor che muove il sole e l'altre stelle*). St Thomas declares that 'every mind naturally desires the vision of the divine substance.'* And Maréchal glosses this by saying that 'we experience God by absence and want; as one who knows water by thirst, God is anticipated by us; we have a prophetic sense of him.'[14] But the implications of this for natural cognition are even more radical. Traditional philosophy held that man's capacity to know God sprang from his natural capacity to know reality. The neo-Thomists stood this on its head and declared that man knew reality because of his innate affinity with God, the plenitude of reality; that he was *capax entis* because he was *capax Dei*; that his very interest in finite things, which is the condition of his getting to know them, is due to his native aspiration for the infinite reality and supreme good.

This doctrine may be placed in a useful context by means of a slight digression. One of the most important starting points of neo-Thomism was in effect a breaking away from the Aristotelian roots of its thought.

---

*Compare St Augustine: 'Thou hast made us for Thyself, and our heart is restless till it rest in Thee.'

Early Christian thinkers naturally took over the human philosophies and world-view they were accustomed to and saw Revelation and the Redemption as something superimposed on the natural world. They preserved the notion that nature had its own proper ends and perfection, but that the supernatural introduced a new dimension; nature unassisted could for example attain a certain virtue, but divine grace alone gave the means of heavenly beatitude; it provided a supernatural happiness beyond the limited happiness which is proper to human nature itself. The neo-Thomists contended that the supernatural – more, the divinisation of man – was built into the very design of the natural world, that, in Fr D'Arcy's words, 'there is no such thing as nature unassisted', nor is there any finite happiness that man can be satisfied with short of the vision of the divine.[15]

A concomitant of this view was the Scotist thesis that the Incarnation was not a consequence of the Fall, as St Thomas is supposed to have taught, but was intended by God from the beginning. Fr D'Arcy cited the opinion of Robert Grosseteste in 1230: 'The Incarnation would have happened even if man had never sinned; it was necessary to complete man's natural glory. Since human nature is capable of union with God, God must from the beginning have intended to crown man's natural endowments by sharing his nature. In this act the natural creation was completed: man became the keystone of the whole natural order which found its consolidating principle in him.'[16]

This truth implied a fundamental revolution in the way of looking at what humanity is. The attainment of union with God is not a superadded gift made to a nature which is inherently unapt for it. Rather is human nature to be defined in terms of that designed end, which is literally its most essential attribute. Fr D'Arcy writes: 'The most real thing in man is that he can be charged with the divine nature.' We can see how this chimes with Hopkins's assertion that all things are 'charged with love, charged with God, and if we know how to touch them, give off sparks and take fire, yield drops and flow, ring and tell of him.'[17] Fr D'Arcy therefore holds that 'human nature is the kind of being that God created in order to divinise it' and that, looking particularly to the Incarnation, 'we ought to define man as a kind of being whom it is possible to deify.'[18]

This philosophy, which puts God so intimately at the centre of the human personality, leads naturally to an acute sensitivity to what the self is. Our Lord's precepts were given because 'he knew what is in man', and those who seek to imitate Him must strive to share that knowledge. St Augustine writes, *ecce intus eras, et ego foris*, and his search for the One within leads him to an exploration and a purification of the self He inhabits. 'The whole of our tasks, brethren, in this life,' he writes, 'consists in healing the heart's eye, through which God is seen.'[19] This exploration of the self leads his followers to another great psychological thinker, Cardinal Newman, to whom Fr D'Arcy came through French channels. Both Blondel and Rousselot showed the influence of Newman's writings at a time when they stirred less interest in England, and the third disciple to be mentioned, the most devoted of them, was the abbé Brémond, whose advocacy of Newman made it necessary for him to leave the Society of Jesus to escape suspicions during the Modernist crisis.

Such suspicions were fed by the wish of the Modernists themselves to annex the Cardinal to their cause; but however fallacious on both sides, the association had brought Newman's philosophical good name to its nadir in Martin D'Arcy's youth. To read what he wrote about Newman in the early 1930s is to realise how far contemporaries were from being accustomed to the adulation that has since been obligatory in treating his memory. What attracted Fr D'Arcy to Newman was not his personality – he criticised him, remarkably enough, for an excess of the Oxford manner – but his extraordinary psychological penetration, in particular in his examination of the human mind in the *Essay in aid of a Grammar of Assent*. As a young man Newman recalled being aware of 'two and two only supreme and luminously self-evident beings, myself and my Creator',[20] and the high value which all through his life he attached to the conscience derived from his sense of its being the voice of God within him. His study of that inner self in his writings was not however what brought him his public fame. He was revered as the harbinger of the Second Spring, but in the first quarter of the twentieth century he was not taken seriously as a philosopher. It was Fr D'Arcy's work to add that stone to the resurgent structure of his reputation.

The last great influence on Fr D'Arcy's early thought, and in this case without the lead of his neo-Thomist teachers, was Gerard Manley Hopkins. Here again the exploration of the soul was the fascination he found. The psychological introspection fostered by the Jesuit training was transmuted in Hopkins by a mind of acute sensibility. In his notes on the Spiritual Exercises of St Ignatius, Hopkins explains this search for the self in the following passage:

Nothing else in nature comes near this unspeakable stress of pitch, distinctiveness, and selving, this self being of my own. Nothing explains it or resembles it, except so far as this, that other men to themselves have the same feeling. But this only multiplies the phenomena to be explained so far as the cases are alike and do resemble. But to me there is no resemblance; searching nature I taste *self* but at one tankard, that of my own being.[21]

What Hopkins means by his word 'selving' is best learnt from one of his most beautiful poems:

> As kingfishers catch fire, dragonflies draw flame;
> As tumbled over rim in roundy wells
> Stones ring; like each tucked string tells, each hung bell's
> Bow swung finds tongue to fling out broad its name;
> Each mortal thing does one thing and the same:
> Deals out that being indoors each one dwells;
> Selves – goes itself; *myself* it speaks and spells,
> Crying *What I do is me: for that I came.*
>
> I say more: the just man justices;
> Keeps grace: that keeps all his goings graces;
> Acts in God's eye what in God's eye he is –
> Christ. For Christ plays in ten thousand places,
> Lovely in limbs, and lovely in eyes not his
> To the Father through the features of men's faces.

At the origin of Hopkins's thinking we may detect Plato's notion of God imposing on matter the likeness of the ideal forms, whose harmony can ring from the apparent dullness of their material vesture. With a strong influence of this Idealist concept, Hopkins defined the self as 'the intrinsic oneness of a being which is prior to its being … A bare self, to which no nature has as yet been added.'[22] This passage expresses the deep sense of the primariness of the self that was shared by Hopkins and Fr D'Arcy, and the latter was to incorporate it in a highly individual way into his theory of love.

These therefore were Fr D'Arcy's philosophical mentors, all of them minds marked by a sensitivity akin to his own and a sense of the closeness of the divine in the material world. The dynamism of the view of human nature which he took and developed from them came from seeing it as straining to break the bonds of the flesh to reach the vision of God, as feeling even in its earthly prison the yearning for divinisation which Christ fulfils. One of Fr D'Arcy's favourite texts was from St Paul's epistle to the Romans: 'For we know that all creation doth groan and travail together to this hour. And not only so, but ourselves, too, who have the firstfruits of the Spirit – we ourselves groan within ourselves while awaiting adoption, the redemption of our body.'[23] The spirit struggling in that quest for a higher world is only half immersed in this lower one. 'Unlike all other animals,' writes Fr D'Arcy, 'man has no element in which he is completely happy; he moves in turn from the passing to the eternal and back again.'[24] He contended, against the obvious, corporeal notion of a man, that 'We are essentially an activity or substantial tendency. We move out from God by His initial stress on our being ... all our life we are being drawn back to Him as our end, the final Love, the plenary goodness whose livery creation wears.'*[25]

The pain of struggling from the lower environment to that in which we have our true home was one Fr D'Arcy knew from the effort of self-purification which is the daily task of a religious. If he celebrated the joy of the goal aspired to, he spoke also of how as it mounts to God 'the soul has to suffer the onslaught of the divine love without knowing its ways, as though God were like a surgeon operating upon it', so that 'many there are who, invited to a complete self-surrender, have held back and remained decent mediocrities, and so lost the golden opportunity of union.'[26]

It was from these premises that Fr D'Arcy set himself the task of constructing his philosophy of human love in the work that of all his books most engaged his feeling, *The Mind and Heart of Love* (1945), on which he was at work throughout the second world war. The first seed of this theme had been planted by Rousselot's *Problème de l'Amour au Moyen Age*, and a further incentive to the undertaking was provided by a large work, *Eros and Agape*, by the Swedish bishop Anders Nygren. The first of its three volumes appeared in English in 1932, and references in Fr D'Arcy's writings show that he was aware of it from the beginning.[27] The duality of Nygren's title reflects the characteristically post-Lutheran polarisation of the human personality which he propounded, and he accused St Augustine of importing the alien Greek notion of Eros, a rational but self-centred love, into Christianity, whose proper ideal should be the self-denying Agape. This was a subject Fr D'Arcy had very much at heart; it is a little unfortunate that his Oxford training channelled the project of writing his own *magnum opus* on love to a large degree into the form of criticising somebody else's. The discussion he devotes to Nygren in *The Mind and Heart of Love* might be described as using a sledge-hammer to show that a nut is cracked; despite its monumentality, the Swede's book did not deserve to have such a structure of discussion built upon it.

A second book that contributed to his thought was brought to his attention by one of his Campion Hall scholastics, Vincent Turner. It was Denis de Rougemont's *L'Amour et l'Occident*, published in 1939. Rougemont drew attention to the fact that the notion of romantic love disseminated by the mediaeval troubadors was not, as was generally assumed, a by-product of the Christian ethos or even compatible with

---

* Compare Hopkins's hymn:

    Thee God, I come from, to thee go

All day long I like fountain flow

    From thy hand out ...

Christianity, but presented an ideal directly opposed to it. For Rougemont however Eros was not the rational, commanding impulse of Greek philosophy and of Nygren's interpretation, but was a dark passion causing man to forget himself for the sake of the beloved. The opposition between these two views was a provocation for Fr D'Arcy to discuss them and try to extract the truth from their disharmony.

The Mind and Heart of Love, which ranges over the concept of love and its history through ancient and mediaeval culture, is Fr D'Arcy at his most erudite and discursive, and some have felt that he planted a garden of such multiple fragrance that one loses the scent of his argument in it. The book's sub-title is *Lion and Unicorn. A Study in Eros and Agape*. The dualities here (and in the phrase 'mind and heart') reflect the aim of studying two contrasting elements in human nature. The lion represents the self-centred impulse, with the desire to dominate; the unicorn's symbolism is given by the mediaeval legend that the unicorn can be lured to its capture by a virgin, for 'no sooner does he see the damsel, than he runs towards her, and lies down at her feet, and so suffers himself to be captured by the hunters.' It therefore represents a submissive and self-sacrificing impulse. Eros and Agape correspond to the same division. A further duality is proposed by the abbé Brémond, who used a parable borrowed from the Catholic poet Paul Claudel depicting *animus*, the mind, in opposition to *anima*, the soul. The two words further suggest the contrast between the masculine and the feminine sides of the personality.

To these contrasting aspects of the self correspond two loves, a concept which goes back to the earliest centuries of Christianity. St Augustine, in a passage which served as a model for St Ignatius's meditation on the Two Standards, had written: 'Two loves built two cities – the earthly, which is built up by the love of self to the contempt of God; and the heavenly, which is built up by the love of God to the contempt of self.' Yet the philosophical question arose, how can love of God really extend to the contempt of self? However purified its character, love must by essence mean desiring what is loved for oneself. Take away that 'selfish' element and you are left with approbation or admiration, but the element of desire implied by love must be annihilated. Rousselot had tackled this problem and claimed to have the solution in the doctrine of St Thomas that man is, metaphorically, a member of God; he is therefore only acting according to his proper nature when he is subserving the whole to which he belongs. In loving God selflessly he is acting by God's own power within him – to use a line from Jacopone da Todi which Fr D'Arcy often quoted, 'Thou art the Love with which the heart loves Thee.'[28] Like other insights Rousselot threw out in his short life, this one needed further development, and Fr D'Arcy may be said to have devoted his life to providing it.

Building on Hopkins's thought, Fr D'Arcy maintained that in its essence selfhood, far from being a handicap to be overcome, is a unique reflexion of God's glory, and that 'We belong most to God by maintaining the very selfhood which He has given us.'[29] It is therefore false to speak as though perfect love must imply the denial of self, and even more to make union with God an extinction of the self, as in the Buddhist Nirvana. The end of love is not self-annihilation but union. Selfishness consists in loving the self in isolation, but in Christian love the self is seen in its sonship to God, while God remains the sustainer and nurturer of the self He has fathered. Love of God for His own sake does not therefore imply the repudiation of the self.

That is not to say that love of God is reached by a self-regarding calculation, either desiring God for His benefits to the self or, more nobly, identifying the self's good with God. The fact remains that perfect love of God must consist in loving Him for Himself, without any shade of self-interest. In the abstract this is objectively right, but psychologically, if love is a true impulse of the personality and not just a submission to an ideal, how is it possible? It is in answering this question that Fr D'Arcy perplexed many of his readers with a distinction deriving Eros and Agape respectively from essence and existence. He took Hopkins's concept of the bare self with no nature added to it and attributed to this essential entity the self-regarding love, which sees the self as an absolute in isolation and therefore has no impulse beyond its own protection and aggrandisement. In possessing existence, however, the self must recognise itself as depending on God; the existential urge is by nature extrovert, since it is concerned with its dependent place in the world of existing things, and in particular with the ground of all existence, which is God.

This perhaps was the stage of Fr D'Arcy's argument that baffled lay readers and tried the sympathy of philosophers. A first difficulty that can be raised is one which Fr D'Arcy himself came to feel. For all his repeated insistence that one undivided self is the subject of both the loves he studies, the very concept of two distinct impulses seems at variance with this. In fact by 1966 Fr D'Arcy had come round to the view that his solution of deriving one love from the essential and the other from the existential side of the self made too deep a division in the human personality.[30]

A more fundamental philosophical objection applies however to the use made of Hopkins's notion of the essential self prior to existence; in Fr D'Arcy's acceptance of it we seem to see the sole relic in his thought of his early flirtation with Idealism. A different school is inclined to find the notion of talking about essence bare of existence an unprofitable one, if not positively mistaken, and one does not need to belong to Gilbert Ryle's school of linguistic analysis to think on those lines. The least that can be said is that it is a shock, after following the rich and luminous philosophy of nature and love built up by Fr D'Arcy, to find it culminate in a doctrine so abstruse and so lacking in inevitability. Its role in resolving the problems he treats is that it points to the need, since man is necessarily both essential and existential, to complement the essential Eros with the existential Agape and thus to a reconciliation between the two, where they had been declared opposed. Yet to learn, after Fr D'Arcy's deep exploration of the nature of the psyche, that an essential impulse requires to be perfected by an existential one is a horrible anticlimax. But for this questionable concept, one can hardly avoid feeling that the logic of his thought would have led him to precisely the opposite analysis: that in a more obvious sense it is the self-regarding love which is the existential impulse, concerned for the preservation and aggrandisement of the self in its primary state of unrealised potency; bringing Blondel's concept into play, however, the self's striving for realisation then leads it to its essential nature, to the state where it is, within its limits, pure act, when it sees face to face and attains the true nature of man as a divinisable being, one whose essential tendency is one of union with his Creator.

The vivid sense of the self which Fr D'Arcy shared with Hopkins and with Newman is at the bottom of his puzzling conclusion; and the whole account given of his line of thought may make it sound excessively self-absorbed. That would be a mistaken impression, and one should not leave it to be thought that Fr D'Arcy, who so rejoiced in human relations, omitted in his Grand Tour of the heart to visit human love. In treating this subject he introduced the third term Philia between Eros and Agape. Here too the sense of God in human impulses is the guiding light of his thought, the conviction expressed in the words of Coventry Patmore which he quotes in another place, that love 'is sure to be something less than human if it is not something more.'[31] One does not however feel that in his study of human love Fr D'Arcy provides a complete philosophy of it. That was not indeed his primary purpose in writing this particular book; but mention of Patmore jogs a suggestion of the fundamental reason: in human relations the prime exemplar must be married love, and within that ideal it is female love in turn that, by its acuteness and sensitivity, and more especially by its qualities of receptiveness and submission, approaches most closely the perfection of the Christian ideal. Fr D'Arcy points out indeed that, where the tendency of the male is to dominate and to make the pleasure of love its own end, the female instinctively looks beyond her mate and her own happiness to her children and to a self-giving for others. This subject of married love was one in which it would have been difficult for a celibate to immerse himself. Yet Fr D'Arcy's inhibition in that respect was a loss, for he possessed a very feminine sensibility that, if he had pursued the theme, would have equipped him to give a view of it of which few moralists have been capable.

The value of Fr D'Arcy's great essay on love is not removed by concepts which are difficult or questionable; and he returned to the theme again and again in the remaining thirty years of his life, in books such as *The Meeting of Love and Knowledge* (1957) and in the countless talks and articles that he produced in England, in America, even in countries like Japan where he welcomed the insights of a wholly different tradition. The value of his quest was in the search to perfect a philosophy affirming that love and truth are one, not because it was pleasant to entertain the thought but because it could be seen as expressing the most inward nature of reality. He thus took Catholic apologetics in England beyond their usual utilitarian scope and onto a more philosophical plane, the inspiration for which had to be sought among French writers. Whether he made any lasting impression with it among his unmetaphysical countrymen may be difficult to say; but surely few speculative schools of thought that have enjoyed a vogue since Fr D'Arcy's day have been of such intrinsic value.

Chapter Six

The War Years

In August 1939 Fr D'Arcy set out on a flying visit to the United States to attend a *Pax Romana* congress in Washington. It was his second visit to the country, the first having taken place in 1935; at that time the appeal for the Campion Hall building fund was in need of stimulation and Fr D'Arcy went to see if the American Catholics could produce more for the project than their English brethren. Sailing in February 1935, he unexpectedly found Tom Burns on the ship, and promptly enlisted him as his Mass server. Burns already had experience of Fr D'Arcy's resolution where his daily Mass was concerned, but the attendance imposed an extra strain on his loyalty when he was obliged to get up early in the morning after late revels in the ship's ballroom.[1]

Arriving in America, Fr D'Arcy gave public lectures in Boston on 3rd March and in New York the following day. He preached a Lenten course at the church of Our Lady of Lourdes in New York; he also made a visit to San Francisco. His activities were cultural as well as religious, and he took the opportunity to promulgate his enthusiasm for Gerard Manley Hopkins, who was still as unknown in America as he had been in England a few years before.[2] In New York his principal contact seems to have been Fr Woodlock's elder brother Tom, who was a well-known figure on Wall Street and a member of a group of notable and active Catholic laymen.[3] This visit provided the first example of Fr D'Arcy's extravagant success in the higher reaches of Catholic society. He was given visitor's privileges at the Century and Harvard clubs in New York and was lionised by the leading Catholic hostesses, Mrs Hoguet in New York and Mrs William Corcoran Eustis in Washington, the latter a recent convert. One of his greatest supporters then and for many years to come was a grandiloquent Irishman called Maurice Leahy, who was prominent in the Oriel Society in New York and lost no opportunity of honouring him. The tour culminated in May with Fr D'Arcy's receiving an honorary Doctorate of Laws from Georgetown University, Washington, with a dinner in his honour attended by the British Ambassador.

The mission that had taken him to America, that of raising funds for Campion Hall, was highly successful. American Catholicism, with its overwhelmingly working-class roots, was avid for European culture; the

Catholic champions of the English-speaking world were held in high regard; and there was enormous respect for the needs of what was billed as 'the first Catholic college to have been founded in Oxford since the Reformation.' Excluded from the Ivy League tradition, American Catholic professionals and plutocrats could affirm their claim to a more ancient civility by honouring savants from the old world. With his wide-ranging erudition and delicate philosophy, Fr Martin D'Arcy seemed the very personification of Oxford culture, and his courtly manners, his Norman pedigree and his ease in every society made him a trophy even to those who did not attain to a complete understanding of him – intellectually or, perhaps, phonetically.*

This visit shortly afterwards involved Fr D'Arcy, quite innocently, in a set-back for Anglo-American Catholic relations. Lord Howard of Penrith was working to bring English and American Catholics closer together, and he asked Fr D'Arcy to join the committee for a dinner he organised for the Calvert Associates at the Breakespeare Club† in July 1935. The party, who were a group of prominent Catholic laymen, were led by the famous editor of *Catholic World*, Fr James Gillis, who had been persuaded to divert them off the route of their pilgrimage to Rome. The leading speaker at the dinner was Hilaire Belloc, who had married an American wife and who had himself lectured in America. Unfortunately Belloc was in a particularly Europe-and-the-Faith mood that evening, and when he came to speak pronounced the opinion that 'between the Europeans and the Americans the gulf is growing wider every year; they have taken different paths and seem to have little in common except that they belong to the same species, man.'[4] Douglas Woodruff, who was to speak next, sought to repair the damage by striking a note of humour, but this proved a serious miscalculation; he was known as the author of *Plato's American Republic*, which had already been interpreted by the humourless as making fun of the Americans, and it was thought that he was up to the same tricks again. The Calvert Associates were furious and Fr Gillis was confirmed for life in his hostility to England.

A contretemps of a more global nature followed Fr D'Arcy's second journey to America. The outbreak of the Second World War forced him to surrender his place to more urgent travellers and he was stranded in the country for an unknown period. At that point Fr George Bull, the head of the Philosophy Faculty of the Jesuit university of Fordham, in New York, suddenly died. He was a friend of Fr D'Arcy's and had invited

---

*Fr D'Arcy spoke with an Oxford accent of antique flavour, appreciably further removed from neutral speech than the standard public-school accent of other Stonyhurst men of his generation. It would take a phonetician to say whether the additional influence was from Oxford or some other source, for example the Irish gentry.

†Named after the English pope Nicholas Breakspear, Adrian IV.

him to lecture on his 1935 visit. Fordham was at that time under the rule of its most famous President, Fr Robert Gannon, who immediately grasped the opportunity. He offered Fr D'Arcy the vacant post and he, having no early prospect of returning to Oxford, accepted it. He continued officially as Master of Campion Hall but for the next year his duties were discharged by the admirable Fr Leo O'Hea, a rather older Stonyhurst contemporary of his who was well known in Oxford as Rector of the Catholic Workers' College.

During the course of the academic year Fr D'Arcy was unexpectedly called upon to do his bit for the war effort one feast day when a British patriotic film was shown in the university after dinner.* When the Jesuit students reacted to it by jeering and barracking, Fr D'Arcy got up from his seat in the front row and walked out. 'He retreated into not a thunderous silence but into a silence that struck like lightning. He was profoundly affronted. He would only speak in answer to the demands of religion, inevitable business or teaching. In the end a deputation of students came to apologise and it was over.'[5]

An incident in Fr D'Arcy's year in America was the controversy over Bertrand Russell's appointment to a Chair at the College of the City of New York. Russell was regarded with particular detestation because of his attack on Christian ethics in his *Marriage and Morals*, and the opposition to his appointment was led by Catholics, who were gaining influence in America as defenders of strict moral standards. A Mrs Jean Kay brought a suit before the Supreme Court in March 1940 to have the appointment annulled, and the Catholic judge, Justice McGeehan, ruled that the appointment would in effect be 'establishing a chair of indecency.' The Jesuit magazine *America* described Russell, more imaginatively but with equal forthrightness, as a 'desiccated, divorced and decadent advocate of sexual promiscuity.' In the middle of the furore Fr D'Arcy was taking part in a radio programme in which the case was discussed. Now Fr D'Arcy yielded to nobody in his sense of the harm done by Bertrand Russell, but in a country like the United States, founded on the principles of free speech, this way of pulling moral boundaries out of a hat struck him as savouring of the kind of lynch law which he deplored later in the McCarthy period. When asked to comment on the case he replied, in his own account, 'I'm not going to answer this question. First of all, Bertrand Russell is an Englishman. I too am an Englishman, and I don't believe in attacking one's fellow countrymen outside one's country. Then again I'm not very keen on this business of hunting down persons, pursuing them and the rest. If you want the principles upon which a case of this sort is

*Patrick O'Donovan, who tells the story, identifies it as *Desert Victory*, but that was not made till 1943, after both Fr D'Arcy's wartime visits to America.

to be judged, I'll be glad to give them to you, but I'm not going to touch persons.'

By chance Bertrand Russell was listening to that broadcast and his gratitude was expressed years later when he met Fr D'Arcy for a BBC discussion programme. He told Fr D'Arcy before it, 'Father, I owe you a deep debt of gratitude. You see, once when I was being hounded you were the only person who would not speak against me.' And a friendship began between them which lasted until Russell's death.[6]

After receiving an honorary degree at Fordham, in July and August 1940 Fr D'Arcy taught a summer course at the University of San Francisco; he then returned to England by way of Lisbon, from which he arrived by air on September 24th, a fortnight before the commencement of the new academic year.[7] The friendships he had made in America resulted for the rest of the war, and long afterwards, in streams of food-parcels sent to him across the Atlantic in such quantities that he had to give some of them away to his friends. They enabled the hospitality of Campion Hall to continue at an unusually high level for the times.

Fr D'Arcy's good relations with the new Provincial, Fr Mangan, were reflected in his being able to secure Fr Basil Gurrin as Spiritual Father at Campion Hall. Basil Gurrin exemplified a type of strongly-marked though unintellectual character that Fr D'Arcy greatly enjoyed. A decided conservative, he modelled himself on the great Stonyhurst Jesuits of the past, forthright men like Peter Gallwey, John Gerard and Bernard Vaughan. Fr Gurrin's devotion to his old school-friend was recorded in a caricature by their fellow Jesuit Fr Sam Dolan. In 1942, during his second absence in America, Fr D'Arcy entrusted to him the revision of the proofs of his new book *Death and Life* as he had done with *The Mass and the Redemption* sixteen years before.

In Fr D'Arcy's absence there had been an official order that material should not be kept in attics where in the event of bombing it might provide fuel for fires, and on his return he was dismayed to find that the Bursar of the Hall, an ex-naval man, had taken drastic action and cleared out the large stock kept in Campion Hall's extensive attics. He was said to have sold the entire collection to a nearby shop for five shillings. Much of what went was the furniture put in the old Hall during Fr O'Fallon Pope's time, but also included were religious paintings and a valuable picture in a gold frame given to Fr D'Arcy by Jack Walton (who had died in 1939). Walking along St Ebbe's shortly after his return, Fr D'Arcy was astounded to see some of these items in a shop window; Jack Walton's picture had his name and donation still inscribed on it. He recovered what he could, but much was lost for good.[8]

Fr D'Arcy resumed his Greats lectures, but university life was suffering the same disruption as during the first war, and there was a good deal of work to be done outside, lecturing, preaching and broadcasting. Still a member of the BBC's religious committee, in 1941 he broadcast on Christian unity and on the Nazi persecution of the Catholic Church, using information that had been smuggled out by Jesuit contacts in Germany. At Oxford he preached and spoke frequently throughout the war at the Catholic chaplaincy, now under the care of Fr Alfonso de Zulueta. The war provided the occasion for renewing contact with Bernard Wall, who had had to close his paper on the outbreak of hostilities and was working at Balliol on war propaganda. With the absence of Isaiah Berlin in America on similar work, his successor as Fr D'Arcy's chief friend among the dons was the amusing and pleasantly unworldly Lord David Cecil, also of New College, who shortly afterwards became Professor of English Literature.

At Christmas 1940 Campion Hall was chosen by the Catholic hierarchy as the venue for a special meeting. In Cardinal Hinsley the Jesuits had the warmest friend of their Order ever to occupy the see of Westminster. He frequently stayed at Stonyhurst for a rest during the war, and he stayed at Campion Hall in 1942 when he visited Oxford to receive an honorary doctorate. One of Hinsley's favourite projects was the Sword of the Spirit movement, aimed at the application of Christian principles to social problems; this enterprise, which was novel in its alliance with non-Catholic groups, aroused little support among the other Catholic bishops or clergy, and Fr D'Arcy was one of the few priests to associate themselves with the movement. On May 11th 1941 he braved the heaviest bombing London had known in the Blitz to speak in Kingsway on the subject of 'a Christian Order in Britain' in a congress presided over by Cardinal Hinsley and the Archbishop of Canterbury, and with an interconfessional group of speakers who included Dorothy Sayers.[9]

In September 1941 Fr D'Arcy left again by aeroplane for America, this time at the request of the Catholic Department of the Ministry of Information.[10] It was hoped that his work might help to influence the Catholic community in the United States, which with its overwhelming composition of Irish and Italians was the most opposed in the spectrum of American opinion to intervention in favour of the Allies. Fr Coughlin, one of its leading publicists, had been promoting quasi-Fascist views throughout the thirties, and Fr Gillis added the weight of *Catholic World* to the anti-interventionist side.* The story of Fr D'Arcy and the film at Fordham illustrates the kind of antipathy that was to be found, while it

---

*In his case, however, this was far from being due to any Fascist leanings. His outspokenness in the opposite sense led to Mussolini's causing his order, the Paulists, to be relieved of their charge of the American parish in Rome.

also suggests that Fr D'Arcy was the owner of more subtle propagandistic talents than some of the British film-makers of the time.

Arriving at Lisbon, Fr D'Arcy was told that his flight to America was delayed by bad weather. He would have been stranded without money but for a fellow passenger, a stranger who on the aeroplane had introduced himself as Hugh Macintosh; he had been a friend of Chesterton and Belloc and had collaborated with them in writing ballads. He immediately invited Fr D'Arcy to stay with him in a hotel in Estoril, where they passed the time sitting on the beach and talking poetry and philosophy. After four days' wait they were told they could continue and in the cold early hours of the morning were embarked in a car to go to the airport. They were both feeling disgruntled enough when a man came up to them asking fussily if they had his bag. 'No, we haven't got your bag,' they answered unsympathetically. As he went away Fr D'Arcy turned to Macintosh and said, 'Who do you think that is?' 'I don't know,' he replied. 'Obviously a greengrocer.' Fr D'Arcy said, 'No, I'm sure you're wrong. I think he's a Balliol man.' 'A Balliol man?' 'Yes, I think with that accent he's a Balliol man.' When they got to the Azores, where they were delayed another three days, Fr D'Arcy heard the same man being paged in the Pan-American Club as Professor Tawney, and realised he was the famous author of *Religion and the Rise of Capitalism*. He went up to him to make amends and said, 'I'm afraid we were a bit stiff.' 'Yes, you behaved very badly to me,' said Tawney. It turned out that he was travelling to give advice in Washington on economic matters, and that his bag contained valuable items over whose loss he was understandably worried.[11]

Residing in New York, Fr D'Arcy became a member of the Princeton Institute of Advanced Study, and in November he made a third visit to California to lecture at the University of San Francisco and elsewhere.[12] With the entry of America into the war in December, his work in the country was done, but getting back did not prove easy. He was kept hanging around in Baltimore, at Loyola University, for three months waiting for a ship,[13] and was eventually put onto an old whaler, where he was allocated the captain's cabin. The ship took twenty days to cross the Atlantic as it dodged German submarines, but Fr D'Arcy was able to find amusement among the dangers.[14] He arrived towards the end of April in Liverpool, where one of his undergraduates from Campion Hall, Vincent Bywater, had been detailed to meet him and spotted him by his distinctive profile crossing a window in the black-out.

A visit of a similar nature was arranged to Spain and Portugal at the end of the year. The official sympathy of both those countries was with their fellow dictatorships, and the British Council was engaged in setting up a programme of cultural propaganda which had considerable success in the educated milieux at which it was aimed. The importance attached to this work is reflected in the choice of the distinguished Hispanist Walter Starkie to direct it, and he for his part thought himself lucky to obtain the help of someone of the standing of Fr D'Arcy, with whom he established a lasting friendship. Leaving England in December 1942, Fr D'Arcy spent over a month lecturing and giving retreats. No doubt the Duke of Alba, at this time Spanish Ambassador in London, had something to do with the expedition, and in Spain Fr D'Arcy's most powerful contact was the strongly Catholic and monarchist Marqués de Oriol, a minister in Franco's government, whose son Lucas had been at Oxford in the late twenties.[15]

During 1942 Fr D'Arcy had been very active lecturing, preaching and broadcasting. In 1943 he resumed the same activity, lecturing to the troops and giving a course at London University. The Sword of the Spirit movement had set up a collaboration with the interdenominational Christian Life Campaign, at whose launch Fr D'Arcy spoke in October. Another ecumenical venture was in September 1944 when he gave an introductory talk on religious art for a conference on The Church and the Artist at the Bishop's Palace in Chichester, again with Dorothy Sayers among his fellow speakers.[16]

His more personal influence is illustrated by an appeal he received from Quintin Hogg while he was serving in the Middle East; at Christmas 1941 he wrote Fr D'Arcy a long letter asking for advice on a crisis that had emerged in his first, childless marriage. His wife had suddenly written to him asking him to redeem a 'promise' to adopt a child, or their marriage would not survive. By an unlucky postal accident, her letter had reached Hogg in two parts, and he had replied reassuring her before realising the nature of her ultimatum. The letter that Fr D'Arcy wrote counselling him in this situation has not survived, but the nature of the guidance he received is suggested by the comment he made about Fr D'Arcy: 'The thing which he always appealed to where I was concerned was the love of the Lord Jesus, which he always assumed that I had, and which, because he assumed it so gently, he really gave me to possess.'[17] His marriage nevertheless proved beyond saving, and its break-up proved one of the most painful experiences of his life.

During the war Campion Hall was able to purchase the adjoining site to the west along Brewer Street, and this inspired Fr D'Arcy to conceive an ambitious plan for the development of the Hall. In 1942 Sir Edwin Lutyens made drawings for a magnificent extension that would have converted the building into a full quadrangle bearing comparison with those of other Oxford colleges. Leaving behind the simple cottage style he had employed in 1934, Lutyens designed the two additional ranges in a full-blown classical idiom that would have made the new Campion Hall unquestionably the finest twentieth-century building in Oxford.

There was a very grand hall, a large new chapel, and a wealth of Lutyens's whimsical touches such as a trefoil-shaped corner room consisting of three apses, with a fourth wall filled by the window onto Brewer Street. The design would have cost hundreds of thousands of pounds to execute, but Fr D'Arcy conceived the enlarged house as a research centre where the American Jesuits, as well as other scholars of the Society, could come to study and have all the resources of Oxford for their work; he envisaged an American being appointed as Minister or Vice-Rector for the overseas community.[18] With the financial sinews of the American provinces and his own contacts in that country he would have had little difficulty after the war in finding the money for the project.

Academically Campion Hall was more or less protected from the ravages of military requirements. With the outbreak of war the Province's house of studies affiliated to London University had had to be evacuated, partly to Oxford, and the number of undergraduates at Campion Hall jumped to twenty-one. If this represented a dilution of quality, the Hall's honour was being sustained as fully as in the past by its leading members. Vincent Turner, after his brilliant Double First, stayed on till 1943 to work for a doctorate in Moral Philosophy, also taking over Fr D'Arcy's duties of lecturing on Aristotle during his absence in America. John Coventry, who was to have a distinguished career in the Order, was one of the undergraduates of this period and gained a First in Classics in 1942. Philip Caraman became in 1941 the first member of the Hall to be President of the Stubbs Society, a university circle of historians.[19] Most of all perhaps of any English Jesuit he was to inherit Fr D'Arcy's mantle as a writer and as a Catholic apologist with wide personal influence.

Evelyn Waugh, however, staying as a guest in November 1943, noted that: 'The talk after dinner was not as good as usual, for there are now a number of secular priests up reading the humanities and these introduced the air of the presbytery. They spoke of impostors who preyed on the devout and each in turn told his story. 'Why Father that is very like what happened to Father Freeman in Bradford ...' and indeed it was all too like. Later Frank [Pakenham] came in with more of the outer air.'[20]

Lutyens was now in the last year of his life, and it is probably to a slightly earlier visit to Campion Hall, in May 1943, that we may assign an exhibition of Evelyn Waugh's Torquemada impulses. Waugh's diary entry recorded: 'Ned Lutyens very gaga, making his old puns and obscenities, but without gusto or relevance.'[21] The story Fr D'Arcy tells is as follows:

Evelyn, in that abrupt way of his, turned to Lutyens and said, 'Ned, isn't it about time you became a Catholic?' Lutyens began to shuffle off as usual. 'Well,' Evelyn Waugh continued, 'you'd better hurry up, you know. Otherwise when you die, you'll begin to burn immediately.' This phrase bewildered him and frightened him beyond words, because weeks after that Ned came up to me and said, 'What? 'Burn immediately,' did he say 'Burn immediately'?[22]

Lutyens died in January of the following year, without having succumbed to Evelyn Waugh's missionary drive, and was buried in Westminster Abbey; Fr D'Arcy was unfortunately prevented by illness from attending the funeral.

In May 1944 Evelyn Waugh sent Fr D'Arcy the manuscript of *Brideshead Revisited*, which he was in the process of completing.* Its theme, as he wrote in 1959, was 'the operation of divine grace on a group of diverse but closely connected characters', one which at that date he conceded was 'perhaps presumptuously large';[23] but at the time of writing the book he regarded it, with some justification, as his master-piece. It is a measure of the importance he attached to this manifesto of his Catholic vision that he wished to have the imprimatur of the man to whom he particularly owed it. Fr D'Arcy's answer was given in a letter of May 23rd: 'I finished the book almost at a sitting & have waited a day to let my impressions settle down. What you want from me is a judgment on the theological and moral points in it, – so I will only say in general that I was deeply moved by the book.'

After suggesting some factual corrections Fr D'Arcy goes on, answering Waugh's request for guidance about how it would be received by a Catholic readership: 'I am sure a number will object to p 118, – because of its open talk about sleeping with a woman as an adventure for young men. The second passage p 233 will be too vivid & coarse a picture for many, & the paragraph on p 244 will be objected to for the same reason – especially 'white breast and narrow loins', – & for the further reason that the last sentence of it looks as if it were justifying & making an ideal of adultery ... I feel pretty certain that most Catholic moralists would say that you had gone over the border in these passages & that they should be put differently.'[†]

Fr D'Arcy wished his criticisms to ensure that the book would have the largest possible readership and to avoid giving 'a handle to new eccle-siastical authorities to start worrying the layman.' (He was presumably

---

*His diary for May 21st reads: 'I have written about 15,000 words in the last week and am in alternate despondency and exultation about the book. Anyway it is very near the end now.' Fr D'Arcy must have been by a long way the first reader to set eyes on the work.

†The first passage objected to is evidently the episode at the 'Old Hundredth' in Book 1, Chapter 5 (cf. below: 'the coarse phrases with the tarts'); the second, in Book 3, Chapter 1, seems to belong to the early stages of Charles Ryder's ship-board affair with Julia; in the third Julia lost her white breast but kept her narrow loins in the published version – this last being a passage which critics have generally agreed in ridiculing.

thinking of the recent appointment of the highly conventional Archbishop Griffin to succeed Cardinal Hinsley at Westminster). He ended: 'I have already said how much I have enjoyed reading what I hope will come to be regarded as a masterpiece.'[24]

The book was printed at the end of the year (Waugh told his wife: 'All the passages, including the coarse phrases with the tarts, which upset d'Arcy have been cut out for the public version'),[25] and Fr D'Arcy received a pre-publication copy as a Christmas present. He wrote back on January 4th 1945:

> 'I want to thank you for a delightful Xmas present the special edition copy of Brideshead Revisited. I feel too close to it to be sure of my own opinion about it but my friends in the Community here to whom I have lent it think it your best piece of work & a superb bit of writing.'

Evelyn Waugh's over-sensitive attitude to his Magnum Opus, as he currently called it, is shown by his grumble to his wife: 'D'Arcy's letter about MO was most unsatisfactory. He says he has not formed an opinion.'[26] Yet Fr D'Arcy's reaction to the Magnum Opus was indeed rather muted. Living in Oxford with a constant supply of American food-parcels, he had perhaps been less oppressed by the 'period of soya beans and basic English', to which Waugh in 1959 attributed the book's gastronomic and verbal excesses. For such an Oxford enthusiast he had responded probably more coolly than Waugh foresaw to the Arcadian depiction of the university in the novel's pages.

Fr D'Arcy developed other literary contacts during these years. In the summer of 1944 he met the rumbustious South African poet Roy Campbell, who had become a Catholic in Spain in 1935 and had been one of the most outspoken supporters of Franco's cause.[27] At Easter 1945 he invited Graham Greene to a party at Campion Hall – evidently their first meeting, since, although Greene's wife and children had been living in Oxford since 1940, he seldom visited them.*[28] On the same Easter Sunday Fr D'Arcy gave First Communion to John Rothenstein's nine-year-old daughter Lucy in the Campion Hall chapel; she had been living in America since the beginning of the war with her mother's parents, who had brought her up in Episcopalian practice, and her reception of the Sacrament marked her return, at her own request, to the faith of her parents.[30]

---

*From this time Fr D'Arcy began to tell people that he had influenced Graham Greene's conversion.[29] The claim can only have originated from some remark Greene made to him (perhaps he had read one of Fr D'Arcy's books at the time of his reception into the Church), since they were both well aware that his conversion had taken place twenty years before this meeting.

Evelyn Waugh records a further stay at Campion Hall a few days before the end of the war, with another of Fr D'Arcy's converts, the writer and journalist T.S. Gregory, among his fellow guests. 'Conversation mostly despondent at the collapse of Europe, the advance of Russia, heathenism. T.S Gregory talking big about our policing Europe. I pointed out that we had not the men to police England, that garrison towns were not centres of good order. Recommended catacombs.★ Father D'Arcy believed he had supernatural guarantees of the future Christianity of Europe.'[31]

Another guest soon afterwards was Quintin Hogg, who was standing in the imminent General Election. Although everybody claimed after the event to have foreseen the result, the truth is that the weight of opinion was for a fairly even outcome; but Lord Hailsham recalls that Fr D'Arcy, characteristically, as he puts it, casting his assertion in the form of a question, said to him, 'Are you quite sure that it is not going to be a landslide for Labour?'[32] The alien world of politics turned out to provide Fr D'Arcy with a more reliable field of prophecy than his own Order, where men were moved in and out of office by less predictable forces.

★Waugh began at this time to maintain that the only proper course for a Christian to take in the contemporary world was to retreat to the catacombs.

Chapter Seven

Provincial

The great Fr Ledochowski died in 1942, after a Generalate in which the Society of Jesus had grown from 17,000 to over 26,000 members. An immediate General Congregation was impossible, and even when the war ended the chaos of central Europe required its postponement for many months. Since the beginning of the war the English Assistant, the Canadian Fr Adelard Dugré, had been living in London, with special powers to deal with the difficult situation, and it was he who decided that the right man to bring the English Province into the post-war era was Fr Martin D'Arcy, who took office as superior on August 2nd 1945. Unquestionably no appointment of an English Provincial had ever been made with a better knowledge of both the Province and the man concerned.

It was also a distinctly unusual appointment. We may take for purposes of comparison the century 1864 to 1964, which can be regarded as the characteristic epoch of the Province. By the beginning of it the English Jesuits had founded all three of their boarding schools and two day schools; the writers' house at Farm Street had just been started and *The Month* was taken over the following year; the houses of study, disseminated from their origin at Stonyhurst, were as they were to remain for sixty years. The main institutional changes that took place during the century were the multiplication of the day schools, the development of the overseas missions and the concentration of the Philosophate and Theologate at Heythrop; otherwise it may be called a time of expansion within substantial stability. The century corresponds exactly to the terms of office of twenty Provincials.

In no other case had one of the Province's leading intellectuals been chosen as its superior. The nearest precedents to Fr D'Arcy's appointment were perhaps those of Fr Alfred Weld (1864–70) and Fr Reginald Colley (1901–4), well-born, cultivated men of humane outlook, but neither of them in the same intellectual flight as Fr D'Arcy. The only two Provincials to serve for more than the standard six years were Fr Edward Purbrick (1880–88) and Fr Henry Keane (1926–34), both of them somewhat narrow-minded, authoritarian and extremely able men who were evidently just what their Roman superiors were looking for. There is a case for saying that the best Provincials were robust, no-nonsense men of effortless authority like Fathers John Clayton (1888–94), Richard Sykes (1904–10) and John Wright (1915–21).★

The appointment of a man like Fr D'Arcy with a view to a more imaginative style of government should have entailed his staying at his post long enough to make a difference; but the nature of the office precluded such a long tenure. A Jesuit Provincial had to spend his time travelling about his Province, speaking to every one of his subjects, priests, scholastics and lay brothers, hearing their manifestation of conscience once a year, and on the strength of the unusual insight thus afforded putting them all in what were hoped to be their proper positions. The headmaster of a single school might consider himself taxed in the apt selection of his staff, but it was the routine task of the Provincial to make all the staff appointments of nine colleges, from the Rectors downward, besides those of the Seminary, Novitiate and other houses. The mere administrative work ensured that it was no office for a venerable father in God, such as the superiorships of some religious orders might tolerate. During the century 1864–1964 Provincials were appointed between the ages of 41 and 58 and were removed between 47 and 61. Fr D'Arcy, at 57, was the third oldest on appointment, and at 61 was the oldest by five months on leaving office. It is highly unlikely that even in the most favourable circumstances he would have been considered for an extension of the ordinary six-year term.

A Provincial discharged his task under strict obedience to Rome, writing regular letters to the English Assistant (Fr Dugré returned to Rome on the advent of peace), and in fact the major superiors were appointed by the General himself, guided by the Provincial's recommendation. At home the Provincial, with his headquarters at Farm Street, was assisted in his government by four Consultors, who met to deliberate once a month, though final decisions rested with the Provincial. In 1945 the senior of Fr D'Arcy's Consultors was Fr Leonard Geddes, a rather grand gentleman of the old school who acted as Vice-Provincial during Fr D'Arcy's two absences from the country. Next came Fr Robert Brown; he had in fact received the rank of Monsignor while Prefect Apostolic of the Zambesi mission, but in accordance with Jesuit custom he used neither the title nor its insignia. He left on a visitation of southern Africa in May 1946 and returned mortally ill, remaining in hospital until his death at the end of 1947. His place as Consultor was thus to all intents and purposes vacant for over two years, until the appointment of his successor, Fr Desmond Boyle, in July 1948, the only change made in Fr D'Arcy's term of office.

★Of Fr Clayton it was reported that his customary way of notifying subjects of a posting was to write a letter saying, 'Dear Fr X, Please go to Y. Yours sincerely, John Clayton SJ.'

Neither Fr Geddes nor Fr Brown had any particular connexion with Fr D'Arcy. That was not the case with his near-contemporary and fellow classicist at Campion Hall Fr Edward Helsham, who was Rector of Beaumont, a tall, serene man who spent almost his whole career in posts of high responsibility. Equally well known to Fr D'Arcy was Fr Henry Sire, whom he had taught at Stonyhurst in 1916–19; Fr Sire was the Provincial's Socius or secretary, and as such was the only Consultor ex officio. His quiet good sense and efficiency kept him in that post for fourteen years (1942–56), and other qualities that endeared him to Fr D'Arcy were tact, impeccable manners and a keen sense of humour. In his role of intermediary between members of the Province and their superior, Fr Basset commented on Fr Sire's 'bewildering gift of siding entirely with each plaintiff without, by so much as an inch, lessening the authority of the Establishment.'[1] His work involved accompanying the Provincial on all his travels, and this let him in for a great deal of driving, since Fr D'Arcy, quite rightly, refused to surrender himself to the ravaged post-war railway system. This burden, however, afflicted Fr Sire less than the occasions when the Provincial volunteered to relieve him at the wheel, since Fr D'Arcy was not only a fearless driver but thought nothing, while travelling at breakneck speed, of abandoning the steering wheel to its devices while he adorned his conversation with expressive gestures.

Fr D'Arcy assumed his office with effortless aplomb. Provincials were generally harassed bureaucrats hard put to it to spare time even for their subjects, let alone for a social life. But Fr D'Arcy's ease in his newly-shouldered duties can be judged from entries in Evelyn Waugh's diaries: (August 13th 1945) 'Father D'Arcy dined with us [at the Hyde Park Hotel]. He has just become Jesuit Provincial. I asked lightly, 'Does this mean you will be next General?' He answered gravely that he hoped not.' Eighteen days later Waugh records meeting Fr D'Arcy at a private view at the National Gallery.[2] On November 25th Fr D'Arcy wrote to him: 'I was at a party the other day at which some of Bloomsbury were present. They were foaming at the mouth over your review of The Unquiet Grave.* I found myself laughing heartily, as I had just read and enjoyed the review.'[3]

Later in the year Fr Martindale found him on brilliant form at a dinner at the Savoy, where the veteran Fr Roy Steuart was also present.[4]

Yet at the same time Fr D'Arcy wrote all his official letters by hand, insisting that a letter was much too personal a thing to be delegated to a secretary. His regular visits to the various houses were looked forward to as perhaps few other Provincials' have been; he was especially loved by

---

*By Cyril Connolly. Waugh comments with mischievous understatement in his diary on November 21st that the review 'seems to have caused a mild sensation in a small circle.'

the lay brothers, a class that tended to be overlooked by the less sensitive type of superior. Add to this his bold vision in the forming of policy and we cannot help being struck by – to cite a favourite text of his – 'the achieve of, the mastery of the thing!'

The impact that Fr D'Arcy had on his new subjects can be felt from a letter that the young Bernard Basset wrote in 1946: 'Saw Father D'Arcy for two hours. He was terrific and our Province is going to alter considerably in his reign ... moreover we have some fifty-eight applicants for the novitiate.'[5] When Fr Basset came to write *The English Jesuits* he dedicated it 'To Father Martin D'Arcy, onetime Provincial of the English Province, who, in his day, gained the love and affection of the present because he had the measure of the past.'

The first problem facing the Province was the severe drop in numbers owing to the demands of the war. The novitiate had been half empty for six years, and from its peak of 909 members in 1939 the Province had dwindled to 820 when Fr D'Arcy took over. The back-log of applicants enabled 51 novices (against a pre-war average of 25) to be admitted in 1946; but it is due mainly to the rare inspiration that Fr D'Arcy gave especially to the younger men that the years 1946 to 1951 saw by far the highest number of admissions in the Province's history, pulling its strength up again by the latter year to 905. But for social changes which were bringing about an inexorable decline in lay brothers' vocations the losses of the war years would have been more than recovered.

It was perhaps in the novitiate that Fr D'Arcy's vision most showed itself. As Master of Novices he appointed Fr Bernard Leeming, who had recently been his Bursar at Campion Hall, and he also made the unprecedented decision to send the young Fr Bernard Basset to perform his Tertianship as Socius to the Novice-Master; at the same time he began writing a regular column for the *Catholic Herald*, and initiated the Sodality Cells movement designed to bring lay people into active religious work in the context of devotion to Our Lady. The year 1946–7 in the novitiate was a quite extraordinary one. The unprecedentedly large intake was composed mainly of ex-Service men who could not be treated like boys fresh out of the Jesuit colleges. Fr Leeming was the ideal choice to handle them. He was a kindred spirit of Fr D'Arcy's, a man of deep interest in people, of great spirituality and of a lively originality. In the circumstances of the time, as his obituarist wrote, 'it needed someone of Bernard's versatility to temper the rigidity of the noviceship.' The essence of the novitiate was a series of 'experiments' to test the individual candidates' capacity to deal with the religious life, and with so many novices under him Fr Leeming was forced to find new experiments to make sure that all got a chance. He stopped sending novices to work in hospitals when he found that Matrons would only set them to wash floors – an apostolate they could exercise equally well at Manresa. One of the novices, Gerard Marsden, wrote: 'He invented an experiment of his own. For weeks he appeared to have hardly seen or spoken to me. Then he called me in and asked how I was. His neglect had been deliberate. "To survive in the Society you must be prepared to meet disinterest and neglect".'[6]

One of Fr Leeming's innovations was to introduce 'open ordo' periods, when the novices had to plan their own day instead of following the routine laid down; his most startling initiative, for the time, was to send groups of four novices to live under canvas among the hop-pickers in Worcestershire, where a Jesuit priest, Fr Webb, conducted a mission. This in particular was regarded with astonishment by the more hide-bound members of the Province, from whom Fr Leeming received a great deal of criticism, and that seems to have been the reason why Fr Leeming's appointment was rescinded after only one year.* Fr Walkerley, who succeeded him, was a more conventional man, though very highly valued in his office, which he held for the next eleven years.

Despite the wartime drop in numbers, in the longer term the Province had appeared to be enjoying a very healthy increase; the pre-war figure of 909 represented a rise of more than 200 since Fr D'Arcy joined the noviciate. Yet the years between the wars had seen a relative slackening of the tremendous achievement of the previous epoch. Until about 1920 it is difficult to fault what the English Jesuits accomplished. Criticisms have been made, perhaps rightly, of the limited proportion of men sent to the missions in the earlier part of the century (though they were far more than any other group except the Mill Hill Fathers, who specialised in missions), and of their training later on; since Fr D'Arcy's career was not personally involved with the missions there is little need to consider that question, and the estimate here given will be confined to the Jesuits' success in sustaining their efficiency and reputation at home. By that criterion the English Province had been brilliantly managed. One might carp at a certain over-engagement in secondary education, and the closure of a new grammar school at Leigh in Lancashire in 1907, after it had swollen to a hundred boys in four years, is a symptom that the superiors had begun to feel they were biting off more than they could chew. The closure of the Province's college in Malta for local reasons in the same year also released manpower for demands in England. The Province however still had an unusually large number of schools on its hands in comparison with the rest of the Society, so that candidates joining it could almost inevitably look forward to a life of schoolmastering. All that

*The decision is presumably to be attributed directly to the General, in whose hand the appointment of Novice-Masters lay.

can be said is that the Jesuits were answering an urgent need in the English Catholic body, and answered it extremely well in both their public and their grammar schools.

A second problem in the early part of the century was that, for historical reasons, the English Jesuits had charge of about forty parishes, engaging the services of some 140 men, work that in other countries was considered outside the scope of the Order. England's missionary status, which was responsible for this undertaking, was officially abolished by the Holy See in 1918, but the first Provincial to grasp the nettle was Fr Henry Keane, who between 1929 and 1933 gave up fifteen parishes – a change that could with advantage have been made a decade earlier, releasing men for more characteristically Jesuit work.

On the positive side, the Province had enlarged the range of its activities. The retreat movement for working men got under way with the opening of the first specialised retreat house in 1909, and at the end of the war Fr Edmund Lester founded Campion House to give schooling to 'late vocations' mainly for the secular priesthood, a work whose value may be judged by the figure of 500 ordinations from Campion House by 1947. Fr Lester also directed a popular eucharistic movement called the Knights of the Blessed Sacrament which attained an international membership of three million by the mid 1930s, and produced a devotional magazine, *Stella Maris*, with a circulation of 47,000. In 1922 the Catholic Workers' College was founded in Oxford to carry on Fr Plater's apostolate for the working class.

Another big project undertaken in the 1920s was of more doubtful advantage. Following the policy for the whole Order, Fr Ledochowski gave instructions for the Philosophate and Theologate to be amalgamated into a single *Collegium Maximum* for which a connexion should be sought with one of the national universities. Fr William Bodkin, the Provincial at the time (1921–6), accordingly bought the magnificent baroque house of the Earls of Shrewsbury at Heythrop, north-west of Oxford, thinking that its proximity would permit an affiliation to the university. It would have been quite foreign to Oxford's policy to grant any sort of status to a Jesuit seminary even in the High Street, let alone twenty miles outside the city; but Fr Bodkin's ignorance of Oxford was exceeded only by that of his Roman superiors, and they authorised the project. The college opened in 1926, receiving the Philosophers from Stonyhurst and the Theologians from St Beuno's. It found itself in an unexpected isolation as much geographical as academic. The discipline appropriate to two separate seminaries proved, it seems, ill adapted to a house where two quite different age-groups were together. Psychologically the greater neglect was perhaps suffered by the young Philosophers, and Fr D'Arcy had enough experience of their troubles as they came on to him at Campion Hall to have developed a marked dissatisfaction with the Heythrop regime, reinforced perhaps by his own memories of seminary life. Of the atmosphere among the Theologians we have the testimony of Fr Frederick Copleston, who went through that part of the course in 1934–8. He describes the students as 'markedly browned off, disinclined, that is to say, to listen to frequent lectures and very critical of their teachers.' One must contrast this description with Fr Martindale's eulogy of the spirit at St Beuno's before the first war. The critical attitude, by Fr Copleston's account, had some justification, for 'in some cases lecturers kept so closely to their textbooks or to stencilled and already circulated 'codices' that one might just as well have read what they had to say in the privacy of one's room ... the lecturers in my day were doubtless learned, but it can hardly be claimed that their matter and manner were such as to arouse an enthusiastic response on the part of their hearers.'[7]

One should not take such criticisms too far. Not all the Jesuit scholastics had the psychological delicacy or the intellectual restlessness that would make them feel these defects. Nevertheless it seems one may say that in founding Heythrop Fr Bodkin had created a college which not only failed to provide the advantages intended but may have been actually worse than what it replaced. To this error we may add his failure to reverse the decline of Stonyhurst, which may also be laid at his predecessor's door but was especially culpable in one who had been a very successful Rector of the college before the war. For all his charming personal qualities, one may perhaps identify Fr Bodkin's Provincialship as the time when the English Province began to falter in its course.

The most far-reaching failure of the Province was the decline of its public schools, and this decline was twofold. Firstly, the entry of Downside (1912) and Ampleforth (1916) into the Headmasters' Conference suddenly undermined the Society's effortless lead in education, to the extent that within a mere twenty years both Stonyhurst and Beaumont dropped out of the front rank and yielded their place to the two Benedictine schools. The first stages of the decline at Stonyhurst have already been described. In 1929 Fr Keane tried to remedy it by cutting short Fr Weld's rectorate and appointing Fr Richard Worsley, who had read Classics with Fr D'Arcy at Campion Hall. His energy brought him within a few months to the Committee of the Headmasters' Conference – the only Rector of Stonyhurst ever to have held that position. But the effect on his hopes of economic depression and falling rolls reduced him to a nervous breakdown after two years and a half. The choice of his successor was the most conservative that could have been made: the now elderly Fr O'Connor was brought back for a second full and inactive term.

Beaumont in the mean time had enjoyed the notable rectorate

(1921–9) of Father, later Archbishop, Aston Chichester, until Fr Weld was granted eight years to reduce that college to the same torpor in which he had left his own. Fr Bernard Swindells succeeded Fr Bellanti as Prefect of Studies at Stonyhurst in 1933, and academically may be considered to have done well with the material at his disposal. The sorry university results of the twenties were bettered, thirteen Oxford and Cambridge awards being won in the five years 1935–9. The low tone to which the school had sunk nevertheless prevented this being reflected in an improvement in Stonyhurst's reputation. Fr Leo Belton, appointed in 1938, was probably one of the best rectors of the years after 1916, but his term of office was almost wholly occupied by the war. By 1945 the task of restoring Stonyhurst to its position of thirty years before was a formidable one. Beaumont, where Fr Boyle had ably held the Prefectship of Studies since 1931, was in better shape,★ and by now carried the Province's chief claim to excellence in education, but its small size (only 170 boys in 1945) did not allow it to face Ampleforth and Downside on equal terms.

Apart from ill-judged and unlucky appointments, the reason for the fall of the Jesuit schools is not too hard to find. There had been a complete failure to gauge the difference that the opening of Oxford and Cambridge made to Catholic education, and the increased demand for graduate masters. At first the Provincial, Fr John Gerard (1897–1900), imagined that the tiny Campion Hall would satisfy all the Province's needs. He had the contempt for London University of a man who had spent his life working under its curriculum, and he immediately discontinued the taking of the London external degrees by Jesuit students. His successors found this too drastic, and the London degrees were resumed on a small scale at St Mary's Hall and later at Heythrop. But in 1925 the English Province, out of 800 members, had only 75 London graduates, most of them elderly, and some fifty Oxford men. That was a completely inadequate proportion for what was mainly an academic body.

This inadequacy should have become apparent when Downside and Ampleforth came panting on the heels of Stonyhurst and Beaumont, and the essential response to it was an expansion of Campion Hall. It is to be noted that both Downside and Ampleforth, just for their own needs, had founded separate houses of study at Cambridge and Oxford respectively; yet the Society of Jesus continued to believe that it could be served by one small Oxford house from which to staff its nine colleges. The policy of gaining prestige by an elite house of studies had initially been a good

★Fr Boyle had set the tone of his leadership in his first public report to the school, when he remarked: 'To report on the work of Rhetoric in the past year is somewhat like being asked to speak about snakes in Greenland. There are no snakes in Greenland.'

one, but to continue with it after the first fifteen or twenty years was a great misjudgment. One has to say that it was a policy which had no stronger supporter than Fr D'Arcy. Free from responsibility for the requirements of the Province, he had looked at the question from the point of view of Campion Hall's prestige at Oxford and the need to avoid seeming to impose on the university. It was an understandable feeling that if fellows of the other colleges were to be asked to take these strange black-clad creatures onto their pupil lists they should be given a stimulating experience to reward them. Yet by the twenties, with senior members like Fathers Martindale, Burrows and D'Arcy himself, Campion Hall was already making a sufficient scholarly contribution to the university to make such diffidence unnecessary. A merely average under-graduate intake would have been acceptable; as it was there were many Jesuit scholastics denied a career at Campion Hall to whom most colleges would have been happy to offer a place.

In 1933 the Province founded a house of studies in Bloomsbury where the London degrees could be taken properly, but it opened with only eight students, who had multiplied to twenty-three by 1938 when the house was transferred to Hampstead. This recognition of the need for more graduates was a partial advance, but the thinking behind it was that only the high-fliers 'needed' Oxford; the experience contrasted unfavourably with that which Downside and Ampleforth offered their young monks.

Ironically, the policy of a very small Campion Hall conflicted with Fr D'Arcy's notion of expanding the horizons of the less sophisticated young Jesuits. As far as university studies were concerned that advantage fell only to a small elite, which constituted a sort of governing class. From 1926 to 1964 all the Provincials without exception were men who had read Classics at Campion Hall, and they tended also to monopolise the higher posts like the rectorship of Heythrop; but they were too small a minority, whose privilege was perhaps not generously looked upon by the remainder. If their circle had been widened, the utilitarian views which damaged the Province in later years might perhaps have gained less acceptance.

The policy of the English Province between the wars exhibits a failure to appreciate that educationally it had become too thin on the ground. Not only did the day schools undergo an enormous expansion at great cost and effort, but in 1935 a new grammar school was taken over in Sunderland, and boarding preparatory schools were opened at Southborne in 1936 and Barlborough Hall in 1939. With the exception of the last, which supported the advance of its parent college, Mount St Mary's, to full public-school status, all these measures may be called steps in the wrong direction, since they represented a quantitative expansion in place of a qualitative improvement; and it may be counted among the achievements of Fr D'Arcy's Provincialship, though they may appear negative ones, that he handed over Sunderland and Southborne to orders of teaching brothers in 1947 and 1948.

To lose the prestige of running the best Catholic schools in the country was a set-back which it would have been worth making a considerable effort to reverse; and perhaps the more serious long-term consequence was in the calibre of entrants to the Order. After Fr Bernard Basset and Fr Philip Caraman, both of them products of the Stonyhurst of the 1920s, it would be difficult to name any members of the English Province who stand comparison with the great figures of the past. By contrast the advance of the Benedictines is symbolised by the elevation of a monk of Ampleforth to the see of Westminster in 1976.

The second and more grievous educational failure was the loss of the schools' religious character. The trend had begun at Beaumont early in the century; until then its discipline and customs were substantially copied from those of its mother college. But with the rectorship of Fr Joseph Bampton (1901–8), Beaumont underwent a radical reform in which it succumbed to the endemic ambition of minor public schools to be mistaken in a bad light for Eton. The consequences to the college's record of vocations were immediate: during the nineteenth century Beaumont had given 36 priests to the English Province in the 39 years of its existence – a perfectly creditable record in view of the school's size. By 1936 however only nine Beaumont boys had joined the Society since the beginning of the century. At Stonyhurst the impulse to copy the Protestant public schools only began to make serious changes after 1916. They were less sudden than at Beaumont, and for special reasons the effect on vocations was postponed for a decade or more. Stonyhurst's contribution to the Province from the mid twenties to the early thirties was in fact outstanding. Part of the credit must go to the charming Fr Michael King, who was Spiritual Father at the college from 1924 to 1931; yet the influence of that saintly old man illustrates the extent to which, in the moral sphere, Stonyhurst was living on its capital of the past. By the middle third of the century the vocations from the Jesuit schools had dwindled to an extent that, in terms of manpower, they were becoming a drain instead of a resource. The claims of the public schools in their heyday to embody the virtues of Englishry, the obeisance to an ephemeral social model, had disabled the Jesuit Order from imparting its own proper formation. It is no accident that Mount St Mary's, the college with the least social pretensions of the three boarding schools, was also the one which retained the best record of vocations. The whole-hearted acceptance of public-school norms by the middle of the century is a lesson for the succeeding generation, when the Catholic schools have surrendered just as unhesitatingly to even worse social influences.

One should not leave the impression that the Province Fr D'Arcy took over in 1945 was in visible decline. It was still by far the largest religious order in England, and figures of the distinction of Fr Martindale, Fr D'Arcy himself, and the many well-known writers and preachers who upheld the fame of Farm Street precluded any dismissal of its quality. Institutionally however the ill-recognised slide of the past twenty or thirty years made it a question whether that quality would be maintained. Fr D'Arcy, aided perhaps by his American experience, viewed the matter in a global conspectus. In 1961 he remarked that for twenty years he had been telling fellow Jesuits that the Society was a burnt-out power;[8] at first he had met only incredulity (and even in 1961, it must be said, the judgment mainly reflects the extraordinarily high standards that the Society had taken for granted in the past); but Fr D'Arcy had already seen straws in the wind such as the growing liturgical movement among lay people in America which, he was convinced, was going to leave behind the type of devotional practice that had been the stand-by of Farm Street's appeal. If the Society was to retain its vitality, it could not remain rooted in well-tried formulas. And if new power houses of influence were to be built, the foundations must be laid in the Province's institutions.

Of the problems described before, that of Heythrop was one of which Fr D'Arcy was very conscious, and glimpses of his efforts to address it will be given in due course. The state of Stonyhurst was another to which he devoted one of his first projects. Since 1940 St Mary's Hall, previously untenanted since the opening of Heythrop, had housed the English College from Rome. With the advent of peace the College was due to return, and Fr D'Arcy proposed to use St Mary's Hall as a house of philosophical studies for laymen. We have seen that in 1923 he had planned a detailed reform of the old lay Philosophers' course of which he had high hopes as a contribution to the Catholic intellectual revival, and doubtless he now harked back to such plans. The notion of sending young men into the fray against the new dragons of positivist analysis might have had interesting repercussions on the English Catholicism of the post-war period. Without access to the Province's records it is impossible to judge the practical difficulties raised by the scheme. Fr D'Arcy cannot have supposed that enough students could be found to fill the eighty rooms of the seminary. In fact his project was nipped in the bud by the Rector of Stonyhurst, Fr Bernard Swindells, who wanted to use St Mary's Hall as a preparatory school to cope with the rising number of boys

Fr D'Arcy's plan seems exposed to strong objections. To revive the course after a gap of thirty years would have been an uphill task, and the barrack-like uniformity of St Mary's Hall was hardly an enticement to residence. It would have been more feasible prospect (once space had been gained by the opening of the new preparatory school) to make available the old Philosophers' quarters at the college, which were far more attractive and more realistic in size. But Fr Swindells, although he had been a lay Philosopher himself the year before Fr D'Arcy, was disposed to see no virtue at all in the scheme.[9] There is no doubt that if the course had been successfully restored, not just as a gentlemen's finishing school but as a real intellectual experience, with able professors, it would have done much to repair Stonyhurst's standing. No such recovery in fact took place. Fr Swindells is generally thought to have been a less successful Rector than Prefect of Studies, but the solution of replacing him so soon (he had taken office in May 1945) was evidently found too drastic by Fr D'Arcy. There is some evidence that he gave Stonyhurst up as beyond recovery and concentrated resources on Beaumont. Here he appointed Fr Boyle Rector in 1947, while he retained his existing office of Prefect of Studies, so that he held the plenary powers of a headmaster; and young men who had Fr D'Arcy's special confidence, like the newly-ordained Fr Christopher Devlin, were appointed to the staff, giving the college something of an Indian summer in the late forties and fifties.

The conditions of the time, however, made the Province's public schools less than the first priority. The Education Act of 1944 had opened the way to an enormous expansion of state schooling, and with six grammar schools in their charge the Jesuits had to respond to the challenge. Fr D'Arcy summoned a meeting of Prefects of Studies which was held under his chairmanship in Oxford in April 1946; it identified teacher training as the prime need, and Fr D'Arcy resolved to found a college that would train students from both the Society of Jesus and other orders. A particular worry was that, with the bureaucratic trend of the time, legislation might soon demand diplomas of education of all masters in schools within the state system, a demand which the Catholic teaching orders were far from being qualified to satisfy.

Fr D'Arcy's first wish was to open the college in the North, where the bulk of the Catholic working-class population was concentrated. The initial thought he had on the subject was punctured by his Socius with a typically practical remark. Driving between Liverpool and Preston, they passed by Scarisbrick Hall, which had just come on the market. Its links with the ancient Catholic family of Scarisbrick and its fanciful nineteenth-century Gothic architecture attracted Fr D'Arcy to it as a home for the new college, and he made a comment to that effect. 'It would take fifty servants to keep a house like that clean,' said Fr Sire, and the idea was dropped.[10]

The next plan was to found the college at Ilkley, near Leeds, and a property was chosen for the purpose. This time the obstacle was one which throws light on the peculiar state of ecclesiastical seclusion inhabited by the religious orders. It was a rare superior who had been a parish priest, with the experience of dealing with the diocesan administration. Fr D'Arcy was no exception to this state of innocence, and it did not occur to him that the permission of the bishop was necessary before starting such a project. It did not occur to any of his Consultors either. To the bishops however this Jesuit self-absorption looked like arrogance, and for a long time they had shown a peculiar sensitivity on that head. When the Bishop of Leeds found out about this plan begun without a by-your-leave, he stamped on it. Fr D'Arcy had to think again. Whether the Bishop was well advised in putting a point of jurisdiction above Catholic educational interests may be left for other historians to judge; but this mistake gave the first grounds for complaint about a lack of practical sense in Fr D'Arcy's exercise of his office.

The march of democracy was in the mean time threatening the house where Fr D'Arcy had taken the Jesuit habit. The London County Council was looking covetously at Manresa House, whose fine grounds it felt could gain a nobler beauty by the building of blocks of flats for the use of the voting public. The eviction of the novitiate and juniorate seemed imminent. In response to this threat Fr D'Arcy conceived the project on which, of all those in his term of office, he most set his heart. It arose from the death of the sixteenth and last Lord Arundell of Wardour in September 1944 and the extinction in the male line of that ancient family. Wardour Castle was offered to the Society of Jesus by his heir, and this offer was one of the first matters awaiting Fr D'Arcy's decision when he became Provincial.

Of all the Recusant families of England, none was more linked with Jesuit tradition than the Arundells. The Society had provided chaplains at Wardour since the reign of Elizabeth. Stonyhurst owed the chief part of its great library to the bequest of the tenth Baron. It was the twelfth Baron who in 1900 had authorised the application of funds to establish the Arundell scholarship, which both Conyers and Martin D'Arcy held in Philosophy. When he died six years later the title passed to a cadet branch and he left his eccentric widow with a life interest in the estate which she abused till her death at the age of ninety-one in 1934. Having no children to benefit, she let the house go to rack and ruin, and she also quarrelled with the Jesuits, obliging them in 1933 to give up the parishes of Wardour and Tisbury which they had served for centuries.

John Arundell, who succeeded as sixteenth Baron in 1939, was a man of sterling character whom Fr D'Arcy had known as a boy at Stonyhurst between 1916 and 1924. As a serving officer he was wounded in the retreat to Dunkirk and taken prisoner, being transferred after an escape attempt to Colditz. While there he fell seriously ill with tuberculosis and was repatriated, but he died only a week after his return to England. The sense of *pietas* to such a family told powerfully in favour of preserving the long Jesuit connexion with the house, and to someone of Fr D'Arcy's aesthetic sensibilities the appeal was irresistible. Wardour Castle was a superb Palladian mansion built by the eighth Baron in the middle of the eighteenth century. With its central domed hall and subordinate wings flanking the main mansion, it is said to have been Evelyn Waugh's model for Brideshead in his plaint for the lost glories of English country-house life. The gem of the house is the chapel, surely the most beautiful Catholic church building in all England, a masterpiece to which Paine, Quarenghi and Soane had contributed their skills. The agent of the English Jesuits in Rome, Fr John Thorpe, had advised Lord Arundell on its design and had contributed the superb altar and a marble relief which before the Suppression had stood in the private chapel of the Jesuit General.

It was Fr D'Arcy's vision to lead the English Jesuit Province into a Renaissance in which beauty should play its part with spiritual and intellectual quickening. Just as at Oxford he had refused to foist an architectural abortion on the university, so now his instinct was that if the Province must leave the beauties of Manresa House it should not be for some nondescript but for an even finer residence. He saw splendid houses as contributing to the aesthetic education of the young men who underwent their training in them, as well as to the polish and social style which ought to be proper to a Jesuit. The establishment of the novitiate at Wardour, for which he began lengthy negotiations with the local bishop, would have been the grand achievement of his Provincialship.

In September 1946 Fr D'Arcy travelled to Rome for the Congregation to elect the new General. We seem to have Christopher Hollis to thank for the story that Fr D'Arcy was himself a front-runner for this post.[11] Certainly he had the advantage, after six years when most Jesuits had been penned in their own countries, of being known to the Americans, and even slightly to the Spanish and Portuguese; but it is unlikely that the Society would have chosen a man of such limited experience of government. The election went to the Belgian Fr Jean-Baptiste Janssens, a model Jesuit, with something of the limitations of a model. The speculations of Fr D'Arcy's friends as to the opportunities if he had been elected instead are to some extent misplaced. Under Pius XII he would have been severely restricted in carrying out a more adventurous policy (he would not, for example, have been allowed to give Teilhard de Chardin the honour that his own conviction prompted), and the hurricane of the later sixties and seventies would have hit him at an age when he had lost the vigour to deal with it. He returned to England to a very different future.

Back in his own Province, Fr D'Arcy's plans for its rejuvenation were taking various forms. In late October he attended the fiftieth anniversary celebrations at Campion Hall. Here the new Master was Fr Tom Corbishley, a brilliant scholar and excellent superior; it seems, though, that Fr D'Arcy looked over his performance at Campion Hall with a jealous eye, and despite their life-long friendship Fr Corbishley sometimes felt his treatment 'cruel'.[12] The reputation of the Hall was being upheld by such senior members as Fr Leycester King, who lectured in the Honours school of Psychology, and Fr P.J. Treanor, who was elected to a research fellowship in astronomy at Balliol. Fr Vincent Turner returned to Campion Hall in 1948 to assume a lectureship in Philosophy. The Province's presence in other universities was being extended by means of chaplaincies. Manchester had been taken on provisionally during the war and was now definitively assumed; together with Liverpool, already in Jesuit hands, it was the only full-time Catholic chaplaincy in any of the provincial universities; there was also a Jesuit chaplain at Glasgow.

Soon after his return from Rome in 1946, Fr D'Arcy received a letter from Fr Vincent Turner, now a fourth-year Theologian at Heythrop. There had apparently been a break-down of the heating system in the Theologians' wing, and according to the authorities the parts to repair it had not arrived. It was now mid November, and the Theologians had begun taking their bedding in the morning to dry it out amid clouds of steam in the central mansion, where the professors lived, and where the radiators were still functioning. The letter was written on a Thursday; at 9.30 on the Friday morning Heythrop received a telephone call from Fr D'Arcy that he would be there for lunch. By 11 o'clock the heating was fully restored throughout the building. When the Provincial arrived the trouble was not mechanical but emotional, to wit the indignant feelings of the scholastics, which Fr D'Arcy applied his gifts of diplomacy to soothing. The Rector, Fr Enright, found himself packed off to Southern Rhodesia, a part of the world to which his career until then had not introduced him.*

The new Rector was Fr D'Arcy's old friend Fr Helsham, who had already held the same office before in 1929–37. Fr Turner considered that the Heythrop professors were among the few individuals who were roughly handled by Fr D'Arcy during his Provincialship, for he was angered by a lack of sensitivity to the problems of the young scholastics under them. But there was little difference he could make, though on the

---

*This was a singular show of authority on Fr D'Arcy's part since the Rector of Heythrop was a superior who received his office directly from the General, and Fr Enright had been appointed as recently as 1945.

academic side he did his best to revivify the studies by inviting distinguished French Jesuits as visiting lecturers. Fr D'Arcy listened sympathetically to a proposal by a scholastic, Bruno Brinkman, to disband Heythrop and return to a separate Philosophate and Theologate, where the students of different age-groups would be more appropriately handled. The official policy of the Society, however, was still for *Collegia Maxima*, and he would have had great difficulty in obtaining consent for such a change. It is due to Heythrop nevertheless to mention at least one outstanding scholar on its staff, Fr Frederick Copleston, whose nine-volume *History of Philosophy* evolved from his teaching there; as an accomplished German speaker, he was also chosen by Fr D'Arcy to go on a series of lecture tours to the British and American zones of occupied Germany in 1947–8.

Among Fr D'Arcy's first appointments in 1945 had been that of Fr Devas as Superior of Farm Street, a veteran of the twenties and thirties and one of the most unconventional and best-loved members of the Community. His great contemporaries were gone or in their last years. Fathers Woodlock and Keating had died in 1939; Fr Steuart lived till 1948. One of the young men Fr D'Arcy sent to begin a new generation was Fr Joseph Christie, a vigorous preacher somewhat in the mould of Fr Woodlock, who was to be one of Farm Street's leading personalities over the next twenty years. Materially the house was in disarray; it had been bombed during the war, and its library, returned from safe-keeping in 1946, was in a state of chaos from which it was gradually recovered largely through the efforts of Fr Philip Caraman. The church had lost its roof, but the government restrictions of the time, which forbade building except for the most essential housing projects, kept it freezing under a makeshift tarpaulin cover throughout the Arctic winter of 1947.

One of Fr D'Arcy's more unexpected achievements was in the matter of the Province's finances. The story goes back to his friendship with Cyril Strauss, an undergraduate at New College in the early 1930s. His interests in art and in Christian philosophy brought him especially within Fr D'Arcy's ambit; but he was killed in action at the end of 1944. A little time after this, while he was still Master of Campion Hall, Fr D'Arcy went up to London to see an alleged Rubens of St Ignatius he had been told of in the shop of an art dealer in Brook Street. While he was inspecting it a tall man in the shop asked him whether he liked the picture. Fr D'Arcy said yes, and the man introduced himself as Robert Strauss, Cyril's brother; he offered Fr D'Arcy the picture as a memorial of their friendship. Robert Strauss was a stockbroker, the senior partner of Strauss Turnbull & Co., and a very rich man. He had a fine country house in Sussex and was himself a collector of great discernment. Over the years he made many gifts of works of art to Fr D'Arcy.[13]

In May 1947 Fr Meskell, the Procurator of the Province (with responsibility for its financial management), came to Fr D'Arcy and told him
that he was losing his adviser on investments. For some years past this
service had been performed by Douglas Woodruff's brother-in-law the
third Lord Acton, who before the war had, in Evelyn Waugh's phrase,
'eked out his rents with a job in a firm of stockbrokers.'[14] On his return
from the war he had tried to devote himself to farming but, frustrated by
the same sort of bureaucratic controls that were keeping the Farm Street
church roofless, suddenly threw it up, bought a property unseen in
Southern Rhodesia and emigrated there. Fr D'Arcy put his Procurator in
touch with Robert Strauss, under whose skilled advice the investments of
the Province rapidly showed a huge growth in value.[15]

Another resource was in the unadvertised largess of Evelyn Waugh.
Campion Hall was still receiving the royalties from his *Edmund Campion*,
and in June 1947 we find Fr D'Arcy writing to thank Waugh for a gift
of 4,500 dollars drawn from his literary earnings, which were then at
their peak – 'a munificent present & on the eve of what happens to be
my birthday. I am so grateful to you for your generosity & feel now that
I can keep on various favourite enterprises in the Province which just
needed some financial help to get going.'[16] In February 1948 Waugh
capped his gift with that of the royalties from the limited edition of *The
Loved One*, and in January 1950 he gave the paperback royalties from
Vile Bodies.[17] If Fr D'Arcy conceived exceptionally grandiose projects
for the Province, he also brought it exceptional sources of wealth to
fulfil them.

At Wardour, negotiations with the bishop over the Society's relations
with the Wardour and Tisbury parishes had been holding up the
purchase, but even before it went through in July 1947 serious problems
had arisen to block Fr D'Arcy's hopes. After a quarter-century of neglect
by the Dowager Lady Arundell the house needed extensive restoration,
and with building restrictions this was going to be impossible. It would
be some years before the house could be used as the intended novitiate.
In May 1947 Fr D'Arcy wrote to Evelyn Waugh offering him Wardour as
a temporary home,[18] but Waugh's *folie de seigneur* did not stretch that far
and the house had to remain empty. The impossibility of moving the
novitiate there was a bitter blow to Fr D'Arcy, and it became necessary to
look for another building to buy. The choice made was Harlaxton, near
Grantham, an elaborate Victorian mansion of more ostentation than
beauty, and the Province had to bear the expense of buying a second
large country house. It seems curious that Fr D'Arcy did not choose
some obviously makeshift home for the novitiate which would be abandoned as soon as the restoration of Wardour was possible. In fact building
work was needed at Harlaxton too, and the novitiate was not able to

move in till 1950. When Wardour remained unused, its acquisition came to be viewed as a romantic extravagance on Fr D'Arcy's part, but if there was an error of judgment it was surely the purchase of Harlaxton, which lacked Wardour's beauty and Catholic history.

Later in 1947 Fr D'Arcy received an appeal from Frank Pakenham, a minister in Attlee's government and charged since that spring with responsibility for the British administration of Germany. The Allies at this time were agreed on the policy of 'pastoralisation', banning the reconstruction of German industry so that the country should never again become an economic power. Pakenham, who saw this policy as immoral, turned to Fr D'Arcy for advice on whether he should resign. But Fr D'Arcy's view of the public influence of his Order did not embrace the resignation of ministers of the Crown on the advice of the Jesuit Provincial, and he threw the responsibility back on Lord Pakenham's conscience. In the event realism obliged the Allies to abandon the vexed policy.[19]

About the same time Fr D'Arcy received an invitation to America from an old friend, Mgr Thomas Shannon of Chicago, who was celebrating his priestly jubilee. Mgr Shannon was a rich and cultivated priest whose munificent works included the building of a beautiful church in his city, and whose anglophile warmth had made him the host not only of Fr D'Arcy but of many English Catholic writers including Chesterton, Douglas Woodruff and others. He offered to pay Fr D'Arcy's air fare to America and back so that he might attend the jubilee. Fr D'Arcy immediately thought of using this opportunity to make a visitation of the Province's mission in British Guiana, which no Provincial had visited since 1913. In the conditions of the time, the General would not have authorised the journey, but Mgr Shannon's generosity allowed it to be made at minimal expense. He set out in November 1947 and attended the sumptuous celebration in which Mgr Shannon played host to Cardinal Stritch of Chicago, together with over a hundred archbishops, monsignori and other dignitaries.[20] Before leaving the United States Fr D'Arcy also received an honorary degree on behalf of Evelyn Waugh at Baltimore, and on December 9th he flew to British Guiana. He, whose visitations were so looked forward to in all his houses, was received with joy by men who had for the most part not seen England for twenty or thirty years. The most eminent of his subjects was Bishop George Weld, who had been Conyers D'Arcy's class-fellow, and whose residence as Vicar Apostolic was next to the Jesuit house. A small colony of old Stonyhurst boys paid Fr D'Arcy honour, and he attended with Bishop Weld the opening of the Legislative Assembly.

After Christmas Fr D'Arcy went on to more arduous exploration, and experienced the first of two close scrapes with death. His destination was the remote mission of Santa Rosa, four hours sailing up the Moruca River, which was the only means of reaching it; he set out early one morning with his assistant, Fr John King, in a long rowing-boat with a small outboard motor piloted by two half-breeds who claimed to know the way. The first stage of their journey took them down the River Pomeroon to its mouth, from where they had to follow the coast westward till they found the mouth of the Moruca. In spite of the motor's breaking down at intervals they reached the sea, where they found themselves approaching large breakers. At this point the boatmen cried out, 'Sharks! Three sharks!' Fr D'Arcy thus tells the story: 'I do not care for sharks but I almost forgot them as an immense wave hit us; then another, and in a few seconds we were being thrown about like a cockleshell and drenched to the skin ... On looking at the boatmen I saw that they were nearly mad with fright, and Fr King and I realised that they had lost their heads and had no idea where the Moruca was. Incompetence on the part of others gives one, I suppose, in time of crisis a kind of Dutch courage ... So the men were ordered to turn in to land and get out of the way of these immense breakers. Somehow or other we managed to do this without capsizing, and reached a little lagoon.' Here they rested and dried themselves in the mid-day sun, and planned to wait till low tide and then return to the Pomeroon. After two or three hours they saw a boat approaching; it was manned by three men who had been sent out as a rescue party by a plantation owner at the mouth of the Moruca: they had passed it unknowingly and he, having heard their motor and failing to see the boat enter the river, had guessed that an accident had happened. The rescue boat was larger and its boatmen more skilled, and they were taken back out into the waves, from which they reached the Moruca in ten minutes. After being treated to rum by the plantation owner they continued on their way and reached Santa Rosa before the end of the day.

The mission of Santa Rosa was served by Fr Henry Mather, whom Fr D'Arcy had not seen since he left England in 1923.* The same charm and dedication that he had brought to the work of a junior Prefect at Stonyhurst were evident in this remote mission. Evelyn Waugh had found him here in 1933 and had been touched by his hospitality and kindness.[21] The reunion now was the happiest of Fr D'Arcy's trip. 'It was so sad,' he wrote, 'to leave this heavenly little place, where all are so friendly and so Catholic.' After a month of journeys as arduous, if none quite as dangerous, as the one to Santa Rosa, Fr D'Arcy flew back to New York at the end of January. In a stay of several weeks he had time to give some

---

*In the best Jesuit tradition, the order for him to set out on what proved to be his life's work came at such short notice that he left in his bedroom slippers, having forgotten to change into his shoes.

retreats and days of recollection, read a paper at Princeton and speak at Georgetown University; an invitation to give a series of lectures at Yale had to be turned down.

It is presumably to this stay in New York, or else the shorter one two months previously, that we should assign Fr D'Arcy's receipt of his most valued art treasure; this was an exquisite fourteenth-century miniature triptych which Fr D'Arcy always referred to as the Travelling Altar of Mary Queen of Scots. His interest in it had first been stirred in 1932, when Lady Lovat drew his attention to it.[22] After three centuries in the possession of the Bavarian royal house it was then being offered for auction. Besides its artistic worth, the piece was of extraordinary interest to someone with a feeling for the Stuart family and for English Catholic and Jesuit history. A Latin inscription round its edge attests its provenance, and was probably added by the Society of Jesus on its acquiring the piece in the late sixteenth century. It names as the previous owner Elizabeth Vaux, almost certainly the wife of the fourth Lord Vaux of Harrowden, whom she married in 1585. A case made for the triptych probably a few years later, when it passed into Wittelsbach possession, had an inscription which takes the ownership a step further back, to Mary Queen of Scots, and the supposition is that Lady Vaux received it from her in the short interval between her own marriage and the Queen's death.* Harrowden is not far from Fotheringay Castle, where Queen Mary was held prisoner, and the Vauxes were prominent Catholics. Elizabeth Vaux herself, a great-grand-daughter of St Thomas More, sheltered Jesuit priests, including Fr John Gerard. The inscription on the edge of the triptych records that she made a gift of it to Claudius Aquaviva when he was General of the Jesuits (1581 to 1616).

The piece came into the possession of Maximilian I Duke of Bavaria shortly before 1617, when it was described in the inventory of his treasures. It had come to him from the family of Fr Aquaviva, the Dukes of Atri, and they had themselves received it from Pope Leo XI, who reigned for a few weeks in 1605. We may be entitled to deduce that Fr Aquaviva had given Pope Leo the triptych as a coronation present and on his death shortly afterwards it was bequeathed back to the General's family. The Stuart interest of the piece was enhanced by the fact that by the twentieth century the Wittelsbachs had inherited the Jacobite claim to the English throne.

The history of the triptych before it came into Queen Mary's posses-

---

*The Latin inscription on the case (which was lost at some point after 1876) appears to mean: 'This image was the companion of the exile and prison of Mary Stuart Queen of Scots; it would have been of her murder also if she had lived.'[23] We seem here to have a specimen of a Bavarian bull, but whatever was in the writer's mind it suggests that the triptych was not a bequest but was given to Lady Vaux before Queen Mary's execution.

sion is not known. It is English work, though with French and Italian influences, made in the middle of the fourteenth century. The triptych, which is small enough to be held in the hand, is intended for private devotion. It is an extremely rare form of work called *basse taille*, with the figures made in enamel on a gold ground, and it retains after six centuries a wonderful luminosity and colour. In 1932, when it appeared for sale, its origin and value were not realised and it was withdrawn after failing to reach its reserve price.[24] It was offered again in 1936, and Fr D'Arcy, by then looking for works of art for Campion Hall, hoped to acquire it, but it was bought by a German collector, Fritz Mannheimer, who initiated the piece's dip into the murkier waters of art collection and dealership. Mannheimer was the head of a Dutch financial syndicate which had made fabulous profits from speculation in foreign exchange, but he went bankrupt and committed suicide two days before the outbreak of the second world war.[25] The triptych, however, with other treasures of his, was kept in safe deposit in a London bank and thus escaped distraint by the Dutch government. During the war the bank, in Bond Street, was destroyed in the bombing of London, and an English sailor looking for loot found the triptych among the rubble and pocketed it. His next posting took him to Cork, where he used the triptych to pay for drinks in a pub; the pub-keeper then presented it to a convent for his daughter's First Communion, and by 1946 it had been acquired by a Dublin art collector, Edward McGuire. Here its history again makes distant contact with Fr D'Arcy through an old friend of his, John Hunt, who with his tough-minded and equally knowledgeable German wife Putzel had operated as a gentleman dealer in London in the 1930s; on the outbreak of the war he had moved to Ireland for his wife's sake. Putzel Hunt saw the triptych in the bedroom of Mrs McGuire, and got her husband to acquire it in exchange for some antique chairs. She swore that at the time she had no idea what the piece was; whether that is true or not must depend on the exact date of the exchange, for the triptych was incidentally illustrated in an article in the *Burlington Magazine* for September 1946,[26] and one can be sure that the Hunts were regular subscribers. When the article was brought to Edward McGuire's notice he realised that he had had by far the worst of the bargain and the resulting quarrel caused something of a Capulet and Montagu feud in Irish society, in which a section of opinion disbelieved Putzel Hunt's protestations.

The *Burlington Magazine*, however, gave the triptych's location as the Residenzcapelle in Munich, and it was not until Mrs Hunt had written to one of the dealers involved in its subsequent sale that the current title to it was discovered. Fritz Mannheimer had left a young widow, born Jane Reis-Brian, who made her way to America and in August 1947 made a second marriage to Charles Engelhard, a man belonging to the same milieu of colossal wealth as her first husband. It may be thought to lend support to the Hunts' claim of innocence that they determined to return the triptych to Jane Engelhard, whom they assumed to be its rightful owner. At this point the mysterious question of Fr D'Arcy's involvement arises. He asserted that, while he knew of the triptych from fifteen years back, he first actually set eyes on it at the Hunts' house[27] – one might suppose on an otherwise unrecorded trip to Ireland in 1947. Did the Hunts ask him, knowing his long-standing interest in the piece, to take it to Mrs Engelhard on his trip to America? There is otherwise no known reason why he should have met the Engelhards, to whom he was introduced in New York by Mrs John Pierrepont.[28] His claim on their gratitude is said to have been that he received Charles Engelhard into the Catholic Church and helped in resolving some canonical problem over his marriage. According to Douglas Woodruff, Fr D'Arcy was presented with the triptych 'to his great surprise' when he went to lunch with the Engelhards one day.[29] But Fr D'Arcy did visit Ireland just after his return from America,[30] and it may be that the triptych had never physically crossed the Atlantic, that the presentation at the Engelhards' lunch was merely abstract, and that it was on this occasion, in April 1948, that he first saw the triptych in the Hunts' house and took possession of it.*

To have such a relic of Mary Queen of Scots was a source of great pride to Fr D'Arcy, and for years he would carry it about with him and produce it from his pocket to show to fellow guests at dinner parties. In 1953 he allowed it to be shown in the Treasures of Oxford exhibition (it technically belonged to Campion Hall) celebrating the Coronation of Queen Elizabeth II; as a result the Dutch government became aware of it and claimed it as part of the estate of the bankrupt Mannheimer. While this claim was disputed the threat of losing the 'Travelling Altar' hung over Fr D'Arcy for some ten years;[32] it is thought that Mrs Engelhard eventually resolved the problem by paying the Dutch government the price of this immensely valuable piece. It is now on permanent loan to the Victoria and Albert Museum.

The affair of the triptych did not exhaust the thrills awaiting Fr D'Arcy on his American journey. He decided that he had done enough flying for the moment and appealed to the President of the United States Shipping Lines, Basil Harris, one of the most prominent Catholic laymen in the country and a great friend of the Jesuits, to find him a cabin on

---

*The words in which Fr D'Arcy describes receiving the piece hint at some such indirect method: 'When I was Provincial & passing through New York the owner of it saw to it that her husband would make a special gift of it to me. This he did & I assigned it to Campion Hall.'[31] Unfortunately at the time when the present book was being written the health of the two surviving people who could have shed light on the matter, Mrs Hunt and Mrs Engelhard, did not permit their being interviewed.

one of his ships. Mr Harris not only obliged but came to bid Fr D'Arcy farewell on board. The experience of the voyage was thus told by Fr D'Arcy:

> We had been about three days out when the sea became roughish. I was just able to say Mass and came down to C deck for breakfast. There were fortunately very few passengers down so early, and the stewards were standing around with nothing to do. Suddenly there was a noise like a bomb and the sea came pouring in. I have no doubt that some thought that we had struck a mine, and there were a few seconds of hurry and scurry. I saw a steward quite near me being carried out and bleeding profusely. Somehow or other the word passed about that some of the portholes had burst open. A wave had hit them and the glass had cracked and burst out in thick jagged splinters. I heard also that a passenger had been badly wounded on the other side of the breakfast room. I rushed round and saw a man covered with blood and twitching in what appeared to be a death agony; so I gave him conditional absolution and then went off to find the steward in the infirmary in case he needed a priest. He, however, though badly wounded was not in danger. The passenger I had seen the day before, a tall American business man, taking a holiday and enjoying himself playing cards with a large cigar in his mouth. He died that night, and on radioing to his widow the Captain found out that he was a Catholic. I buried him at sea.[33]

Arriving back in England at the beginning of March, Fr D'Arcy found himself with an urgent situation that had arisen in connexion with Manresa. About the time of his departure to America, it had been discovered that the best chances for the teacher-training college he was still planning would be in conjunction with London University, whose regulations could moreover accommodate very well the Juniorate and Philosophate studies of the Society. Preliminary discussions were therefore held with Professor Lauwerys of the Education Faculty in January 1948.[34] At that point the London County Council issued its expected compulsory purchase order on Manresa House and its grounds. To avert this, the best hope was to plead that the house was needed as a teacher training college (a function higher in the LCC's priorities than a novitiate), and to seek recognition as quickly as possible from London University and the Ministry of Education. But the purchase order had a deadline of June 30th 1948 within which to appeal. Fr Meskell quickly wrote to Fr D'Arcy and received his permission to proceed on those lines by the middle of the month. The Vice-Provincial, Fr Geddes, was well placed to direct the business as Rector of Manresa. A meeting with

London University's Institute of Education on February 10th successfully got the negotiations afoot.

At this point however the Jesuit plans were again threatened through failure of communication with the episcopate. Putting Manresa to its new use meant that the move of the novitiate must be arranged without delay, but astonishingly the plans to buy Harlaxton had been initiated without consultation with the Bishop of Nottingham, who reacted with the same indignation as his brother of Leeds. Admittedly a novitiate might seem more of an internal Jesuit matter than a training college, but it is extraordinary that with the Ilkley fiasco to warn them Fr D'Arcy and his Consultors did not take care to observe the formalities.* With another humiliating rebuff facing him, Fr D'Arcy, now back in England, turned to the Province's warmest friend in the hierarchy, the aptly-named Archbishop Amigo of Southwark. It was his personal intervention with Bishop Ellis of Nottingham that smoothed over the difficulty; the purchase of Harlaxton went ahead in June.

A more complicated obstacle arose with Cardinal Griffin. Fr D'Arcy wrote to him on April 15th explaining the Jesuit plans, which envisaged Manresa taking not only its own students but those of other teaching orders. The Cardinal considered that this was a matter for the whole hierarchy to pronounce on, but Fr D'Arcy had timed his letter just too late for the annual Low Week meeting of the bishops (again an ignorance of diocesan routine may have been the reason). Cardinal Griffin refused to decide without his bishops. Worse still, the Cardinal now went into hospital, so that further consultation would be indefinitely delayed. What made the situation particularly embarrassing was that the Jesuits, in getting their plans started, had contravened the agreement that the Ministry of Education had made with the Catholic Church that all such projects would go through the Archbishop of Westminster. When Fr D'Arcy wrote to the Minister, he had to ask him not to mention to Cardinal Griffin what was being done. The only way to overcome the Cardinal's refusal (once more Archbishop Amigo helped to arrange this) was to send an urgent circular to all the bishops asking their opinions. When their answers were received, Cardinal Griffin at last gave his permission, on June 12th, and the Society's negotiations with the Ministry of Education became above board.

In the mean time measures had been taken against the London County Council's purchase order. By an admirable stratagem it was

*As ecclesiastical blunders go, this may be contrasted with the one committed by Fr D'Arcy's successor when Harlaxton was opened in 1950. He neglected to obtain the canonical erection as a novitiate, with the result that all the vows taken there were invalid; the mistake was not noticed till Harlaxton was closed again in 1957, when a *sanatio* had to be issued to validate the vows of the past seven years.

decided to approach the lawyer who normally acted for the Council in its expropriations and invite him to act for the Society of Jesus. He advised that the best chance of success was to come to a compromise with the Council, whereby it purchased rather less than two thirds of the estate and the nucleus with Manresa House remained in the Society's possession. This agreement was reached before the Council's deadline, and the Society obtained the full market price for its property.

The teacher-training college at Manresa opened in 1949, while the novitiate was still there. Its institution entailed a reorganisation of the Jesuit training, and the work of planning the studies was largely in the hands of Fr Conyers D'Arcy, who was Prefect of Juniors. The Juniorate was shortened from two years to one, which was made to correspond to the first year of the teacher-training course. The scholastics then went on to Heythrop for two years' Philosophy as before. For their third year however they came back to Manresa, their Philosophy being accepted by London University as a special subject as prescribed by the education course. The scholastics then stayed on at Manresa for a third year of teacher training, which included practice in various Catholic day schools, an experience which had hitherto been absent from the Jesuit training; at the end of this third year they received their teachers' certificates. The course was intended for non-graduates, who simply required a teaching qualification, but there was also a one-year course for graduates. At first Manresa had only Jesuit scholastics, but it soon began to take other students as well. London University welcomed the incorporation of a college specialising in Philosophy as a component of the education course, and the contribution made by the Jesuit professors to its Philosophy faculty was much valued. From the Society's point of view, however, it is difficult to be convinced by this complicated scheme, whose essential defect was the attempt to squeeze a three-year education course into the already lengthy Jesuit training. Nevertheless we should remember that in the atmosphere of *dirigisme* that then prevailed it was feared that without that qualification the Jesuits might soon be debarred from staffing their own colleges.

By the time Fr D'Arcy got back from America in 1948, he found his position as Provincial compromised by an unlucky development. In the election of new Assistants that took place at the General Congregation of 1946, the post of English Assistant had gone to the Irishman Fr John Hannon, a charming man with whom Fr D'Arcy was immediately on the best of terms. He invited Fr Hannon to make a visitation of the English Province, which he did in February 1947, gaining universal popularity. Fr Hannon however died in July of the same year. As was required in such a case, the General wrote to the Provincials concerned for their views as to a successor. It is not known whom Fr D'Arcy recommended, but the two obvious English candidates were the last two Provincials, Fathers Bolland and Mangan. Fr D'Arcy felt it necessary to give particular warning against the choice of the former, whose negative cast of mind and abrasiveness in personal relations had already been too apparent in his government of the English Province. Unfortunately, with the unreliable postal system just after the war the General's letter was delayed; when it reached England Fr D'Arcy had already left for America; its chasing him and his reply took further time, and in the interval Fr Bolland had already been chosen as Assistant. One of the first things that arrived on his desk was a letter from Fr D'Arcy explaining in detail why he was unsuited to the post he held.[35] Fr D'Arcy's whole style as a superior was one with which Fr Bolland was instinctively out of sympathy, and the insight into the opinion Fr D'Arcy held of him was not calculated to soften the rigour of his supervision. It was also an unlucky chance that Fr Bolland's main career had been spent at Heythrop, an institution with which Fr D'Arcy's relations were cooler than with any other house in the Province. It was among his own old colleagues at Heythrop, if anywhere, that Fr Bolland was going to find the jaundiced views of the Provincial's management that would bolster his own hostility.

Fr Bolland's obituarist wrote: 'His habit of spotting weak points and drawbacks seemed to paralyse him when it came to action, and there was a tendency to reject out of hand ideas and standards which had not formed part of his own experience.'[36] Only the official correspondence would reveal to what extent this failing hampered Fr D'Arcy's further projects; one can see it displayed however in the way Fr Bolland handled one of Fr D'Arcy's more imaginative schemes. At the General Congregation of 1946 Fr Janssens, in his address after being elected General, stressed to his hearers the urgency of using every modern means of communication in promoting the Order's work. Fr D'Arcy was impressed by this instruction and came home searching for ways of implementing it. Television had scarcely made its way into British homes at that date, and the major tool of advertising seemed to be photography. On his next visit to Heythrop therefore Fr D'Arcy asked a first-year Theologian, John Gillick, if he would be prepared to begin studying photography with a view to working directly under the Provincial in this new apostolate as soon as he completed his Jesuit training. In the mean time an account was opened for him with the Province Procurator, a camera was bought, and he was to begin doing what he could at Heythrop.

The Rector of Heythrop at that time was still Fr Enright, who was not an admirer of Fr D'Arcy's and represented the school of thought in the Province which disapproved of the lotus-eating life of Campion Hall. He objected to the plan, but he soon afterwards made way for Fr Helsham, and Mr Gillick began some experimental projects which included making a film-strip of the Mass. The fate of Fr D'Arcy's conception was demonstrated in 1954, when it was intended that Fr Gillick, as he was by then, should accompany Fr Brodrick to Spain to make illustrations for the latter's book on St Ignatius. When permission was requested, Fr Bolland wrote back demanding to know by what right Fr Gillick possessed a camera. The photography project went into eclipse until 1958, when Fr John Coventry, on becoming Provincial, sought to revive it, and explained Fr D'Arcy's intention to the General. An enterprise called Manresa Press Photographics was started in 1960, with Fr Gillick in charge, but the renaissance proved illusory: after three years the project was dropped.[37]

1948 saw the beginning of another of Fr D'Arcy's new schemes, the revival of *The Month*. That journal had been just ticking over since the death of the great Fr Keating in 1939; Fr D'Arcy quickly fixed on the man to save the situation, the young Fr Philip Caraman, but he was still in his training years. As soon as he finished his Tertianship in 1948 Fr D'Arcy appointed him editor, and early in September wrote to Evelyn Waugh asking his help.[38] Waugh had several meetings with Fr Caraman, who told him of Fr D'Arcy's conception of the new *Month* as an equivalent of *Horizon* 'with Catholic thinking instead of fluff',★ a wide-ranging review of literature and the arts.[39] With Fr Deryck Hanshell, whom he requested as assistant editor, Fr Caraman brought out the reformed journal in January 1949, and Fr D'Arcy did its first number proud with one of the finest articles he ever wrote, *The Clown and the Philosopher*; it was the work of a hand firmly on the pulse of the post-war trends in philosophy and a quite remarkable production for a man who had held an arduous administrative post for the past three years. Evelyn Waugh contributed extracts from his current novel on St Helena's life and later that year a short story, *Compassion*, based on his experiences in Yugoslavia, which was subsequently incorporated in *Unconditional Surrender*. The early numbers had contributions by Christopher Dawson, John Rothenstein, Graham Greene, Professor E.W. Tristram and Fr de Lubac. In September *The Times Literary Supplement* devoted some space to an account of the chief items since the beginning of the year, and remarked, 'it would be hard to point to a livelier monthly review ... and harder still to indicate one which had carried out more consistently a precise and civilised intention.'[40]

Fr D'Arcy was keeping his literary contacts warm all this time. His

★*Horizon* was from 1939 to 1949 the organ of Bloomsbury, edited by Cyril Connolly and regarded as the leading literary review of the time.

appeal to Evelyn Waugh for *The Month* came shortly after a meeting noted in the latter's diary: 'Father D'Arcy dined with me. Full of love but ill and scatterbrained.'[41] It was in the following year that he made friends with Edith Sitwell. He had apparently met her at Oxford in the thirties, but their real acquaintanceship came about through Roy Campbell, who was now the talks producer for the BBC, and whom Fr D'Arcy was seeing increasingly more of since their meeting at Campion Hall. Edith Sitwell had been mortally offended by a critical review of her work by Geoffrey Grigson, and correspondingly charmed by a defence of her included in an article by Campbell in the *Poetry Review* for August 1949. According to Edith Sitwell, Campbell actually came to blows with Grigson in the BBC canteen. She wrote to David Horner early in October: 'The Campbell-Grigson affair has caused a sensation in wide circles. Fr D'Arcy's eyes (I met him at the Campbells') gleam with an unchurchmanlike interest -(the Campbells are Catholics)- the Spanish ambassador is enthralled.'[42] If Fr D'Arcy's interest came from an expectation that Edith Sitwell's growing friendship with the Campbells might bring her to the Catholic Church, he was to be proved absolutely right, for the Campbells were her godparents when she was received in 1955.

We must return to Jesuit affairs. A great friend of Fr D'Arcy's in the Province was Fr Francis Vavasour, the very efficient Procurator of Stonyhurst. Though his parents had emigrated to New Zealand, where he was brought up, he belonged to a Stonyhurst family well known to Fr D'Arcy – his uncle Oswald Vavasour had been a contemporary of Conyers, and he was a cousin of Fr Robert de Trafford, both of them being members of ancient families of Catholic baronets. Francis Vavasour had come to England in 1926 to join the Society of Jesus and had not gone back since then. After thirteen hard-working years at Stonyhurst Fr D'Arcy considered that he deserved a chance to see his family again; but any sort of travelling was very grudgingly allowed by Rome at this time, and permission for a journey to the Antipodes was out of the question. Perhaps remembering Fr Bodkin and his own trip to Budapest, Fr D'Arcy told Fr Vavasour to go and say nothing to anyone. In the normal course of events there was no reason why news of such a thing should have got to Rome, but the jealous ear listening there had, it seems, a resentful mouth in England feeding it. An Assistant had no power to dismiss a Provincial under him; he could only advise the General, and to recommend dismissal Fr Bolland needed concrete offences to show. Now he had one. On February 14th 1950 Fr D'Arcy received a letter removing him from his post, and basing its reasons explicitly on evidence that had been proffered against his conduct. It seems hardly credible that such delations would have been made spontaneously by any member of the English Province, and we may be safe in thinking that they had been solicited by Fr Bolland from senior figures in his confidence.

The letter of dismissal listed three main reasons for the step. The first was the scamping of visitations to the major houses (and this has been interpreted as evidence that the delations came from Heythrop); the second was the granting of too much freedom to young priests; and the third, in the recollection of Fr Vincent Turner, who saw the letter, was administrative remissness.[43] The timing of the dismissal was a deliberate public reprimand. Although in theory Jesuit superiors could always be removed at a moment's notice, in practice the appointments of the English Provincials had followed the breaks of academic years. The most recent precedent for a dismissal like Fr D'Arcy's had been in December 1900, when Fr Gerard had been removed after trying to protect Fr George Tyrrell from censure. Fr D'Arcy called Fr Caraman to his room at Farm Street and was in tears as he showed him the letter, speaking of the disgrace inflicted on him. At last he said, 'I'm glad I don't know who my enemies are; it makes it easier for me to pray for them.'[44]

Fr D'Arcy's fall from office provoked the dismay of virtually everybody in the Province. Fr John Coventry, himself a future Provincial, has said, 'It was the blackest day of my life when I heard he had been taken off.'[45] No Provincial of this century has governed with such vision, has exercised such public influence, has so inspired his subjects or been so loved by them. Fr D'Arcy's greatest projects failed of achievement: the plan for the new Campion Hall was made impossible by the building restrictions of the time; the purchase of Wardour was made to look pointless by the later failure to bring the house into use when its restoration became permitted. There were also some undoubted blunders, like the one over the training college at Ilkley. But when due subtraction has been made, no Provincial in a full term, let alone in four years and a half, started so many vital enterprises or gave his subjects such hope for the future. Whether the Province needed Fr D'Arcy's more ambitious plans may be a matter for debate, but it certainly needed the kind of broad and generous vision that he brought to his office; the lack of it was to be sadly visible during his own lifetime.

It should be sufficiently obvious from the many admirable religious described in these pages, or even the merely ineffective ones, that Fr Bolland was wholly unusual as a specimen of Jesuit superiors. It is quite wrong to represent Fr D'Arcy, as has been done by some, as a man defeated by the typical narrowness of the Roman bureaucratic mind. There can be no doubt at all that if Fr Hannon had lived Fr D'Arcy would have continued his Provincialship with a free hand and completed it with honour. Criticisms that Fr D'Arcy failed to communicate adequately with Rome and explain his plans are also wide of the mark. Given Fr Bolland's particular disposition of mind no efforts at persuasion could well have affected the result.

Six years later, in February 1956, Fr Bolland stepped off a tram in Rome and his gown caught in the automatic door as it closed. The tram started off, dragging him along the ground, and a wheel crushed his leg. He died nine days later in hospital. It was an ironic destiny for a man who had halted the plans of men of great spirit and enterprise that he should have ended his days taken whither he would not by a mere tram.

Chapter Eight

The American Epoch

Outside the Society of Jesus Fr D'Arcy's friends were not alive to the public reprimand implied by his dismissal, but they knew that he had suffered a hard blow, and a group of his closest friends organised a dinner to show support for him. Evelyn Waugh and Tom Burns were the prime movers, and they asked Frank Pakenham, who was then Minister for Civil Aviation, to chair it. The dinner was held at the Hyde Park Hotel on July 24th 1950 and revealed the breadth and distinction of Fr D'Arcy's circle of friendship; it was attended by the French, Italian and Irish Ambassadors, some half-dozen members of the two Houses of Parliament and a host of people of eminence in the literary and intellectual worlds. After a speech by Lord Pakenham, T.S. Eliot proposed the toast, and was followed by Douglas Woodruff, who made what Evelyn Waugh called 'the funniest & most felicitous speech I have ever heard from anyone. That was the high spot. Poor D'Arcy's reply was not good. He told some footling funny stories & then fell into a rhapsody of self-pity.' Nevertheless the occasion 'achieved its primary end in giving D'Arcy a sense of being surrounded by love & sympathy.'[1]

As the last remark shows, Fr D'Arcy's friends, outside and within the Society, were surprised at how hard he took his dismissal. His feeble form at the dinner was the symptom of a depression that left his spirit crippled for years. There was enough of the substance of failure in his record to make his dismissal sting, where injured merit could have been borne more easily; no-one is the best judge of his own achievements, especially when they are measured above all in human warmth and inspiration. The touch of vanity which Fr D'Arcy had never found needful to extirpate from his dandyish character was a hostage to such rough handling as he had received. In a fairy-tale, a great-souled prince crossed by a malignant dwarf would carry on undaunted, but he would not be hampered by certain circumstances, such as a vow of obedience, in which Fr D'Arcy found himself. Not that vows were necessary to ensure his loyalty and discretion. 'He loved the Society more than anything on earth', Fr Vincent Turner wrote.[2] There was no question of a public fuss or even an uncooperative sulk; nor did he allow a hint to emerge of the personal hostility behind his removal, and he thus allowed talk of mismanagement and failure to cloud his reputation.

In October the British Council asked him to give a lecture tour in nine Italian cities, including Rome. Whether on his own initiative or under obedience, it seems that he had a meeting in the Curia, presumably with the General himself, and that it was far from affording him solace, for when he stayed with Mary Herbert at Altachiara a few days afterwards she found him very depressed.[3] This may, though, have had something to do with the fact that he fell ill there; on his return he wrote to Evelyn Waugh with unexpected cheerfulness: 'I have had a most delightful tour of lectures in Italy, perhaps the most pleasant since the Hellenic Cruise many years ago.'[4]

Fr D'Arcy's official appointment on ceasing to be Provincial was as a writer on *The Month*, and he placed himself wholly at the disposal of the editor, Fr Caraman. It was a humble position for a man of his past career, though it must be said that there were not many posts of authority for which his age then suited him. Perhaps the most appropriate would have been that of Superior of Farm Street when Fr Devas retired after a stroke that June, and he would surely have given the office something of the same imaginative public character that Fr Corbishley did a few years later; one cannot know whether Fr Bolland would have blocked, or did block, such a modest recompense.

There was an impression in some quarters in America, and perhaps in England, that Fr D'Arcy was in disgrace. That was not so as far as the English Provincials were concerned: the three who held office till 1964, Fathers Helsham, Boyle and Coventry, were all personal friends and fully in sympathy with him. Nor was it true at a more popular level: in 1953 a provincial congregation elected Fr D'Arcy the Province's sole representative at a special assembly of the Society in Rome – a rebuff to Fr Bolland's disapprobation which that official might digest as he wished. Publicly, Fr D'Arcy was, with the aged Fr Martindale, the Province's leading celebrity, and visible signs of it kept cropping up as thickly as they had in the thirties. In July 1950 his picture appeared in *Vogue* as one of Great Faces of Oxford. He was photographed by Eisenstaedt at Farm Street and the portrait was printed in *Life* for January 14th 1952 in its Portfolio of Distinguished Britons – the only churchman and only Catholic in the selection. Already in 1948 he had been elected a member of the Athenaeum under a special rule for the admission of men of high public distinction. In 1952 the Stonyhurst Association elected him President, the only priest since Cardinal Vaughan to have received such a token of admiration, and he had the pleasure of supporting Fr Vavasour in the first year of his highly able Rectorship. His attendance at the Rome meeting of the Society in 1953 was followed by a visit to Malta, which sparked his interest in its Knights, and in October 1954 he was received as a Conventual Chaplain *ad honorem* of the Order of Malta, the first English Jesuit ever to attain that distinction; the only other until recently was Fr Vavasour, who was admitted two years later.

In the early fifties Fr D'Arcy's depression had not yet been lifted by such marks of esteem, and the circumstances of the day helped to make optimism difficult. The Catholic revival in England that had seemed so bright between the wars was losing its impact; its brilliant young converts were growing middle-aged and were not finding successors. The intellectual tide in favour of form and authority had ebbed, a good illustration of the new climate being the way Evelyn Waugh was treated – and behaved – as a reactionary survival embattled in squirearchical seclusion. The institutional Church was also at a low ebb; the Archbishops of Westminster between 1944 and 1963, Cardinals Griffin and Godfrey, were perhaps the most mediocre incumbents in the history of their office. At Farm Street a similar judgment is applicable to Fr Devas's successor as Superior. In the wider field, in February 1950 Mr Attlee's government still had another twenty months to run, and the country was in the atmosphere of drab bureaucratic control that provoked George Orwell to write *Nineteen Eighty-Four* and Evelyn Waugh to write *Love Among The Ruins*; the descent in Europe of the Iron Curtain, which sharpened their pessimism, was all the more ominous to an observer whose primary values were religious.

The stable, civilised world, lit by classicism, to which Fr D'Arcy's mind went back seemed barely recognisable among the rubble, and the philosophical scene mirrored the political. Across the Channel the *vague* was Existentialism, which Fr D'Arcy saw as a desertion of the rational standards that must be the mark of a civilised culture; the fashion for Freudianism backed this tendency by sanctioning the surrender to man's brutish passions, the impulse of the barbarian, and by the denigration of his higher powers. In England the dominant system in the universities was the Logical Positivism which had been launched by A.J. Ayer in *Language, Truth and Logic*, with his claim to put all religious and moral values outside the scope of meaningful discussion. Ayer's thesis was that statements only possessed significance if it was possible to verify them by factual observation; otherwise they were literally nonsense. Reviewing the book in *The Criterion* in 1936, Fr D'Arcy had remarked, 'he seems on his own principle to be talking nonsense', and he described Ayer's ostensible empiricism as 'a masked metaphysic with an unverifiable criterion of verifiability.'[5] Sixty years later, the Positivists have themselves recognised the justice of this criticism, but in the interval their canons of linguistic analysis dominated and stultified British philosophy. The self-absorbed futility of the verbal games to which they confined human thought seemed to Fr D'Arcy all the more frivolous in the threatened post-war world, of which he wrote: 'The new universe floated by the scientists drifts away into a black cloud; the world of art becomes a private dream, and statesmen have to compound with slavery. It is not enough just to complain that one group of modern philosophers spends its time sharpening the language of communication, that another group is 'committing itself' in an absurd world, proud in its anguish and holding fiercely to its one last possession, the will; while a third is summoning the forces of the self to the world's aid. The part of wisdom is constantly to dress our days as they come to 'a dexterous and starlight order.'"★[6]

As Jesuit Provincial, Fr D'Arcy had seen himself as armed with power to combat such forces, but stripped of that power he lost his optimism. Slowly however opportunities were offered him to make his philosophy felt. In January 1951 he went on a five-month American lecture tour that took him to New York, Boston, Chicago and the Catholic university of Marquette, where he received his third honorary degree. He went from an exhausted world to one which seemed to be the harbinger of the future, and the Catholic scene in America was, above all, bursting with vitality. Between 1940 and 1963 the number of Catholics in the United States jumped from 21 million to 44 million; vocations to the priesthood and the religious life were soaring. Fr Coughlin had been succeeded as a famous radio publicist by Mgr Fulton Sheen, who took Catholic apologetics into the television age, and Patrick Scanlan at the *Brooklyn Tablet* wielded a comparable journalistic influence. In Cardinal Spellman, Archbishop of New York from 1939 to 1967, the Church had an exceptionally powerful spokesman, with strong links with the worlds of politics and finance.

Of all the historic achievements of the Catholic Church there is none more neglected today than its advance in the post-war years. The peculiar American contribution to that growth inspired an article which Evelyn Waugh wrote in 1949, *The American Epoch in the Catholic Church*. He noted in it: 'It seems that in every age some one branch of the Church, racial, cultural or national, bears peculiar responsibilities towards the whole. Vitality mysteriously waxes and wanes among the peoples. Again and again Christianity seems dying at its centre. Always Providence has another people quietly maturing to relieve the decadent of their burden.' In the sixteenth century Spain was perhaps the power-house; in almost every century since the conversion of Clovis the honour might seem to belong to France. That could not be said of the French Church after

---

★ The quotation is from G.M. Hopkins, *The Bugler's First Communion*. The philosophical allusions, if they be found too cryptic, are to linguistic analysis, Existentialism and Psychoanalysis.

1945, racked with self-accusation and controversy. Instead, in Evelyn Waugh's words, many were 'turning their regard with hope and curiosity to the New World, where, it seems, Providence is schooling and strengthening a people for the historic destiny long borne by Europe.'[7]

The character of this florescence however was set by a social context that was unintellectual and, by origin, working-class. In 1947 it was observed that there was not a single Catholic bishop in the United States whose father or mother was a graduate. Truman Capote's description of Fr D'Arcy as 'a sort of Monsignor Sheen to the intelligentsia' carried an implication about the quality of Mgr Sheen's audience. And the whole tone of the popular figures mentioned above reflected the Irish clerical tradition behind them, absolute, autocratic and philistine. A typical product of it was Joe McCarthy, and the McCarthy era, in which Fr D'Arcy's return to America immersed him, could be identified as a stronger sign of Catholic triumph in American public life than the election of John Kennedy as President in 1960. One satirist described it as a time when 'the Harvard and Yale sons of the old Protestant aristocracy were regularly investigated for un-Americanism by certified products of Fordham and Notre Dame.'

Fr D'Arcy's apostolate in America occupies a place apart in that Catholic achievement, the dominant ethos of which was not one he found sympathetic, for all its Irish roots; the circles he typically moved in tended if anything to be explicitly hostile to it. He belongs rather to a surface current of that tide, one confined to the intellectual and moneyed world, but reflecting the energy of the larger surge on which it flowed. Fr D'Arcy's invitations to America were, like those of Christopher Dawson or Evelyn Waugh, symptoms of the continuing avidity of American Catholics to listen to the English Catholic writers. It was to some extent a policy of prestige. For university society, to attend Fr D'Arcy's lectures when he visited was to mark a claim to membership of the intellectual *gratin*. The delicate philosophical musings on the human heart, the explorations of the Christian tradition in art or of the poetry of Gerard Manley Hopkins, were the caviar of university fare. His contribution was wholly individual; he linked himself with no school or party, whether English or American, and his role essentially, in a society where the words 'Catholic intellectual' seemed almost an oxymoron, was to personify a Christian humanism drawing for its stock on the wealth of the European past.

In 1951 Fr D'Arcy resumed contact with the sculptor Frederick Shrady, whom he had known briefly as a young student in Oxford in the late twenties. In 1954 Shrady made his bust of Fr D'Arcy which is in the Metropolitan Museum in New York, and presented a replica of it to Campion Hall. His Austrian wife Maria, whom he had married after the war, herself a poet of religious sensibility, was chiefly responsible for elaborating the artist's way of life in a beautiful house on the European model in the Connecticut countryside, which was a centre of a lively circle of Catholic writers and artists. Fr D'Arcy stayed here innumerable times in the remaining twenty-five years of his life. The Shradys' friend Paul Horgan has written of his delight in children, with whom he was known, on entering a house, to sit down and immerse himself in conversation to the complete oblivion of his adult hosts; the Shradys with their beautiful children, whom he watched grow up over the next twenty years, became for him a second family.

In New York perhaps Fr D'Arcy's closest friend was the former seminarist and FBI man Matt Murray, who as the owner of the lucrative parking service at the New York tracks was in a position to help him develop a latent taste for race-going. Murray was closer to the more demotic strain in American Catholicism, which Fr D'Arcy found socially if not intellectually congenial. A legacy of his introduction to bar-room circles was his addiction to sweet Manhattans;* he would order them on every possible occasion, and two of these under his belt at the start of an evening warmed him up for his happiest conversational flights. They struck a note of indulgence in his character which some people found surprising, though Tom Burns saw the mark of a true ascetic in the unaffected enjoyment of simple pleasures.

Fr D'Arcy's friendship with Charles and Jane Engelhard developed strongly after their gift of the Mary Queen of Scots triptych, and they used to wait for his journeys to America to conduct the christenings of their successive daughters. Charles Engelhard cleverly built up a fabulous fortune from the export of South African gold, which he brought out of the country in the form of objets d'art such as dishes and pulpit tops to evade the restrictions on bullion exports. A former bomber pilot, he kept up his flying interests by forming a fleet of private planes, headed by a converted jet airliner. He was a friend of Ian Fleming and served as the inspiration for Goldfinger, a creation which Engelhard enjoyed to the point of nicknaming one of his air stewardesses Pussy Galore. His South African links caused him to be attacked in the sixties as a quasi-Fascist, but he was in fact an influential Democrat and one of the leading contributors to John Kennedy's presidential campaign. Through him Fr D'Arcy got to know President Kennedy, to whom he pronounced a personal tribute on English television the day after his assassination. It was also through the Engelhards that he met the Duke and Duchess of Windsor. The Engelhards' main houses were a Rhenish schloss in New Jersey and a marble-floored extravaganza called Pamplemousse at Boca

*A cocktail of whisky with vermouth.

Grande, Florida. Despite the nouveau-riche ostentation of these places, Charles Engelhard was an art-collector of intelligence and wide curiosity. In the late fifties he expanded his interests to racing and was later the owner of the famous Nijinsky.

Fr D'Arcy's second long stay in America in this period was for an academic appointment at Georgetown, which was the flagship of the Jesuit university system. Georgetown was then under one of its greatest Presidents, Fr Edward Bunn, whose special gift was the detection and exploitation of unemployed talent in other Provinces. He invited Fr D'Arcy to teach at Georgetown for the full semester from January to June 1954, and Charles Engelhard paid his passage. His stay again included lecturing visits to New York, Chicago and other places. He would punctuate his teaching commitments with forays through the country, being received by his friends with the typical generosity of well-to-do Americans. Besides the Engelhards, Fr D'Arcy's close friends among the very rich included Mrs Robert W. Johnson, of the well-known chemical company, who gave him some of her most delicate Dior dresses to be made into chasubles, and Mrs L.D. Cavanagh (a niece of the celebrated Duchess Brady), with whom he used to stay at Easter-time. Fr Haller, who was the Bursar at Georgetown in these years, has recalled how he would come back from such trips with a sheaf of cheques for the university treasury, sometimes of as much as $30,000.[8] At one moment he would be found staying in the Engelhards' sumptuous apartment in the Carlton Towers in New York, at the next insisting on travelling the long journey from Boston to Chicago by bus instead of air.[9] In both cases the Society was saved money, and Fr D'Arcy took luxury and discomfort with equal insouciance.

Fr D'Arcy's next American appointment was for a semester at Notre Dame, Indiana, from January to May 1955.[10] While here, in April, he received a letter from Edith Sitwell, who had come across him while on an American lecture tour the previous year, and who now wished to enter the Catholic Church. Fr D'Arcy wrote back expressing his pleasure and telling her, 'I had felt God's love moving in your last volumes of poetry.'[11] As he had still several weeks to go before his return to England, he put her in touch with Fr Caraman, who gave her instruction. Fr D'Arcy was present at her reception at Farm Street in August. Edith Sitwell wrote for him a poem, *His Blood Colours my Cheek*, which was published in *The Month* in 1958.

In the early fifties, while his visits to America were still sporadic, Fr D'Arcy made a number of other trips abroad. He was by now one of the most respected philosophers on the European circuit and was invited to congresses such as one held on Lake Maggiore in autumn 1952, where he spoke on 'The Power of Caritas and the Holy Spirit'. Walter Starkie invited him back to Spain the following January, when he saw the Duke of Alba, then in retirement and in the final months of his life, for the last time. In June 1954 he was at a congress in Florence 'for Peace and Christian Civilisation', the brain-child of the idealistic Mayor of Florence, Giorgio La Pira. He wrote to Maria Shrady: 'On the journey [back from America] I found myself oddly unwell. It turned out on getting here that I am allergic to penicillin & I had been poisoned by it. So I went off to Florence with misgivings, but the place lifted me up. The Congress was an immense affair ... The confusion was exasperating though usually very funny.'[12]

A growing interest in Eastern culture was stimulated by a journey to Japan in 1953, just after the Madrid visit. The trip was an exchange visit between Columbia and Tokyo universities, and Fr D'Arcy travelled via America in a party of two Englishmen and seven Americans. He was, with Mrs J.D. Rockefeller, the guest of honour, and the stay included a lunch with the British Ambassador, an audience with the Emperor, and lecturing in five Japanese universities, besides visits to Hiroshima and Nagasaki. He was interested to meet Zen Buddhists, who told him how on rising from bed they practised archery, concentrating their minds on the target till the self was forgotten, and then the arrow flew straight to the target.[13] He fell ill again on this visit, and Patrick O'Donovan, who happened to be in Japan covering the Korean War, lied him into an American military hospital and claimed to have saved his life. He was nevertheless well enough to go on to Hong Kong and India before returning home.

He was dismayed to find that intellectuals in Japan had completely rejected their traditional culture and lacked any real interest in philosophy, being consumed with a feverish zeal for whatever was the latest in any field. He liked to illustrate the trait with an anecdote: 'I was snubbed beautifully one day, at the university in Kyoto. It was during a reception, and I was chatting with a Japanese professor. Did I know Bertrand Russell, he asked. I said that we were quite good friends, although this did not mean that I agreed with all of Russell's views. "Ah yes," said the Japanese, "but he is up to date".'[14]

A sequel to Fr D'Arcy's brush with the East was described by Gerard Noel when he was editor of the *Catholic Herald*. He had brought some friends to meet Fr D'Arcy at the Connaught, the small but luxurious hotel opposite Farm Street church, in whose discreet bar Fr D'Arcy used to consume many of his Manhattans. While they were sitting there Kenneth Tynan walked in and Noel beckoned him over. He started to talk of Zen Buddhism. 'It so happened that Fr D'Arcy had recently returned from Japan, and knew a surprising amount about the subject … A fascinating battle of wits ensued and the two participants agreed to differ with enormous mutual respect. The stammered but fluent 'periods' of Ken were taken up (but never cut short) by the rapier-like thrusts of Fr D'Arcy, backed not only by a vast background knowledge but also by enough mental agility to keep traditional and humane Christianity in double harness with the modern complexities of Zen Buddhism.'[15]

As appears above, by 1953 Fr D'Arcy considered himself a good friend of Bertrand Russell. Given their two public clashes before the war this was an odd friendship, but we earlier saw its origin in Russell's gratitude for Fr D'Arcy's refusal to join the lynch mob against him in America in 1940. This debt, acknowledged at a BBC dinner in the early fifties, brought Fr D'Arcy dividends in the subsequent broadcast. It was a philosophical Brains Trust in which Fr D'Arcy and another Catholic were pitted against Bertrand Russell and A.J. Ayer. The result is thus described by Fr D'Arcy: 'The first question was from Sweden: 'Is there any rational argument for the existence of God?' Ayer immediately started to answer in the negative, and then I came on. Russell leaned back and after a while said, 'D'Arcy's got a good point there, D'Arcy's got a very good point there.' The next thing they got onto was moral evil. I was asked to begin that subject, and I gave the ordinary Catholic view. Ayer immediately said, 'Completely unintelligible. That means nothing.' And Russell: 'Oh, no, no, that's a very good position. I rather incline to agree with what D'Arcy said on that subject. Oh, no, no, no, Ayer."' Russell then invited Fr D'Arcy to dinner, where they resumed their purring, and Russell confessed to an interest in mysticism.[16] It was typical of Fr D'Arcy that he began to entertain hopes for a change of heart on Bertrand Russell's part, and appealed to a passage from his Autobiography for evidence of a belief uncannily similar to his own: 'Nothing can penetrate the loneliness of the human self except the highest intensity of the sort of love the religious teachers have preached. Whatever does not spring from this motive is harmful and at best useless. Seriously, the unmystical, rationalistic view of life seems to omit all that is most important and most beautiful.'[17] Despite such sentiments, Russell denied Fr D'Arcy what would certainly have been his most spectacular conversion.

Another BBC broadcast Fr D'Arcy made with A.J. Ayer in August 1957 was singled out by the latter as one of the few examples of the genre whose influence on public opinion might have been more than evanescent. The participants on this occasion were Fr D'Arcy and Lord David Cecil for Christianity, Ayer and Julian Huxley for unbelief. 'The first question put to us,' writes Ayer, 'was whether we believed in the Devil. 'No,' I said immediately, 'and not in God either,' giving my reasons as briefly as I could. Father d'Arcy responded with less than Jesuitical urbanity★ and a lively discussion followed in which the Anglican David Cecil joined forces with the Roman Catholic d'Arcy and Julian Huxley gave me his powerful support. Later in the programme we were asked whether we believed in original sin and Father d'Arcy said he did.' Ayer refrained from raising the related doctrines of Adam and Eve and the Immaculate Conception, but the impact made on him by Fr D'Arcy's advocacy was evidently limited, for when the latter thanked him after the programme for not bringing up those doctrines Ayer took away the impression that he would have found himself incapable of defending them. This happened to be the last time Fr D'Arcy was invited to appear on the Brains Trust, a fact which the loyal Frank Pakenham attributed to Ayer's machinations; but he relayed Fr D'Arcy's response: 'Oh no. Freddie Ayer is a gentleman.' Perhaps this reported platitude conceals a more pointed expression of Fr D'Arcy's belief: 'The Devil is a gentleman.'[18]

Fr D'Arcy's writings in the nineteen-fifties show the construction of an intellectual response to a post-war world overshadowed by the advance of atheistic communism. Before the war he had written some forthright things about communism, asserting, 'seldom in history has a more childish philosophy held the attention of man' and that, 'The doctrine is a damnable one, appealing as it does to the vivid discontents of the simple and the poor in order to rob them of Christianity, of their God and their human dignity.'[19] In 1956 he published *Communism and Christianity*, which begins with a description of the Marxist philosophy; probably no-one has ever written a more objective exposition of that subject, but Fr D'Arcy never believed that taking a dispassionate view of a question meant being incapable of reaching a strong judgment on it. He continues with a review of Christian history which is not polemical; nevertheless, coming after the unrelieved materialism of the Marxist analysis, no comparison could be more eloquently drawn than by his sublime summary of the action of divine grace in human affairs. Fr D'Arcy saw a society whose Christian harmony had been shattered, first by the Reformation, and then in its remaining territory by the advance of rationalism and by the French Revolution. In successive ages Catholic reactions – the Counter-Reformation and the Catholic revival of the nineteenth century – had seemed to give hope that the destruction could be repaired; but their hope had not been fulfilled. The first world war had destroyed the old order, and with it the illusion of a continuing Christian civilisation that had clung to its back.

Between the wars Fr D'Arcy had again imagined that a Christian

---

★In Sir Isaiah Berlin's recollection, Fr D'Arcy's reply gave a not-too-veiled hint of his conviction that Ayer was one of the leading agents of the Devil's work.

restoration was gathering strength. The spiritual disorientation left by the recent cataclysm and then the retreat of secular liberalism before the violent Right seemed to show that the tide of history was turning again; it was an opportunity that could be used by Christians as much as by Fascists and National Socialists. This hope was again destroyed by the second war; its legacy was half a world imprisoned in communism and the other half penetrated with deep cultural evils. For all the cries of woe uttered by thinkers over the centuries, he felt that the crisis could now truly be seen as greater than ever before in Christian history.[20] And yet even in that gloom he saw hope, not just for a stemming of the tide but for a full rebuilding of Christian civilisation.[21] Never tied down by a negative view, he saw it as the Church's function to spy out the opportunities, both in the Christian legacy of the contemporary world and in its new features, and make use of them to recapture men's hearts. He pointed to signs that the Church itself was finding the vitality for this task: firstly, the retreat of a merely institutional understanding of the Church in favour of a new interest in the doctrine of the Mystical Body, signifying the abiding incarnate presence of God in human society; secondly, the liturgical movement among the laity, encouraged by the hierarchy, and expressing the community of that Mystical Body.[22]

The pre-eminent Catholic thinker of the time who gave him cause for hope was Teilhard de Chardin, whom he knew personally in these years. True, he felt serious reservations about Teilhard's philosophy and made a number of specific criticisms: his evolutionary vision seemed dependent on attributing to inanimate nature an inadmissible quality of consciousness, and involved a distortion of the true pattern of history, in which human liberty and the real conflict with evil failed to be given their due place; more fundamentally Teilhard's view of Christ's headship over all things seemed to Fr D'Arcy a premature synthesis 'too narrowly apprenticed to scientific evolution.'[23] He thus found Teilhard's an imperfect philosophy, but the excitement it had for him was that here was a Catholic priest, a respected scientist, producing a theory that pointed to a luminous harmonisation between Christian philosophy and science, the learning par excellence of the day. If such a synthesis could be perfected there might be a Christian conquest of contemporary culture comparable to the triumph of the scholastics in mediaeval thought.

The enemy to be defeated was nevertheless a formidable one, and in England the self-confident Catholic team, backed by some of the period's most representative thinkers, of which Fr D'Arcy had formed part in the thirties was now fragmented and finding little resonance for its views outside the Catholic body. In 1939 Wyndham Lewis had cited Fr D'Arcy as one figure people might choose if asked to name a man typical of the age (other candidates he offered, according to party, were Freud and the

Nazi ideologue Dr Rosenberg), adding that nothing was more modern than the New Catholicism. In the fifties Lewis and most right-wing thinkers were in eclipse. The acceptance of the kind of rationally-based apologetic that Fr D'Arcy stood for was drastically shrunken. In place of reasoned argument there was a great fog of irrationality to contend against, and with irrationality a descent into barbarism. This reversion, with its turning to the base passions, especially those of sexual licence, and the misprizing of the highest powers of the human spirit, was the element which most depressed him in the trend of the times.

At a less philosophical level, by the mid fifties Fr D'Arcy had more or less recovered his personal equanimity after the blow of his dismissal. Farm Street was a congenial home, now under the superiority (1953–8) of Fr Leo Belton, a saintly and courteous man who had been his near-contemporary at Stonyhurst. Fr D'Arcy's deep love of the Order whose life he had embraced received first expression in his affectionate engagement in his own religious community. The house was living through another great period, perhaps without quite the weight of historical scholarship of the early years of the century, but surely equal in its pastoral energy. Though the community of writers were not primarily involved in the church's pastoral work, there were many calls on Fr D'Arcy, as there had been before 1945, to give sermons, retreats and the like both in London and round the country, and he remained one of the leading figures in the Society's work. Fr Basset was not far away at Southwell House, now the Province's London retreat house, and his enthusiastic personality was making a wide public impact; the First Friday vigils at Southwell House drew crowds, as did special acts like the centenary of Our Lady of Lourdes in 1958, when the Albert Hall was packed to capacity twice in one night. At Farm Street itself Fathers Brodrick and Caraman were at the height of their literary productivity in these years, and the latter was pushing forward with his great editorship of *The Month*, to whose finances Fr D'Arcy's own literary earnings made a notable contribution.

Fr Joseph Christie was much in demand as a preacher and lecturer in England and in America, and was soon appearing on television; his pulpit dialogues with Fr Brodrick at Farm Street recalled the D'Arcy-Woodlock dialogues which had filled the church in the twenties and thirties. Fr Christie was in the habit of going to Fr D'Arcy for his insights, but one day at tea-time the latter returned the compliment by asking him for hints for a forthcoming wedding sermon. 'Don't use any ideas in *The Mind and Heart of Love*,' said Fr Christie. 'I've already used them all.' 'Only those you understood, Joe,' was the reply. Fr D'Arcy's dearest companion in the house was Fr Basil Gurrin, whom he had brought here in friendship in 1948. Lower down the scale, another great friend was the Farm Street receptionist, Pat Ryan, an imposing figure who was sometimes mystified to find himself addressed as 'Your Grace' by awed visitors, to whom Fr Sire had mischievously confided that he was an archbishop in mufti.

Intellectually, Fr D'Arcy was still at the height of his powers, though two of the levels at which his mind operated can be illustrated by incidents of 1956. Evelyn Waugh records a visit to Dublin in February. He was bidden to dinner at the Kildare Street Club by Billy Clonmore (since 1946 sixth Earl of Wicklow) with the news that Fr D'Arcy was there. 'It was not, it transpired, the anniversary of Billy's reception, nor very near the date. I can only think Father D'Arcy was in Dublin on other business and proposed the dinner. We sat in the public dining room and had an excellent dinner with many good wines. I sat between Father D'Arcy and [Terence de Vere] White ... Poor Father D'Arcy's memory is so defective that he begins anecdotes and forgets their point, loses every name.'[24] Six months later Fr D'Arcy lectured at a summer school in Oxford and gave a talk on Gerard Manley Hopkins which was so moving that at the end of it his class burst into spontaneous applause.[25]

Fr Christopher Devlin had been teaching at Beaumont and simultaneously writing for *The Month*, and in 1956 published his edition of the notebooks of Gerard Manley Hopkins. In the same year he was sent as a missionary to Southern Rhodesia. A farewell dinner party held by his brother, the distinguished judge Sir Patrick Devlin, in his flat in Gray's Inn Square, was attended by Fathers D'Arcy, Brodrick and Caraman, and was a happy occasion; but Fr Devlin returned four years later with terminal cancer, and the reunion in the same flat in May 1961 was a sadder one, with Fr Devlin bedridden after a recent operation. Lady Devlin wrote: 'Of all his brothers in Religion probably Fr D'Arcy was the dearest to Christopher. It was, then, also fitting that he was the last one Christopher saw.' Fr Devlin was sent to a nursing home in Scotland and died that October.[26]

Fr D'Arcy was entering a time of life increasingly punctuated by the deaths of friends. Roy Campbell had been a lively companion in the early fifties, when Fr D'Arcy used to go to the parties held in the basement of his house in Camden Grove, where artists and writers such as T.S. Eliot and Evelyn Waugh were frequent partners in hilarity. Campbell went to live in Portugal in 1952 and was killed there in a car crash in April 1957.[27] Fr D'Arcy celebrated his requiem at Farm Street; among the friends of Roy Campbell present was Bernard Wall, who after the war had resumed his journalism as editor of *The Changing World* and *The Twentieth Century*, and had just brought out his *Report on the Vatican*, unusual in that period for its critical view. Another death of 1957 was that of Ronald Knox, at whose own request Fr D'Arcy preached the funeral sermon in Westminster Cathedral.

The year 1957 saw a special General Congregation of the Society (not called for the election of a new General), which set out with ambitions for reform but whose most memorable decree was to forbid Jesuits to smoke. Fr D'Arcy's addiction to this habit prompted one journalist to name him as one of the better-known likely victims of the order, so that in a postcard to Evelyn Waugh he subscribed himself: 'From one whose habit of sin, – now incurable – has been publicised in the papers.'[28] Waugh had in fact been supplying him with cigarettes for a number of years, enabling him to dispense with his old custom of rolling his own. Fr D'Arcy thought that his venerable age would exempt him from the ban, but the question was resolved by an attack of bronchitis early the next year which put him in hospital for a time and made abstention a matter of health.[29]

The indirect consequences of this Congregation brought Fr D'Arcy three grievous blows to his personal feelings and his pride in the English Province. The preliminary meeting of the Province held at Easter passed a resolution to break up Heythrop – the policy that had tempted Fr D'Arcy during his Provincialship – with a view to establishing the Philosophate at Wardour and the Theologate at Manresa. Involved in this policy was the decision to close down the teacher training college which Fr D'Arcy had founded at Manresa, while Heythrop was earmarked as a combined Novitiate and Tertianship.[30] The restrictions which had prevented the use of Wardour had long been removed, and there would at last have been something to show for its purchase.

It has already been pointed out that the 1949 plan for teacher training at Manresa was a cumbersome one, and its ill effects had not taken long to be shown. Admittedly some change needed to be made. Whatever Fr D'Arcy thought, however, of the implicit criticism of his scheme, he was justified in arguing that outright closure was not the answer. Manresa was not purely a Jesuit concern but had been increasingly offering training to students from outside the Society; its closure after such a short time offended the Catholic hierarchy, the other religious congregations affected, and above all London University, which was infuriated by the cavalier repudiation of its commitments by the Society.[31] This decision taken on grounds purely of internal Jesuit advantage was by itself an ominous decline in the Province's standards of public policy.

Secondly, however, the plan for the division of Heythrop was soon overruled, and one of the principal reasons given was the expense of the works needed to move the Philosophate to Wardour.* Heythrop

---

*It would be interesting to know whether any attempt was made to enlist Fr D'Arcy's influence in fund-raising for the sake of a house whose restoration he had so much at heart. It is worth noting, purely to indicate the value of the gifts made to him, that the price of the Mary Queen of Scots triptych amply exceeded all likely building expenses at Wardour.

remained as it was, Harlaxton was closed in 1957 and the Novitiate was brought back to Manresa. Four years later this decision was reversed and Manresa, after exactly a century in the Province's service, was sold to the London County Council; but for a second time the opportunity of bringing Wardour into use was rejected, and the house was sold to a non-Catholic girls' school, the Novitiate being reinstated at Harlaxton.

Thus in two important respects Fr D'Arcy's policies as Provincial were repudiated. But these were venial offences beside the third aspect of the reorganisation: to supply the loss of the training course at Manresa, it was decided to send virtually all scholastics to Campion Hall to take diplomas of education. An annexe was quickly built on (Lutyens's splendid plans for enlargement received their death-blow: there was no question of their being implemented in part, and a functional block was designed), and the number of residents went up from between thirty and forty to between fifty and sixty, many of them well below the normal standard for university admission. From being an elite institution, Campion Hall came to be seen as an easy back door into Oxford.

It was argued before that the expansion of Campion Hall ought to have taken place forty years earlier; but the policy required was a judicious enlargement to admit men who could acquit themselves respectably in the degree courses. To throw the house open without selection for teacher-training purposes was quite a different thing. To Fr D'Arcy, whose ideal had always assumed the highest standards, the plan was an abomination. Its horror was increased by the fact that it was brought in by men who had long been close to him and who ought to have known better, Fr Desmond Boyle as Provincial, a distinguished Campion Hall graduate, and Fr Tom Corbishley, who was both Master of the Hall and, from 1957, Vice-Provincial. Of the latter Fr Vincent Turner, who knew him from the first years of his Mastership, asserted that he was in no way Fr D'Arcy's inferior either as Master or as Rector.[32] Those who remember his less exciting later years might see more justice in the quip of one of his undergraduates: 'Poor old Tom! Jack of all trades and Master of Campion Hall.' The inglorious policy with which he closed his term of office originated in Rome, but both he and Fr Boyle may be blamed for failing to put up an adequate opposition to it.

In the downward slide of the English Jesuit Province, the degradation of Campion Hall marks a new departure: a deliberate act of policy that actually damaged the prestige of the Province (the foundation of Heythrop had been grandly conceived, even if misconceived). The utilitarianism and disregard for the service that the Society gave to others were symptoms of a growing narrowness of view. The decline from the days when Fr D'Arcy conceived a vision addressing broad wants of the post-war world was a sharp and rapid one; sadly, it was only a foretaste of what was to follow.

Alienated from the Province's policies and from his superiors,[33] Fr D'Arcy was now spending an increasing amount of time in America. With his next visit there from January 1958 to May 1959, he began a decade in which, while returning periodically to Farm Street, he spent much more time (86 months against 40) in America than in England, his longest stay being eighteen months in 1962-3. He celebrated his seventieth and eightieth birthdays there, the first with a large reception given for him in Washington by Mrs Barrett McDonnell and the second with a dinner given by the Engelhards at the New York club 21, with the Duke and Duchess of Windsor among the guests. The universities he lectured at included Boston College, Columbia, Cornell, Fordham, Georgetown, Loyola (Baltimore) and Loyola (Chicago), Minnesota, Notre Dame, Princeton, the University of California, the Wesleyan University in Connecticut, and Yale. In 1960 he was elected a member of the American Academy of Arts and Sciences, he received doctorates from Laval University in Quebec (1962) and Duquesne University in Pittsburgh (1967), and honours for Catholic philosophy which included the Loyola Gold Medal from Chicago in 1963 and in 1967 the Aquinas-Spellman Medal of the Catholic Philosophical Association of America.

Fr D'Arcy's celebrity status in the United States had perhaps been given its accolade when in March 1957 he was asked to say the prayer for the opening of the Senate. The prayer he composed began as follows:

> O Father of everlasting wisdom, who hast taught us to say that 'the Lord is my light, whom then shall I fear?' and whose good pleasure it is 'to reign in our understanding blissfully,' grant to Thy servants now gathered together in the august Senate of the United States of America to 'beat from their brains the thicky night' and be enlightened by Thy daybreak.*[34]

Experts may pronounce on whether the brains of the United States Senate have ever been prayed for in quite that manner, and others on whether the prayer was effective.

Truman Capote gave his impression of Fr D'Arcy's American fame in *Observations*, published in 1959. The text, accompanying a gangster-like portrait by Richard Avedon, spoke of 'the worldly, impossibly erudite Darcy who ... year after year bustles, a rusty-black, miser-like figure,

---

* The quotations are respectively from the psalm *Dominus illuminatio mea*, Julian of Norwich, and Hopkins's translation of the hymn *Jesu dulcis memoria*:
  Light us, Lord, with Thy daybreak,
  Beat from our brains the thicky night.

always pinched and poor-looking, between continents,* beseeching the rich in support of Catholic good-works, lecturing the already Enlightened and, as a sort of Monsignor Sheen to the intelligentsia, converting to the Faith many of the century's cleverest minds... A mentally modernized Savonarola, Darcy is swift in pursuit of man's soul, the undyable self is his concern.'

Retreats such as one he gave in Washington in Holy Week 1961 for a group of prominent men in government and other professions were a means by which his influence reached the highest circles. Of his impact in social settings, Matt Murray tells a story of inviting Fr D'Arcy to dine in his New York apartment with Corliss Lamont, a millionaire who devoted his time to advocating atheism and who wrote a number of books such as *The Illusion of Immortality*. Murray knew well the power which Patrick O'Donovan described in his obituary of Fr D'Arcy: 'When he took off in conversation, about the reality of the Devil or the splendour and mystery of the Mass or of the utility of beauty in the service of God, the talk was a prolonged firework.' He told Fr D'Arcy beforehand to let Lamont speak and not to begin his reply until he gave the signal. Lamont expounded his views over dinner until half past nine, and then Murray gave the sign arranged. Fr D'Arcy spoke until half past eleven, a wonderful sermon on the concept of God and the destiny of the human soul. Corliss Lamont was left speechless; his wife said, 'Father, if I am dying, I want you at my bedside.'[35]

Fr D'Arcy's ubiquitous presence at the grandest parties was often cited as evidence of his avidity for high life by people who were unaware how often he was bored and exhausted by such functions.[36] The initiative came from the numerous hosts whose reunions he ornamented. His food intake had always been minuscule and was even more so now that he had entered old age; so there was no gourmand motive behind his presence at well-stocked tables. An example of the kind of gathering he preferred is given by his meeting with William and Patricia Abell in Washington in October 1960. Fr Bunn, the President of Georgetown University, was dining at their house and on the spur of the moment suggested that they would enjoy meeting Fr D'Arcy. Called out at nine o'clock in the evening from the university, Fr D'Arcy immediately accepted the invitation, and there developed one of his warmest friendships. William Abell has written: 'Perhaps the facet of Father D'Arcy which was most unusual and moving to me was the spontaneity and ease with which he spoke of Christ. He was the only person it has been my privilege to know who

---

*Matt Murray has a memory of taking Fr D'Arcy to the airport, where Truman Capote accosted him and engaged him in conversation. If he had met him in a New York drawing-room he would have found him his more public elegant though emaciated self.

would frequently refer to 'my beloved Jesus' in a personal, tender, totally unaffected and moving manner.'[37] Fr D'Arcy's reminiscences, taped at the Abells' home during his visits over the winter of 1960–1, were published by Mr Abell in 1991 under the title *Laughter and the Love of Friends*, aptly commemorating a lifetime's friendships from Hilaire Belloc in his prime to young men and women growing up in the later twentieth century.

Chapter Nine

Via Dolorosa

When the Second Vatican Council opened in December 1962, its programme of *aggiornamento* agreed in some leading respects with Fr D'Arcy's own views on future aims and past defects in the Church: in the latter class he included a backward-looking habit, an excessive legalism and a colouring of Jansenism, or failure to comprehend the richness of divine grace by minds overloaded with concepts of sin and retribution.[1] Familiar from his youth with the too-rare apostolate of a Charles Plater, and with the Society's work in a slum parish like Cowcaddens, he had also criticised from an early period the laggardness of Catholics in taking up work for the poor.[2] In ecumenism he could have been called a pioneer, as one of the few Catholic priests to associate themselves with Cardinal Hinsley's Sword of the Spirit collaboration during the war. His relations with non-Catholics had always gone on assumptions of amity and courtesy which were foreign to some Church leaders★. On the other hand he had listened to too many converts from the Church of England to regard union with it as a particularly valuable gain, and personal co-operation seemed to him a more useful aim than schemes of ecclesiastical rapprochement. The Council showed itself disposed to take up the liturgical movement, which he regarded as one of the strongest contemporary signs of the life of the Church. Above all, of course, he valued the liberalisation of policy which gave honour to theologians like Teilhard de Chardin and Henri de Lubac, men whose thought he regarded as signs of the Church's intellectual vitality. Added to Pope John XXIII's warmer style of Church government and reaching out to contemporary society, these developments gave new life to his conception of a Catholic revival that would, even at this late hour, restore Christian civilisation.

Fr D'Arcy did not however indulge in the Pentecostal expectations voiced by some advocates of the Council; in fact his first fear was that it might prove just another manifestation of the Church's bureaucracy in action. When its promise of real reform was delivered he was agreeably

---

★*The Irish Times* for 2 February 1967 has a letter referring to an incident some years earlier when Archbishop McQuaid of Dublin refused Fr D'Arcy permission to speak at the non-Catholic Trinity College.

surprised. Although at the closure of the Council in December 1965 the ferment aroused was already provoking disquiet, the danger he saw was that extremists would provoke a reaction and a clamp-down by ecclesiastical authority.[3] He had nevertheless been aware for some time of a darker current in the reform movement. In 1961 he spoke to William Abell of 'a certain new phase' of Modernism, 'different, but interesting and slightly dangerous';[4] by the mid-sixties he would not have spoken so mildly. He saw the vogue for thinkers like Bonhoeffer as promoting a secularisation of religious thought, the very opposite of the recovery of the spiritual which he affirmed as the most desperate need of the time.

Whatever the hopes for the Church at large, they were not being fostered by events in the English Jesuit Province. At Easter 1963 Fr Caraman was dismissed as editor of *The Month* in consequence of what appears to have been a petty office jealousy. Fr D'Arcy's strongly expressed protest by letter from America achieved nothing.[5] With the exception of Fr Peter Hebblethwaite, who held the post for some years before leaving the Society, Fr Caraman was the last editor of *The Month* to enjoy a national reputation. In 1965 his disgrace was deepened when he was stripped of his office as Vice-Postulator for the canonisation of the English Martyrs and sent for some years to Norway, that being as far in the direction of Siberia as the arm of the English Province extended.

Early in 1964 Fr Gordon George arrived in England, appointed by the General to carry out a visitation of the English Province. One of the main problems he had to deal with was the over-extension of manpower. From their peak of 905 in 1951, the numbers of the Province had by now declined to 874. This was not quite as serious as it might seem, since much of the decrease was due to the fall in lay brothers' vocations, which could be made up by employing paid servants; nevertheless thirteen years' decline after a century and a quarter of strong growth was a measure of the stagnation into which the Province had drifted.

The utilitarianism, to call it no worse, of Fr George's approach was shown in the solutions he proposed. The matter of the lay brothers was tackled by measures apparently aimed at assimilating their qualifications and training to those of a secular business firm. A more startling decision however was that just before he left England, in July 1965, he ordered the immediate closure of Beaumont, and here we find a worse fault in his armoury than utilitarianism. Fr George, a Canadian, came to his task with a determination to strike a blow at the gentlemanly airs of the old country, and no doubt Beaumont, out of the Province's three public schools, particularly focused his objections. Occupying an elegant eighteenth-century house which had once belonged to Warren Hastings, and in close proximity to Windsor, it presented a paradigm of the aristocratic life. For a good many years it had been the Province's best school; the past three Provincials, Fathers Helsham, Boyle and Coventry, had all been previous Rectors of Beaumont, interrupted in their succession by Fr William Clifford, who as a baronet of ancient Catholic family had given the school an added note of social distinction. In 1961 Beaumont had celebrated its centenary and a fund of nearly £100,000 raised for the occasion had paid for its enlargement, numbers having grown by 100 since the end of the war.

The reason alleged for the closure was the shortage of manpower, but the different motive behind it soon became apparent. Fr George forbade any sort of consultation; when the Rector of Beaumont tried to announce the closure to the parents in a conciliatory manner, Fr George overruled the proposed circular and substituted a more aggressive message of his own.[6] He then departed for Rome, his work done, putting himself outside the range of the public outcry provoked by his order. As Visitor he had been invested by the Society's Constitutions with the full powers of the General, and his freedom of action was increased by the death of Fr Janssens in October 1964 and the seven months' interregnum until the election of his successor. When Fr Coventry's term of office came to an end in October 1964, Fr George himself appointed the new Provincial, Fr Terence Corrigan, a weak man from whom no resistance to his views was to be expected.

Despite assertions made against Beaumont's viability, its closure forestalled excellent prospects, whether under Jesuit or other management. Though small, Beaumont was well situated to expand as a day school, in accordance with the trend of the time. Mgr Gilbey, just then bringing to a close his highly successful chaplaincy at Cambridge, offered himself as Rector of Beaumont with a view to its being taken over by secular priests and lay masters, but his proposal was refused; it would have satisfied the aim of saving Jesuit manpower, but it would have defeated Fr George's real object of destroying a public school. The blow to the Jesuits' position in education was a double one, since the Benedictine former preparatory school of Worth immediately rose to fill the educational vacuum left in southern England.

The bad feeling caused by this act is said to have been the most traumatic experience of Fr Arrupe's first months as General; nevertheless it was one which he could have avoided by overruling the decision. A comparison with Fr Bolland is pertinent here: he may have blocked valuable projects, but he destroyed nothing, and indeed no action of such extremism would have been considered at the time. The closure of Beaumont is an example of the readiness of the Catholic Church in the nineteen-sixties to adopt unhesitatingly any measure, however damaging, that bore the stamp of modernity.

Not much more comfort was to be drawn from the fate of the remaining Jesuit schools. From 1963 to 1972 Stonyhurst was under the head-mastership of a coarse and abrasive man more successful in imparting his socialist than his Christian faith, and he set in motion the trend that led to a largely non-Jesuit Board of Governors, an overwhelmingly lay staff and a lay headmaster. The worse secularisation however was in the character of the school. The devotions that had permeated its life were allowed to lapse; Stonyhurst lost its last resemblance to the nursery of religious vocations that Fr D'Arcy had known as a boy;* the Sodality of Our Lady disappeared in 1967, after 358 years of unbroken existence. Of all the manifestations of that generation's neglect of Marian piety, perhaps none hurt Fr D'Arcy so much as this one, which reduced to a historical curiosity the day in 1902 when he had consecrated himself as a perpetual servant of the Virgin Mary.

An important policy adopted by the Province at this time was to turn Heythrop into a Pontifical Athenaeum which would take students from various dioceses and a number of the smaller religious orders. In this character Heythrop acquired the power to grant degrees; its Chancellor was the Archbishop of Westminster, Cardinal Heenan, the Jesuit Provincial becoming Vice-Chancellor, and the college entered upon its new life in 1965, with the authorisation and support of the Holy See and the English Catholic hierarchy. Almost at once, however, Jesuit numbers began to fall sharply, and in 1970 the decision was taken to close Heythrop and incorporate the Philosophy and Theology studies as part of London University; compensation had to be paid to the orders which had just built halls of residence at Heythrop in expectation of the ambitious venture. It would be superfluous to point to the closure of Beaumont as an example of the Society's ignoring of outside interests, but a second flagrant example was now given within five years of the first. The English Jesuit Province was somewhat in the position of a runner in a race who, after lopping off a foot, proceeds to improve on the situation by amputating the rest of the leg.

More generally the Province, like other sectors of the Church, was displaying a terror of opposing the current of the age. The situation that Fr D'Arcy had known in his first eight years in the Society was replicated, with the difference that it was now not Modernism but tradition that was being marginalised. Thus Fr Deryck Hanshell was removed as Master of Campion Hall in 1965 and despatched to Canada; Fr Joseph Christie, the last remaining star of the Farm Street pulpit, was sent to America in 1967; the Province's best-known theologian, Fr Joseph Crehan, was prevented from publishing the final volume of his *Catholic*

---

*In 1991, of forty-four old Stonyhurst boys then in the Society of Jesus, only seven had entered since 1964.[7]

Dictionary of Theology, so that it remained truncated three quarters of the way through. At Farm Street Fr James Brodrick alone spoke out consistently against the prevalent moral cowardice, but his failing health soon caused him to be moved to a nursing home. With Fr Caraman in Norway and Fr Basset assigned to a parish in the Isles of Scilly, the Province passed within a few years into a state of total eclipse.

When he came back from America in August 1966, Fr D'Arcy found these unwelcome changes brought sadly close to home. The Superior of Farm Street had been changed earlier that year, when Fr Corbishley's six-year tenure of the post was completed. Fr Corbishley had been an old friend and a man of civilised intellect; Fr D'Arcy held him less to blame than the Provincial for the rape of Campion Hall, and at Farm Street he had exercised his office in a particularly distinguished way, introducing the social practices of Oxford to the extent of holding dinners for eminent figures such as Archbishop Ramsay, Harold Macmillan and Sir Alec Douglas-Home. With his successor however the barbarian tendency in the Society of Jesus took over, and Fr D'Arcy reported to Maria Shrady that 'this Church and House are being transformed into faces of Medusa.'[8] The removal of Fr Basil Gurrin to another house was an especially hard blow to him. One of his less appreciated companions at Farm Street was Archbishop Roberts, a former Archbishop of Bombay who suffered in his eyes by comparison with his predecessor, the saintly Alban Goodier. Archbishop Roberts's taste for baiting the official Church received public display in 1964, when he clashed with the English hierarchy on the subject of contraception. In point of fact Fr D'Arcy too thought that a modification might be made in the Church's teaching on that subject, but he based his view on possible medical advances rather than on Archbishop Roberts's accustomed guying of authority. When Fr Christie publicly called Roberts a heretic at a meeting in Cambridge in 1967 Fr D'Arcy reported the incident with some relish to Maria Shrady.[9]

These irritations were added to an increasing distress at the way the reform movement in the Church was tending. Fr D'Arcy's first cause for regret was in the field of liturgy. Reforms in the Mass were prescribed by the Council late in 1963, and the practices of the more advanced liturgists began to be extended in the succeeding months. Of these the most unwelcome to Fr D'Arcy's thinking was the innovation of Mass facing the people, or to speak more properly the replacement of the traditional altar by something tending in greater or lesser degree towards a Communion table. Fr D'Arcy's convert Evelyn Waugh had run some way ahead of him in these matters, and he found the modest reforms of the time so abhorrent that he wrote to Fr D'Arcy asking whether, in his country retreat, he could avail himself of the rule exempting Catholics from their Sunday obligation if they lived more than three miles from a church. Fr D'Arcy wrote back on August 8th 1964: 'I can well understand how nerve racking & almost unbearable a Mass in the future in a small & modern Church might be with the priest facing the people. But I think it a terrible loss to miss the central act of our faith, and the divinely instituted means of worshipping God in Christ and through his Church, so I do hope you manage to put up with what may seem appalling.'[10]

The difference between Fr D'Arcy and Evelyn Waugh was that the latter had been hostile from the start to lay participation in the liturgy; Fr D'Arcy by contrast regarded it as the means of bringing the laity to an understanding of the divine Sacrifice, and the dialogue Mass received from him a warm welcome. As early as 1926 he had enlarged in *The Mass and the Redemption* on the importance of the role of the laity in the Mass, some thirty years before that message became fashionable in ecclesiastical circles.

The exchange between Fr D'Arcy and Evelyn Waugh has been used by Auberon Waugh to allege an estrangement between the two. Writing in *Books and Bookmen* in 1973, he reported that his father had 'insisted on identifying the "blue chin and fine, slippery mind" which had introduced him to Catholicism as being responsible for its collapse.'[11] At the source of this tale, Auberon Waugh has admitted, is 'an echo of a memory of [Evelyn's] saying he did not wish to see D'Arcy again.'[12] The use Auberon Waugh made of this memory bore less relation to fact than to his annoyance at Fr D'Arcy's failure to mention Evelyn's loyalty to the old Mass when writing recently about his religious faith. Evelyn Waugh's remark would have been characteristic, but was hardly a serious reaction to being denied permission to avoid Mass. Both Fr D'Arcy himself and Christopher Sykes discounted the supposed quarrel,[13] though it is true that Waugh's rural isolation and Fr D'Arcy's prolonged visits to America prevented their meeting again; even their correspondence was limited to a single exchange of letters in September 1965, when Waugh dismayed Fr D'Arcy by the despair he expressed at the state of the Church. Yet just before he died, on Easter Sunday 1966, Waugh had received a copy of Fr D'Arcy's intellectual autobiography *Facing God*, which he was looking forward to reviewing.

Fr D'Arcy expressed himself on the liturgy in one of his last books, *Facing the Truth*, published in 1969, in which he devoted three chapters to the subject. In a gentle criticism of the innovations, he complained of the banalisation of the profound meaning of the words of the Mass by minimalist translation. He also challenged the current orthodoxy among liturgists that Mass in the early Church had been said facing the people – a view now abandoned by scholars. Fr D'Arcy pointed out that in early churches the altar was set in a curtained space reproducing the veiled

Holy of Holies of the Jewish Temple. He emphasised the need to express, as both ancient Jewish and Catholic tradition did, the presence of God in His dwelling house. The trend towards stripping grandeur and beauty from churches and from the celebration of the Mass was one he felt particularly strongly about, and he used to denounce the 'rags' that were typically used to celebrate Mass instead of the rich vestments suited to the service of the King of Kings. Against the loquacity of the modern liturgy he liked increasingly to quote the text, 'Be still and know that I am God.' A favourite passage of his from Newman was one describing the Mass: 'It is not a mere form of words – it is a great action, the greatest action that can be on earth. It is not the invocation merely, but if I dare use the word, the evocation of the Eternal. He becomes present on the altar in Flesh and Blood, before whom angels bow and devils tremble. This is the awful event which is the scope, and is the interpretation of every part of the solemnity. Words are necessary, but as a means, not as ends; they are not mere addresses to the throne of grace, they are instruments of what is far higher, of consecration, of sacrifice.'[14]

Paul Horgan wrote at this time of the reverent absorption in the divine mystery which characterised Fr D'Arcy's manner of celebration: 'Who may ever hear him say his daily Mass, at his usual side altar at Farm Street, there knows him best ... The celebrant comes walking slowly, alone, bringing the veiled chalice. He is deep in contemplation, seeing nothing about him. He mounts the altar steps and seems tall. He enters the mystery with a lifetime's humble habit. He enters the holy of holies to lead us after him.'[15]

The core of the desecration was however, in Fr D'Arcy's view, the congregation-centred doctrine of the Mass that was superseding the understanding of it as the divine Sacrifice. This type of error he had denounced as early as 1926, when he wrote: 'It would be wrong to ... think that the Mass has no purpose save to bring down our Lord to be our food. That would be to turn upside down the meaning of sacrifice – to put man before God.'[16] The effect of this central distortion on the life of the Church could not but be grave, for in the conviction which he reiterated in 1961: 'There is one place whence all spirituality draws its life and forms of inspiration, and that is the altar of God. The Mass is the furnace of divine love and it is the maker of sanctity.'[17]

Facing the Truth was the only book Fr D'Arcy wrote in specific response to the changes brought by the Vatican Council. It contains one chapter in which he made use of the new freedom to put forward his own theory of Christ's self-consciousness. He argued against the quasi-Docetist view that many had considered obligatory till then, that Our Lord exercised full omniscience in His earthly life, and urged that His consciousness was essentially a human one; the implications for Fr

D'Arcy's favourite subject of self-consciousness in the case of one who knew himself as both man and God were a problem which he would no doubt have discussed many years earlier if Church attitudes had permitted it.

A chapter on 'The Immutability of God' seems mainly intended as a reply to Karl Rahner's perky conclusion that 'God is immutable in himself, but mutable in another.' Fr Rahner's provocative treatment of theology stirred Fr D'Arcy to some of his very few criticisms of fellow Catholics. In another work he took exception to Fr Rahner's famous pronouncement that the definition of a doctrine was a beginning and not an end – 'a somewhat unfortunate description, because it seems to suggest that we can start all over again with a defined doctrine, as if nothing had already been properly stated.'[18] In fact he was shocked that a man like Karl Rahner should use his outstanding talents less to illuminate Catholic doctrine than to throw it into the melting pot.

A further subject discussed in *Facing the Truth* was that of freedom of conscience. The appeal widely made to Newman as a champion of religious freedom provoked Fr D'Arcy to point out that what Newman meant by conscience was quite different from the misuse of the term by those who made it a private judgment entitled to set itself up against authority. He quoted the words of Newman: 'Conscience is a stern monitor but in this century it has been superseded by a counterfeit, which the eighteen centuries prior to it never heard of, and could not have mistaken for it, if they had. It is the right of self-will.'[19]

Finally Fr D'Arcy answered those who proclaimed that with the Vatican Council the Church had thrown off the legacy of its Constantinian establishment and the Roman notions of authority allegedly derived therefrom. Again he quoted Newman in one of his Anglican sermons, challengingly titled *The Christian Church an Imperial Power*, in which he marshalled an array of Old Testament texts to prove that power and authority are integral to the nature of the Church: 'If we will be scriptural in our view of the Church, we must consider that it is a kingdom, that its officers have great powers and high gifts, that they are all charged with the custody of Divine Truth, that they are all united together, and that the nations are subject to them. If we reject this kind of ministry, we shall in vain go to Scripture to find another. If we will form to ourselves a ministry and a Church bereft of the august power which I have mentioned, it will be one of our own devising; and let us pretend no more to draw our religion from the Bible. Rather we are like Jeroboam who made his own religion.'[20]

In his writings on the Catholic Church Fr D'Arcy had consistently defended the traditional posture of authority which was now being repudiated. In *Catholicism* he wrote: 'It will speak well for a religion [in its claims of divine foundation] if it is superlatively authoritative and oracular, walking the earth like a god, never altering its stride, never looking back, and never stumbling.'[21] In *The Life of the Church*: 'One may venture to say that of all the characteristics of the Catholic Church, her *uncompromisingness* in doctrine is, for all minds not weakened by the prejudices of a passing hour, the most gloriously attractive. Even if the history of the modernist controversy be considered only from the most purely philosophical point of view, the wisdom of the Roman Church and her profound knowledge of man is strikingly evident. On the approach of the great wave of sentimentalism and voluntarism that threatened to carry all before it, a short-sighted opportunism might have counselled yielding a little before the current, letting the vessel tack a little towards the quarter whence the wind seemed to be blowing. But she who for so long and amid so many tempests had been the fisher of men knows this world as an old fisherman knows his lake; she understood that that momentary weakness would have imperilled, for the sake of a few ephemeral results, the whole day's catch.'[22] Even over-strictness was therefore excusable: 'It is natural and logical that the Church should, as the steward of Christ, prefer to be thought narrow-minded than risk the loss of one soul for whom its Lord died. This care and discipline will, however, vary in different ages according to the general sanity or insanity of an age, and in a serene epoch there would be little check on freedom.'[23] Needless to say, he did not consider the nineteen-sixties a sane or serene epoch.

However little at home he was beginning to feel at Farm Street, Fr D'Arcy was still much in demand in America. He was off again there at the beginning of 1967, and made annual journeys for the next eight years, though his visits were now of only half the year or less. His circle of acquaintance continued to expand. From the early sixties he had a growing friendship with Paul Horgan, one of the leading Catholic writers in the country, who had received the Pulitzer Prize for *Great River* in 1954. He was Director of the Center for Advanced Studies at the Wesleyan University, and here at his invitation Fr D'Arcy spent the spring semester of 1965. He was allocated an excellent apartment where he was expected to prepare his own meals. The admirable gadgets with which the place was equipped would have baffled his unmechanical genius at any time in his life, and in February he was reporting to a friend in England that starvation stared him in the face.[24] As he survived the experience, we may deduce that he asked Dr Horgan to move him onto a less independent regime.

On the West Coast, Fr D'Arcy's friendships included Bing Crosby and Bob Hope. His intimacy with the latter was the work of the very Catholic Dorothy Hope, who devoted persistent efforts to converting her husband and asked Fr D'Arcy to stay with them many times, with a lively faith in his superior influence. His work in that cause was hampered by Bob Hope's habit of leaping up in the middle of every conversation to keep track of the numerous television programmes in which he had a proprietary interest.[25]

Also from the early sixties Fr D'Arcy found a great friend in Bishop John Wright of Pittsburgh, perhaps the most cultivated figure in the American Catholic hierarchy, who was transferred to the Curia as a cardinal in 1969. Cardinal Wright exemplified a school of thought that was very much Fr D'Arcy's own, having played a distinguished part as a leader of the reforming tendency in the Second Vatican Council; yet by the early nineteen-seventies he was so dismayed at was being perpetrated in the Council's name that as Prefect of the Sacred Congregation of the Clergy he was actively encouraging young men to enter Archbishop Lefebvre's seminary in Switzerland. This convergence of view together with his personal qualities was the basis of a warm sympathy which was to be manifested at the time of Fr D'Arcy's death.

A new admirer won by Fr D'Arcy in the late sixties was a young Jesuit scholastic from Chicago, Donald Rowe, whose artistic interests took him to England in search of works of art for the gallery he wished to establish at Loyola University. Fr D'Arcy was the only Jesuit he encountered with the same appreciation of the arts, and he resolved to name the gallery after him. Jane Engelhard paid for the gallery, which was opened with Fr D'Arcy's presence in January 1969. Artistic and literary circles were a milieu in which Fr D'Arcy could still find happy escape from the troubles of the time. He continued to receive many gifts of works of art and enjoyed the respect of august figures such as Sir John Pope Hennessy, one of the Oxford undergraduates he had befriended in the 1930s and now Director of the Victoria and Albert Museum.

The contemporary youth culture and its long-haired votaries neither carried Fr D'Arcy away nor intimidated him. When Lord Hailsham asked him what he considered the most striking characteristic of the young he replied in a tone of infinite compassion: 'Oh, their diffidence, of course.'[26] Paul Horgan recalled an incident presumably from the Wesleyan University: 'In the most sceptical and conscientiously rude student gatherings he has been known, merely by walking through the door and down the aisle to the dais, with his head nodding, his gaze downward, his thoughts already gathering in a sort of gently audible musing, to compel the assembled students to rise out of respect and remain standing until, astonished, he invites them to be seated.'[27]

Fr D'Arcy's facility for communicating with the young had not left him in the age when he discussed the merits of the early talkies stars. By the late fifties he had become a keen television watcher, sitting up in the

Farm Street recreation room till the end of broadcasting and using the programmes as a peg for lively conversation with one of the younger members of the Community.[28] At the age of eighty he discussed hippies and pop music on television with Lord Hailsham. His scrap-book shows that his fancy was caught by a newspaper cartoon about streaking, a fashion which invaded England in 1974. Humour apart, though, his considered judgment on his times was filled with pessimism. He saw the permissive sixties as the triumph of the barbarian advance which he had feared since the second world war, and in Los Angeles in 1971 he warned of the Antichrist, 'the libidinous ape, the great deceiver who calls lust love, avarice fulfilment, peace the loosening of all ties of loyalty, and who invites surrender to immediate gratification.'[29]

Within the Church, the terminology of the time segregated Catholics into conservatives and progressives. By this division Fr D'Arcy would have been a progressive hitherto, his chief mentors, like Fathers Rousselot, de la Taille and Teilhard de Chardin, being generally claimed for that team. He had never, though, been tempted to value a theory by its novelty vis-à-vis established thought, irrespective of its content. The pervasion of this attitude in the Catholic Press was an unwelcome development of the time, and Fr D'Arcy was grieved to find a leading example in one of his own pupils. In 1967 Douglas Woodruff retired as editor of *The Tablet* and was succeeded by Tom Burns. Any personal pleasure Fr D'Arcy may have felt was displaced by the policy Burns followed over the next nine years. Those who resisted the new lines supported by *The Tablet* were viewed as suffering from an intellectual arthrosis which was perhaps understandable but which had no contribution to make to the debate of the time. The figures thus dismissed included, within Fr D'Arcy's own circle, Christopher Dawson, Arnold Lunn, T.S. Gregory, Robert Speaight, Christopher Sykes and Bernard Wall, in fact most of the liveliest spokesmen for Catholic belief in the previous generation. Fr D'Arcy himself, Burns decided, had developed a closed mind in his old age.[30] Their continuing relations demonstrate Fr D'Arcy's ability to keep a friendship, like those with Bertrand Russell and A.J. Ayer, with people who he privately considered were doing grave moral harm. Personally, he continued to find more congenial company with Douglas and Mia Woodruff at Marcham Priory.

The change in *The Tablet* was only one example, in Fr D'Arcy's understanding, of a one-sidedness that was overtaking Catholic intellectual life and stultifying the promise of the early and middle sixties. For a more poignant expression of the same view we may turn to Frank Sheed, one who had identified himself with particular enthusiasm with the aims of the Second Vatican Council, and who, looking back in 1974 to the vigour and optimism of English Catholicism in his youth, contrasted it with the squandered opportunity of the present: 'Why did the bright promise of the twenties, thirties and even forties, fade away into the sadness of the seventies?'[31] Fr D'Arcy had a longer historical view than Sheed, and did not believe that the Church's brain had begun to function in the nineteen-twenties; but he had lived through the same revival and played a great role in it, and the bathos to which it had been brought was, no less for him, a personal sorrow.

Developments in the English Jesuit Province were following a parallel line: in 1967 the editorship of *The Month* was conferred on Fr Peter Hebblethwaite, who made his unflattering attitude to the Vatican authorities such a note of his subsequent career. By 1976 he had left the priesthood to marry and *The Month* was being edited by a layman. The community of writers which had flourished at Farm Street for a century had become extinct. But the crisis in the Province by now went well beyond such matters. The move of the scholasticate from Heythrop to London marked a step in the transformation of the traditional training in which Fr D'Arcy and others could only find cause for grief. Fr Vavasour, who was quartered with the scholastics in London, described their regime in a letter of 1970:

> The Society in England, especially here in this house, has virtually ceased to exist. All religious dress, rules, customs, beliefs, have been abandoned & I find myself with one old brother & an aged & crippled Fr Somerville having to struggle on trying to live the Society's life as it was taught to us while those about us have thrown overboard everything ... They are a law unto themselves, get up when they like, stroll into breakfast half dressed in hippy clothes, unwashed. No prayer or Mass, no attempt at any of our customs e.g. reflection during breakfast taken in silence ... I alone still wear a gown, & because I rise at 5.00, say office, Mass (Tridentine rite) & make a meditation of a kind ... I find myself sent to Coventry.
>
> Superiors seem bent on doing nothing about it all. Poverty & Obedience have long since disappeared. One young man brought his girl friend into supper the other evening with contempt for glances of disapproval from old men. There is nothing left to one but to pray & persevere from day to day.[32]

Between 1964 and 1976 over a hundred members of the English Province abandoned their vows, some of them in scandalous circumstances. At Campion Hall the undergraduate body almost disappeared in the mid seventies through mass defection. Recruitment likewise fell drastically,* and the numbers in the Province plummeted from 874 to 652. A circular letter from the Provincial in 1974 warned: 'Unless we attract many more novices the Province will be reduced, in the not too distant future, to a body of about a hundred men.'[33]

For priests like Fr D'Arcy and Fr Vavasour it was a natural blow to their esprit de corps to see the Province they had joined when it seemed the strongest warship in the Church's fleet reduced within a lifetime to the appearance of a badly holed vessel, adrift without a compass. It was, far more, a cause of deep pain to see the abandonment of the religious observances in which they had been trained. Yet the woes of the English Province paled before those which Fr D'Arcy's visits to America offered to his eyes. The fall of Heythrop may be set against that of Woodstock, the oldest and most famous of the Society's seminaries in the United States. It was moved to New York in 1970 to the tune of the same homilies on the need for urban involvement, and closed in ignominious circumstances a few years later. The Provincial who had ordered the move, Fr Sponga, left the Church to marry his secretary, and the Rector who had headed the college in New York, Fr Cardegna, also left the priesthood.[34]

An item in Fr D'Arcy's scrap-book apparently from 1974 figures a photograph cut out from a newspaper: it shows a circus elephant standing on its head and has been captioned by Fr D'Arcy, 'The New Look and Stance of the Society of Jesus.'[35] The reference is to the General Congregation of that year, which saw the high tide of the Marxist fashion that had gained favour especially among the Order's trans-Atlantic members. The elephantine humour is perhaps a sign that Fr D'Arcy did not really think it a laughing matter. The Congregation was checked in its course by the intervention of the Pope, but the tide was not turned until in 1981 Pope John Paul II suspended the Society's regular government and appointed a personal delegate pending the election of a new General. The numbers of the Order fell from over 36,000 in 1965 to 28,000 in 1976, wiping out the entire gains made since the second world war; and in longer consequence the loss was greater, since the defection was overwhelmingly among the younger men and in new recruitment.

The orthodoxy of the time rejected the values which had governed most of Fr D'Arcy's lifetime. According to the new teaching houses of formation were not to be isolated havens of piety but must be immersed

*Admissions of novices during the seventy years that Fr D'Arcy was in the Society can be divided into six fairly well-marked periods: 1906–18, average 17 (only 1918 being really exceptional with 8); 1919–39, average 25; 1940–45, average 11; 1946–51, average 36; 1952–67, average 21; 1968–76, average less than 7.

in the secular community; fine country houses should be shunned as signs of elitism; a house of studies at Oxford was uncomfortably tainted by the same sin, and it was an embarrassment that the English Province had any public schools at all, let alone its former three. The traditional ways of the Society were to be severely questioned, and social consciousness must be the lens through which all policies and individuals were viewed. The value of these notions will be easier to assess when the two models are judged by their respective achievements; but it remains that Fr D'Arcy was the epitome of the tradition that was being rejected: an aristocrat, a public-school man, a believer in country houses, an elitist in academic ideals, a philosopher who had never ceased to urge the paramountcy of the spiritual, and yet a figure whose distinction hampered attempts to discredit the ideals he embodied. The Society's contemporary unease with this relic of its past has spilt over to deceive the unwary; thus we find in the latest biography of Evelyn Waugh that Lady Selina Hastings, who has taken at their face value the Jesuit obituaries of 1976, roundly describes Fr D'Arcy as 'an unashamed tuft-hunter', his outlook dominated by nostalgia for 'the great houses and ancient lineage of the old Catholic nobility.'[36]

His personal prestige was, however, the least of Fr D'Arcy's concerns, and wider troubles were making even the vagaries of his Order a secondary one. For him the real tragedy was the destruction of those keen hopes for the revivification of the Church, and through it of the world, that had animated him in the fifties and early sixties. The fate of the liturgical movement was a special example: he had seen it as a movement that would bring the laity into a deeper understanding of the divine Sacrifice and thereby to a deeper sense of the Mystical Body of Christ and of the penetration of the sacred in the secular world. In that lost period the aim of the movement was to spread among the laity a love and understanding for the liturgy as it was, not to turn it into something else. The fanatics already discernible among the liturgists had not however escaped Fr D'Arcy's notice. In 1960, when liturgical change had barely begun, he wrote: 'If the fanatic be as scornful of old practices as the artist of the shop products which adorn so many churches and chapels, the old conservative can retort that this exclusive love for what is liturgical is a monomania, a pleasure of the mind or taste, but of insufficient help to the will.'[37]

His fears were more than fulfilled when liturgists in the sixties began to promote the concept of the Mass as an assembly of the faithful, at the expense of its character as the sacrificial mystery, and to refashion its liturgy accordingly. In place of the stronger bond with the sacred for which Fr D'Arcy looked, the consequence was to be displayed in an alienation which in England has brought a forty per-cent decline in Mass attendance in the last thirty years. That statistic was hidden from Fr D'Arcy, but the idea that participation in the Mass, let alone understanding and love of it, would be achieved by removing beauty, ceremony and reverence seemed to him one of the many unopposed fallacies of the time. As the new language of theology gained ground, the very concept of the Mystical Body was obscured by that of the 'People of God', a pre-Christian notion further devalued by overtones of 'We the people'.

The culminating blow was the new order of the Mass introduced in 1969-70, which was the complete rejection of the traditional principles Fr D'Arcy had tried to defend. Having watched the liturgical radicals manoeuvre into position during the fifties, he was not beguiled by the official line that the reforms of the next decade represented the Church's mature liturgical scholarship.* In his published work his criticisms were restrained, but to friends like Maria Shrady he spoke of 'the modern copying of Protestantism and Iconoclasm' and of 'these semi-sophisticated barbarians who now twist the office of the Church and the Liturgy about.'[39] He himself continued to say the Tridentine Mass to the end of his life, and refused invitations to public celebrations that would have obliged him to use the new rite.

Fr D'Arcy had no hesitation in identifying the tide that had engulfed the Church with the Modernism which had been too tyrannically suppressed when he was young. Then authority had been crudely used, now it was being abdicated; the first error had injured the Church, but the second was destroying it. The hopes of a Christian revival dissolved, as it became evident that the Church, far from finding ways to convert the world, was entering probably the gravest internal crisis in its history. The future he saw now was one of huge loss of faith, a great contraction of the Church and terrible suffering as a new Dark Age supervened both in civilisation and in the life of the spirit. If he had lived to see the reign of John Paul II he would not have regarded his efforts to stem the tide as more than a holding operation. Only when the Church had re-learned its divine commission would it be able to impart the vision of the spiritual once more to a world abused by material illusion. The grief that had become Fr D'Arcy's dominant feeling was expressed to Philip Ingress Bell who came to see him at Farm Street and who remembered the sadness with which he told him, 'My soul is sick, Philip – sick.'[40] He

---

*Compare the comment of the monastic historian David Knowles in 1971: 'It was also a great disaster that the original liturgical movement was first of all in the 1950s allowed to get into the hands of rabid liturgical purists, and then since 1963 exploited by those who used liturgical scholarship as a blind for de-sacralising and de-catholicising the liturgy.'[38]

ceased to conceal at this time that he longed for death.

Even in these last years, though, the condition of a sad, defeated old man was not one for which Fr D'Arcy's nature fitted him; the influence he continued to exert in America on visits till his eighty-sixth year is a testimony of that. Fr Vincent Turner wrote: 'Perhaps the most remarkable of all his characteristics was his flame-like quality, a lambent ardour of spirit that animated him into extreme old age. It was nourished by a deep personal religion, a spirituality very simple and entirely traditional, Christo-centric and eucharistic, behind all the dazzle and the quicksilver, and it survived the transformations of the world he had loved into a world that he could not much admire.'[41]

Fr D'Arcy's alarming but wirily resilient health had been showing danger signs for some years. In July 1970 he suddenly fell ill on a visit to Liverpool and was in hospital for some weeks for a prostate operation. He told Maria Shrady that he had no intention of dying in that city, whose boyhood memories had few charms for him,[42] and he was well enough to return to his restless schedule by October, attending the canonisation of the English Martyrs in Rome on the 25th, and dashing back to give a sermon on 'The Magnitude of Faith' as University Select Preacher at Oxford on November 1st. In May 1973 he fell 'from a height' in New York just before returning to England and badly hurt his foot, but made the flight all the same. In February 1974, back in America, he had to have an operation for a detached retina. That was the last journey he made. When he returned to England in May he was already very frail, and the last eighteen months of his life were spent at Farm Street. In June 1974 he lost in Fr Basil Gurrin his oldest friend in the Society.*

During the course of 1975 he suffered three brain spasms,[43] and the main relic of his old public schedule was his preaching of the seventh annual Hopkins sermon, 'Christ's Mastery' at Farm Street in June. By the time of his 88th birthday in 1976 he was more or less confined to the house and was being looked after by Brother Harkess. He was due to enter the hospital of St John and St Elizabeth for an operation, and chose to do so on September 20th because Brother Harkess went on retreat on that day. He was found unable however to undergo the operation; he then developed bronchitis and could not be moved back to Farm Street.[44]

Cardinal Wright, on his way from Rome, came to visit him in hospital and told him that he was going to America to perform the wedding of the

---

*Of his other two class-fellows, Henry Mather had died in 1963 in British Guiana and Robert de Trafford in 1969 after thirty years at Heythrop. Conyers D'Arcy died in February 1967 while his brother was away in America.

Shradys' daughter Maily. 'I can't do anything for her,' said Fr D'Arcy, 'but give her a kiss from me.'[45] He was visited by the Superior of Farm Street, Fr Copeland, to whom he said that he wanted to go back to Farm Street to celebrate the Feast of Christ the King with the Community. He spoke of his love of Our Lord under that title which went back to his days at Stonyhurst, when he had shared it with Basil Gurrin. Fr Copeland told him that the feast, which had formerly been at the end of October, had been changed to November, and was glad to have this excuse to postpone his return, which was by now impossible. On the eve of the Feast of Christ the King, Saturday November 20th, Fr Copeland came to visit him again and spoke to him for a while. Fr D'Arcy thanked him, and as he made towards the door called him back and continued the conversation; this happened three times. The last time Fr D'Arcy asked Fr Copeland to confirm that the next day would be the Feast of Christ the King, and on being reassured thanked him a third time. 'I believe also,' wrote Fr Copeland, 'he felt he was called by Christ the King to celebrate this feast with Him in Heaven, and I think he was simply asking me to confirm for him that it would be so soon.' Fr Copeland then gave him Extreme Unction.

In America that same Saturday afternoon the wedding of Maily Shrady took place, and before he began the ceremony Cardinal Wright told her of the death-bed commission he had received and gave her the kiss that Fr D'Arcy had asked him to pass on to her. At almost the same moment, it seems, in London, at eleven in the evening Fr D'Arcy died, an hour before his beloved Feast. Fr Copeland wrote: 'You will know that the centre of the Spiritual Exercises of St Ignatius, the centre from which they took their origin, and the foundation on which the Society of Jesus is built is the meditation called by St Ignatius 'The Call of Christ the King.' The timing of Father D'Arcy's death, was it not the most tender, intimate, and personal touch of the Friend for his friend?'

The kingship of Christ was for Fr D'Arcy no mere figure but a reality in which the divine will was recognised as the sovereign principle in human society. He saw the acknowledgment of that principle in the ages which he looked back to as the model of Christian Faith. He had begun his ministry full of hope that the time had come to restore that sovereignty; if it was despised in the world, the Church, firm in vision and purpose, kept its ideal alive and could still teach the world to acknowledge it once more. Such hopes had survived in him for the greater part of his life, until he saw the Church herself bow before the world over which she should have proclaimed the divine kingship. If it had been possible for Fr D'Arcy to give way to utter despair he would have done so in the last half-dozen years of his life. Yet it has been said that true tragedy is only permissible to the pagan mind, for the Christian retains

the promise of divine grace which forbids him to see hope as lost; and Fr
D'Arcy saw the future as Gerard Manley Hopkins had done when he
looked over a world which had turned its back on God:

> Though the last lights off the black West went,
>   Oh, morning, at the brown brink eastward, springs –
> Because the Holy Ghost over the bent
>   World broods with warm breast and with ah! bright wings.

Notes

Abbreviations

Autobiog.:   Manuscript autobiographical notes by Fr D'Arcy in the Farm Street Archives.

Bib.:   Bibliography of Fr D'Arcy's works.

BM: British Museum manuscript collection, letters of Fr D'Arcy to Evelyn Waugh, 1944-65 (these had not yet been catalogued in 1994)

FS: Archives of the Farm Street headquarters of the English Jesuit Province (114 Mount Street, London W1Y 6AH)

Georgetown: Manuscript collection of Georgetown University, Washington (unless otherwise stated the source is the Frederick and Maria Shrady papers)

Hailsham: Lord Hailsham's funeral address on Fr D'Arcy, Campion Hall archives.

Hist. Dom.:   MS journal of the house, Campion Hall archives.

Int.:   Author's interview with the person stated.

LLF: *Laughter and the Love of Friends* (ed. William S. Abell), Christian Classics Inc., Westminster, Maryland, 1991

LN: *Letters and Notices* (newsletter of the English Jesuit Province)

Obit.:   Obituary of Fr D'Arcy in *Letters and Notices*, (Nov. 1977) p.188-202.

Self-Port.:   *Fr D'Arcy, A Self-Portrait* (programme for Thames Television, September 1971)

Treasure Hunting: Manuscript by Fr D'Arcy in the Campion Hall archives, Oxford.

Chapter 1

1 *Burke's Landed Gentry*, D'Arcy of Stanmore and Gorteen, gives the ancestry of Fr D'Arcy's line down to the late 18th century. See also *Dictionary of National Biography*, Thomas Lord Darcy and other members of the family.

2 *Dictionary of National Biography*, Robert D'Arcy, 4th Earl of Holderness.

3 In the D'Arcy pedigree (see Note 1) Francis D'Arcy is merely mentioned as having married and died before 1780. The genealogist Martin J. Blake wrote: 'Catherine ffrench married a D'Arcy of Gorteen, and their eldest son, Anthony, married Clare Kelly.' (National Library of Ireland, Blake Papers, MS 10,791–2, P.2). According however to *Burke's Peerage* (Barons ffrench of Castle ffrench), Catherine, the 4th daughter of Thomas ffrench, married Thomas Clutterbuck, and an unnamed 5th daughter married a D'Arcy of Gorteen. The two authorities can be reconciled if we suppose that Catherine ffrench first married Francis D'Arcy (who died after only a few years of marriage) and then Mr Clutterbuck. This and other family information has been kindly supplied to me by Miss Zita Kelly, a descendant of Nicholas D'Arcy of Ballyforan.

4 LLF, p.200–1. If Fr D'Arcy was accurate in calling her a great-aunt, this must have been Nicholas D'Arcy's sister Catherine, about whom, however, no other information has come to light.

5 Autobiog., which gives details of Fr D'Arcy's father's and mother's families.

6 FS WU/3 (collection of documents relating to Valentine and Madoline D'Arcy)

7 According to the Law Lists, Valentine D'Arcy had resumed chambers and begun increasing court activity in the Northern Circuit by 1893.

8 FS 40/5/2: a letter of Conyers D'Arcy to his brother in summer 1908 mentions: 'Mother has not been [in Bath] for 16 years ago – come November!'

9 F.E. Smith, 1st Earl of Birkenhead (1872–1930), Lord Chancellor; Gordon Hewart, 1st Viscount Hewart (1870–1943), Lord Chief Justice; Sir Rigby Swift (1874–1937), elected Recorder of Wigan in 1915 (a post for which Valentine D'Arcy seems to have applied unsuccessfully). For the effect of these three on the Northern Circuit see the article on the last in *Dictionary of National Biography*.

10 Self-Port.

11 Ibid

12 Stonyhurst Magazine, Vol. 32 (1954), p.46–7, reminiscences by the journalist J. Jeffries of his schooldays, 1891-98.

[13] Vyvyan Holland, *Son of Oscar Wilde* (1954), Chap.5.

[14] Autobiog.

[15] As Note 12.

[16] LN Vol. 25 (1900), No.131, p.351.

[17] As Note 13.

[18] C.C. Martindale, *Charles Dominic Plater SJ* (1922), p.25.

[19] As Note 13.

[20] Quoted by Fr D'Arcy from memory in Bib. No.127, p.57. It is in fact a conflation of stanzas 22 and 23 of *Sospetto d'Herode* in *Steps to the Temple* (1646).

[21] Stonyhurst Magazine, Vol.9 (1904), p.80.

[22] Bib. No.12, p.401.

[23] Treasure Hunting.

[24] Self-Port.

[25] For the Sodality and contemporary Stonyhurst life see G. Gruggen and J. Keating, *Stonyhurst College, Its Past History and Life in the Present* (1901).

[26] Ibid p.26.

[27] Marylebone Cricket Club, the most famous cricket club in England.

[28] The history and life of the Philosophers are described in H.J.A. Sire, *Gentlemen Philosophers* (1988).

[29] Bib. No.42, p.322.

[30] Int. Fr D'Arcy December 1972.

[31] Bib. No.9, p.442.

[32] Ibid The first is the logical principle known as Occam's Razor, the second means: 'That on account of which something possesses a particular property, itself possesses that property to a higher degree.' (e.g. sugar sweetens tea because it is itself sweeter).

[33] As Note 30.

[34] Bib. No.86, (2nd edition) p.10.

Chapter 2

[1] For the history of the English Province see Bernard Basset, *The English Jesuits* (1967).

[2] Full information year by year is given in LN and the *Catalogus Provinciae Angliae*.

[3] Denis Meadows, *Obedient Men* (1954), p.47.

[4] Madeleine Devlin, *Christopher Devlin* (1970), p.26, quoting his *Life of Robert Southwell* (1959), p.43.

[5] Catholic Encyclopaedia, Vol.14, article by Fr John Hungerford Pollen, *Society of Jesus*.

[6] As note 3, p.66.

[7] Ibid, p.44.

8   John Rothenstein, *Brave Day, Hideous Night* (1966), p.133.
9   LN Vol.37 (1922), p.170.
10 LLF, p.13–14.
11 FS 40/5/2.
12 Philip Caraman, *C.C. Martindale* (1967).
13 Bib. No.127, p.13–14.
14 LLF p.92–3.
15 As Note 3, p.140.
16 Ibid, p.202.
17 Bib. No.127, p.58.
18 Ibid, p.59.
19 The story is told in Self-Port. and in various of Fr D'Arcy's writings.
20 In Alfred Miles, *The Poets and Poetry of the Century* (1893), Vol.8.
21 Gerard Manley Hopkins, 'Ribblesdale'.
22 Bib. No.39, p.315.
23 Self-Port.
24 LLF p.24 and 71.
25 Evelyn Waugh, *Brideshead Revisited* (1945), Book 1, Chapter 1.
26 For these three encounters see LLF, p.162, 203 and 27.
27 Bib. No.127, p.59.
28 LLF, p.28.
29 Bib. No.127, p.60.
30 Self-Port.
31 LLF, p.154; also p.32.
32 Bib. No.127, p.13.
33 As Note 12, p.200.
34 LLF, p.88–9.
35 FS WU/3.
36 Michael de la Bedoyère in Catholic Profiles, *Catholic Herald*, 25 May 1945.
37 Obit, p.189–90.
38 Bib. No.2.
39 Campion Hall archives, Fr Hannan in 'The Death of Fr D'Arcy'.
40 Bib. No.1.
41 LLF, p.89–90 and 95.
42 Bib. No.14.
43 C.C. Martindale, *Charles Dominic Plater* (1922), p.223–4 and FS 31/1/D'Arcy.
44 Hügel's letters are printed in *The Month*, Vol.42 (1969), p.23–26.
45 Bib. No.27, p.57.
46 C.C. Martindale, *Charles Dominic Plater* (1922), p.99–100.
47 Bib. No.10, p.40 and 48.
48 Bib. No.16, p.108.

[49] Bib. No.12, p.402.
[50] Bib. No.127, p.15.
[51] Bib. No.27, p.53.
[52] Self-Port.
[53] Hailsham.
[54] LLF, p.36.

Chapter 3

[1] LLF, p.37–8.
[2] Bib. No.127, p.14.
[3] T. Burns, *The Use of Memory* (1993), p.14.
[4] *The Tablet*, 8 February 1993, p.175 (review of LLF).
[5] Burns's obit. of Fr D'Arcy in *The Tablet*, 27 Nov. 1976. The nearest I can find to the quotation given is two sentences on p.457 of *Les Yeux de la Foi* (*Recherches de Science religieuse*, 1910, No.5): 'L'amour, l'hommage libre au Bien suprème, donne de nouveaux yeux. L'être, plus visible, ravit le voyant.' Burns was not given the whole essay to translate, as he seems to imply.
[6] Bib. No.12, p.409.
[7] Bib. No.127, p.14.
[8] As Note 6.
[9] Bib. No.9, p.442.
[10] Ibid, p.549.
[11] A letter complaining of the way this punishment was applied appeared in *Stonyhurst Magazine* Vol.21 (1931), p.428. The author can testify that things were the same in the 1960s and 70s.
[12] LLF, p.39–40.
[13] Madeleine Devlin, *Christopher Devlin* (1970), p.18.
[14] Self-Port., and letter of Henry John (National Library of Wales MS 22782D fol.35–6).
[15] LLF, p.42–3.
[16] Ibid, p.43.
[17] Philip Caraman, *C.C. Martindale* (1967), p.193.
[18] National Library of Wales MS 22782D fol.37.
[19] Quoted in Michael Holroyd, *Augustus John*, (Penguin revised edition, 1976) p.667.
[20] Obit,, p.190.
[21] LLF, p.43.
[22] Diaries of Evelyn Waugh, 8 July 1930.
[23] As Note 5.
[24] Walter Drumm, *The Old Palace* (1991), p.72.
[25] Louis MacNeice, *The Strings are false* (1965), p.128.

[26] Earl of Birkenhead, *The Prof* (1961), p.169.

[27] Bernard Wall, *Headlong into Change* (1969), p.169.

[28] LLF, p.146–7.

[29] Hailsham; also his article in *The Catholic Herald* July 1968.

[30] Elizabeth Longford, *The Pebbled Shore* (1986), p.54.

[31] Evelyn Waugh, *Ronald Knox* (1959), p.309.

[32] Bill Boni in *The Spokesman-Review* (American paper), 31 July 1960.

[33] Lord Longford, *Avowed Intent* (1994), p.80.

[34] *The Letters of Wyndham Lewis* (ed. W.K. Rose, 1963), p.171–3 & 236.

[35] Auberon Waugh, *Will This Do?* (1990), p.21.

[36] LLF, p.191–2.

[37] Lord Hailsham in *The Catholic Herald* July 1968.

[38] As Note 3, p.42 and 53.

[39] Robert Speaight, *Fr D'Arcy at Oxford* in *The Month*, Vol.125 (June 1968), No.1210, p.337 40.

[40] Alan Pryce-Jones, *The Bonus of Laughter* (1987).

[41] Georgetown, Christopher Sykes Papers: Fr D'Arcy to Sykes 4 February 1964, quoted by Sykes in his BBC broadcast of August 1967, Reminiscences of Evelyn Waugh.

[42] As Note 37.

[43] Evelyn Waugh, *A Little Learning*, (1964).

[44] Patrick O'Donovan's obit. of Fr D'Arcy in *The Catholic Herald*, 26 November 1976.

[45] LLF, p.170.

[46] Int. Sir Isaiah Berlin 5 July 1994.

[47] A.J. Ayer, *Part of My Life* (1977), p.89.

[48] As Note 13, p.30.

[49] As Note 19, p.659.

Chapter 4

[1] Details of the plans are given in Fr D'Arcy's manuscript notes 'The New Campion Hall' in Campion Hall archives and in LLF, p.49–52.

[2] Obit. p.195–6 (the writer is Fr Vincent Turner).

[3] Robert Speaight, *Fr D'Arcy at Oxford* in *The Month*, Vol.125 (June 1968), p.337–40. The comments also sound much like others which Fr Turner made in Obit.

[4] Quoted in Michael Davie (ed.), *The Diaries of Evelyn Waugh* (1976), p.800.

[5] National Library of Wales MS 22789E fol.5, Fr D'Arcy to Augustus John.

[6] T. Burns, *The Use of Memory* (1993), p.21.

[7] Stanley Parker writing in *The Oxford Mail* 29 October 1942.

8 National Library of Wales MS 22781D fol.76 and J. Rothenstein, *Brave Day, Hideous Night* (1966), p.133.

9 As Note 1.

10 LLF, p.135.

11 Artemis Cooper (ed.) *Mr Wu and Mrs Stitch* (1991), p.30–33.

12 LLF, p.170.

13 FS WU/3.

14 Obit., p.191.

15 Evelyn Waugh, *The Hospitality of Campion Hall* in *The Tablet*, 26 October 1946.

16 John Rothenstein, *Brave Day, Hideous Night* (1966), p.131.

17 Hist. Dom.

18 Treasure Hunting, for this and succeeding paragraphs.

19 Bib. No.39, p.352.

20 Bib. No.55, p.157.

21 Quoted by Robert Speaight, *The Life of Eric Gill* (1961), p.176.

22 FS 40/5/2.

23 As Note 19.

24 LLF, p.169.

25 As Note 16, p.131.

26 Catholic Profiles in *The Catholic Herald*, 25 May 1945.

27 Bib. No.60, and cf. Georgetown, Fr D'Arcy to Maria Shrady 18 October 1966 saying that Rothenstein's book 'gets my views all wrong.'

28 Obit. p.196.

29 Hailsham.

30 T. Burns's obit. of Fr D'Arcy in *The Tablet* 27 November 1976.

31 As Note 16, p.132.

32 As Note 15.

33 As Note 31.

34 FS 40/5/2 has the drawing. Fr D'Arcy's recollection of the joke in LLF p.53 may have been distorted by a feeling at the time that *ars longa, vita brevis* would have been a wittier comment.

35 Int. Sir Isaiah Berlin, 5 July 1994.

36 Evelyn Waugh, *Ronald Knox* (1959), p.244.

37 BM, Fr D'Arcy to Evelyn Waugh, 18 June 1958.

38 As Note 36, p.265.

39 Christopher Hollis, *Oxford in the Twenties* (1976), p.123.

40 A debating society, not a students' union; also the most important undergraduate club in Oxford.

41 LLF, p.148.

42 Ibid, and Oxford Union records.

43 Adrian Hastings, *Some Reflexions on the English Catholicism of the late 1930s*, in A. Hastings (ed.) *Bishops and Writers* (1977).

[44] David Pryce-Jones, *Evelyn Waugh and his Circle* (1973), p.51, and Elizabeth Longford, *The Pebbled Shore* (1986), p.148.

[45] Int. Lord Longford, 22 March 1994.

[46] Lord Longford, *Born To Believe* (1952), p.96.

[47] Lord Longford, *Avowed Intent* (1994), p.81.

[48] Ibid, p.80.

[49] LN Vol.52, No.312 (1956), Obituary of Fr Bolland.

[50] Int. Fr John Coventry, 23 March 1994.

[51] As Note 49.

Chapter 5

[1] Bib. No.132.

[2] Bib. No.34, p.16 (1958 edition).

[3] Bib. No.32, p.575.

[4] Quoted in Bib. No.86, p.294 (1954 edition).

[5] As Note 2, p.191.

[6] Ibid, p.72–3.

[7] Bib. No.100, p.305.

[8] Quoted in Bib. No.81, p.25.

[9] As Note 2, quoted on p.201.

[10] Ibid, p.63.

[11] Bib. No.28, p.203.

[12] Bib. No.112, p.17.

[13] As Note 2, p.65.

[14] Quoted in Bib. No.121, p.65.

[15] Bib. No.27, p.12.

[16] As Note 1, quoted on p.49.

[17] Quoted in Bib. No.114, p.265.

[18] As Note 3, p.566, 574 etc.

[19] Quoted in Bib. No.129, p.178.

[20] J.H. Newman, *Apologia Pro Vita Sua*, 1864.

[21] Quoted in Bib. No.80, p.87.

[22] As Note 7, quoted on p.308.

[23] St Paul's Epistle to the Romans, Ch.8, v.22–3.

[24] As Note 2, p.206.

[25] As Note 15, p.18.

[26] Ibid, p.83, 85.

[27] Bib. No.45, p.28.

[28] As Note 2, quoted on p.208.

[29] Bib. No.52, p.91.

[30] As Note 19, p.87.

[31] Quoted in Bib. No.60, p.1295.

Chapter 6

1 T. Burns, *The Use of Memory* (1993), p.138, and Int. T. Burns 29 March 1994.
2 Hist. Dom. (1935), FS 40/2/7 and 40/5/2, and LLF, p.139–40.
3 LLF, p.74. There is a photograph from this time of Fr D'Arcy with Woodlock in FS 30/1/D'Arcy.
4 Bernard Wall, *Headlong into Change* (1969), p.22, and LLF, p.115–16.
5 Patrick O'Donovan's obit. of Fr D'Arcy in *The Catholic Herald*, 26 November 1976.
6 LLF, p.149–51.
7 FS 40/2/7 and Hist. Dom. (1940).
8 Treasure Hunting.
9 *The Tablet*, May issues, 1941.
10 Hist. Dom. 1941–2.
11 LLF, p.159–62.
12 FS 40/5/2.
13 BM, Fr D'Arcy to Evelyn Waugh 28 October 1947.
14 Self-Port., FS 40/2/7, and Stanley Parker in *The Oxford Mail*, 29 October 1942.
15 FS 40/2/7, Int. T. Burns 29 March 1994, and *Twin Circle* (American magazine), 16 May 1971.
16 Hist. Dom. (1943), Bib. No.82, *Banbury Guardian* 14 October 1943, and FS 40/2/7.
17 Hailsham. Other information comes from Int. Lord Hailsham 14 April 1994 and from Lord Hailsham's biographer Mr Geoffrey Lewis.
18 LLF, p.55–8.
19 Hist. Dom. 1941–4.
20 Diaries of Evelyn Waugh, 2 November 1943.
21 Ibid, 29 May 1943.
22 LLF, p.54.
23 Preface to the 2nd edition of *Brideshead Revisited*.
24 BM, Fr D'Arcy to Evelyn Waugh 23 May 1944.
25 Mark Amory, *The Letters of Evelyn Waugh* (1980), Waugh's letter to his wife 9 January 1945.
26 Ibid, 10 February 1945.
27 Peter Alexander, *Roy Campbell, A Critical Biography* (1982), p.203.
28 John Rothenstein, *Brave Day, Hideous Night* (1966), p.152.
29 The claim first appears in an interview Fr D'Arcy gave to the Spanish magazine *Foco*, 3 January 1953, on his visit to Spain.
30 As Note 28.
31 *Diaries of Evelyn Waugh*, 18 April 1945.
32 Lord Hailsham in *The Catholic Herald*, July 1968.

Chapter 7

[1] LN Vol.77, No.358 (1972), p.223.

[2] *Diaries of Evelyn Waugh*, 31 August 1945.

[3] BM Fr D'Arcy to Evelyn Waugh, 25 November 1945.

[4] Philip Caraman, *C.C. Martindale* (1967), p.224.

[5] *Stonyhurst Magazine*, Vol.46, No.485 (1989), p.209, obit. of Fr Basset. The reference to 58 novices dates the letter to mid 1946.

[6] LN Vol.77 (1972), p.106.

[7] Frederick Copleston, *Memoirs of a Philosopher* (1993), p.67–71.

[8] LLF, p.81.

[9] Details of this plan are all from the author's conversation with Fr D'Arcy in December 1972.

[10] As Note 1.

[11] Very similar paragraphs to this effect appeared in the *Bath and Wiltshire Chronicle* for 23 May and the *Bath Weekly Chronicle* for 25 May 1946, and had no doubt been fed to them by Hollis, who was Member of Parliament for Devizes; cf. his obit. of Fr D'Arcy in *The Times*, 22 November 1976.

[12] Obit., p.197.

[13] Treasure Hunting.

[14] Evelyn Waugh, *Ronald Knox* (1959), p.248.

[15] LLF, p.47.

[16] BM, Fr D'Arcy to Evelyn Waugh, 16 June 1947.

[17] FS 40/2/7.

[18] BM, Fr D'Arcy to Evelyn Waugh, 20 May 1947.

[19] Int. Lord Longford, 14 April 1994.

[20] The account of the journey is taken from LN Vol.56 (1948) p.161–88.

[21] *Diaries of Evelyn Waugh*, 23 January to 4 March 1933.

[22] Treasure Hunting. Details in the Victoria and Albert Museum papers on the Campion Hall triptych and from information provided by Mr Claude Blair. A history of the triptych is given in *The Campion Hall Triptych and its Workshop*, by Marian Campbell, in *Apollo*, June 1980, p.418-23.

[23] Victoria and Albert Museum Papers: *Exili comes et carceris imago haec Mariae Stuardae Scot. Reginae fuit fuisset et caedis si vixisset.* The version given in Marian Campbell's article in *Apollo* (see Note 22) is slightly altered.

[24] Note by Douglas Woodruff in *The Tablet*, 11 December 1976.

[25] Germain Seligman, *Merchants of Art* (1961), p.159-62.

[26] *Burlington Magazine*, September 1946, *A Ducciesque Tabernacle at Oxford*, by Edward B. Garrison, with Plate II opp. p.218.

[27] Victoria and Albert Museum papers.

[28] Letter of Mrs Engelhard's secretary to the author, 1 June 1994.

[29] As Note 24.

[30] *An Irishman's Diary* in *The Irish Times*, 23 April 1948.

[31] Handwritten note by Fr D'Arcy from October 1973 in Campion Hall archives, 'Fr D'Arcy Correspondence (c.1968–75)'.

[32] In 1961 he wrote that he was in danger of losing the triptych: Georgetown, Fr D'Arcy to Maria Shrady, 19 June 1961.

[33] As Note 20.

[34] The affair is described in LN, Vol.58–9, p.1–24.

[35] Int. Fr Philip Caraman, 20 April 1994.

[36] LN, Vol.62, No.312 (1956). Obit. of Fr Bolland.

[37] LN, Vol.91, No.404 (1993). Article by Fr Gillick.

[38] BM, Fr D'Arcy to Evelyn Waugh, 6 September 1948.

[39] Martin Stannard, *No Abiding City* (1992), p.220.

[40] Quoted in G.A. Beck (ed.), *The English Catholics 1850–1950*, p.502.

[41] Diaries of Evelyn Waugh, 29 August 1948.

[42] John Pearson, *Façades* (1980), p.410.

[43] Obit., p.198.

[44] As Note 35 for this and other details of the dismissal.

[45] Int. Fr John Coventry, 23 April 1994.

Chapter 8

[1] Mark Amory, *The Letters of Evelyn Waugh* (1980), letter of 26 March 1950.

[2] Obit., p.199.

[3] Int. Lady Helen Asquith, 19 April 1994.

[4] BM, Fr D'Arcy to Evelyn Waugh, 28 October 1950.

[5] *Philosophy Now*, in *The Criterion*, Vol.XV, No.LXI (July 1936), p.582 and 597.

[6] Bib. No.110, p.104.

[7] Evelyn Waugh, *The American Epoch in the Catholic Church*, in *The Month*, November 1949.

[8] Int. Fr Haller, 17 May 1994.

[9] Georgetown, Fr D'Arcy to Maria Shrady, 16 December 1967 and Int. Fr Francis Sweeney SJ, 24 May 1994.

[10] Georgetown, Fr D'Arcy to Maria Shrady, 27 November 1954 to 19 May 1955.

[11] Quoted in Victoria Glendinning, *Edith Sitwell* (1981), p.315.

[12] Georgetown, Fr D'Arcy to Maria Shrady, 6 August 1954.

[13] Bib. No.102.

[14] Article by Bill Boni in *The Spokesman-Review* (American paper), 31 July 1960.

[15] Gerard Noel in *The Catholic Herald*, 3 September 1971.

[16] LLF, p.151.

[17] Quoted in Self-Port.

[18] A.J. Ayer, *More of My Life* (1984), p.142.

[19] Bib. No.56, p.42 and 45.

[20] Bib. No.114, p.268.

[21] Bib. No.113, p.211. 'As we still live upon the ground of a Christian culture, there is no antecedent reason why the church should not bring an intellectual concord into society, as it did in the dark ages, but now with a much more complicated and rich material to work upon.

[22] As Note 20.

[23] Ibid, p.254–5 and 262.

[24] Diaries of Evelyn Waugh, 9 February 1956.

[25] Fr T. Corbishley in *The Catholic Herald*, 21 September 1956, and Christopher Hollis in *The Catholic Digest*, 1962.

[26] Madeleine Devlin, *Christopher Devlin* (1970), p.208.

[27] P. Alexander, *Roy Campbell, A Critical Biography*, 1982, p.221, and Bernard Wall, *Headlong into Change*, 1969, p.181.

[28] BM, Fr D'Arcy to Evelyn Waugh, 16 September 1957.

[29] Georgetown, Fr D'Arcy to Maria Shrady, 8 February 1958, and BM, Fr D'Arcy to Evelyn Waugh, 26 May 1959.

[30] The project is outlined by Fr John Coventry (Provincial 1958–64) in Francis Edwards, *The Jesuits in England* (1985), p.249.

[31] For Fr D'Arcy's view see LLF, p.56–7.

[32] Obit., p.197.

[33] BM, Fr D'Arcy to Evelyn Waugh, 21 January 1963.

[34] *Congressional Record*, 18 March 1957.

[35] Int. Matt Murray 19 May 1994.

[36] Int. Mrs Barrett McDonnell 18 May 1994 in particular connexion with her 70th birthday reception for Fr D'Arcy.

[37] LLF, p.xiii.

Chapter 9

[1] Self-Port.

[2] Bib. No.27, p.73.

[3] Bib. No.127, p.19.

[4] LLF, p.60.

[5] BM, Fr D'Arcy to Evelyn Waugh, 21 January 1963.

[6] LN Vol.89, No.394 (1988), *The Closure of Beaumont*, by Fr Thomas Dunphy (the Rector concerned), p.43–7.

[7] *Stonyhurst Magazine*, Vol.47, No.487 (1991), p.8–25, and cf. No.488. Two members of foreign Provinces are not included in this reckoning.

8   Georgetown, Fr D'Arcy to Maria Shrady, 9 December 1966, and other complaints 15 August and 17 September.

9   Ibid, 6 March 1967.

10   BM, Fr D'Arcy to Evelyn Waugh, 8 August 1964.

11   *Books and Bookmen*, Vol.19, No.1, Issue 217 (October 1973), p.11.

12   Letter of Auberon Waugh to the author, 10 February 1994.

13   Georgetown, Christopher Sykes Papers. Exchange of letters between Fr D'Arcy and Sykes, 17 and 28 November 1973.

14   Quoted by Tom Burns in his obit. of Fr D'Arcy in the *Stonyhurst Magazine*, Autumn 1977.

15   Paul Horgan, Fr D'Arcy and the Ages of Man, in *The Month*, Vol.225, No.1210 (1968), p.341–3.

16   Bib. No.16, p.45.

17   Bib. No.119, p.8.

18   Bib. No.132, p.26.

19   Bib. No.131, p.13.

20   Ibid, p.37 and (for the full quotation from Newman) Bib. No.60, p.1275.

21   Bib. No.17, p.17.

22   Bib. No.39, p.331.

23   Bib. No.57, p.222.

24   FS 40/3/6.

25   Int. Matt Murray, 19 May 1994.

26   Lord Hailsham in *The Catholic Herald* July 1968.

27   As Note 15, p.342.

28   Information from Fr Cyril Barrett, a member of the Farm Street Community in 1961–2.

29   Quoted by Bill Loughlin in his obit. of Fr D'Arcy in *The Tidings* (Los Angeles paper), 26 November 1976.

30   T. Burns, *The Use of Memory* (1993), p.140.

31   Frank Sheed, *The Church and I* (1974), p.103.

32   Letter of Fr Vavasour to A.W. Sire (the author's father), 28 October 1970.

33   LN Vol.80, No.367 (July 1975, quoting letter of 16 November 1974).

34   James Hitchcock, *The Pope and The Jesuits* (1984), p.28 and 46.

35   FS, Fr D'Arcy's scrapbook.

36   Selina Hastings, *Evelyn Waugh* (1994), p.224. The passage is closely based on Fr D'Arcy's Obit.

37   Bib. No. 119, p.8.

38   Quoted in Adrian Morey, *David Knowles* (1979), p.39.

39   Georgetown, Fr D'Arcy to Maria Shrady, 17 November 1967 and 19 May 1975.

40   *Stonyhurst Magazine*, Autumn 1977, obit. of Fr D'Arcy.

[41] Obit.

[42] Georgetown, Fr D'Arcy to Maria Shrady, 23 July 1970.

[43] Ibid, 13 November 1975.

[44] The account of Fr D'Arcy's death circulated by Fr Copeland is the source for the last weeks.

[45] Int. Maria Shrady 19 May 1994.

Chronological Bibliography of Fr D'Arcy's Writings

The order of composition (where known) takes precedence over that of publication.

1. *The 'God' of Mr Wells* (review of *Mr Britling Sees It Through*) in *The Month* Vol.129, No.634, p.304–12, April 1917
2. Preface to *Idols and Idylls* (schoolboy essays by P. Ingress Bell) 1918
3. *The Idea of God* in Father Cuthbert [Hess] (ed.), *God and the Supernatural*, 1920, p.44–81
4. *Theories of Asceticism* (review of two books) in *Blackfriars* Vol.1, No.10, p.603–11, January 1921
5. *Philosophers in Congress* (account of philosophical congress in Oxford, September 1920) in *The Month*, Vol.137, p.129–37, February 1921
6. *The Problem of Evil* (Catholic Truth Society pamphlet) 1922
7. *The Task before Catholic Philosophy* (account of philosophical congress at the Sorbonne, December 1921) in *The Month*, Vol.139, p.293–302, April 1922
8. *Conspectus praesentis status Philosophiae in Anglia* in *Gregorianum*, Vol.3, p.578–85, 1922
9. Two letters urging the restoration of the lay philosophy course in the *Stonyhurst Magazine*, Vol.16, No.242, p.442–3 (December 1922, signed No. 18) and No.244, p.549 (March 1923, signed Philosophus)
10. *A Theory of the Mass* (on Maurice de la Taille's *Mysterium Fidei*) in *Irish Ecclesiastical Record*, Vol.21, p.39–49, (January–June 1923)
11. *Bernard Shaw's St Joan* in *The Month*, Vol.144, p.97–105, August 1924
12. *The Philosophy of Art* in *Blackfriars*, Vol.5, No.55, p.401–13, October 1924
13. *Immanuel Kant* in *Dublin Review*, Vol.175, p.161–70, October–December 1924
14. *The Mystical Element of Religion* in *Catholic World*, p.745–52, March 1925
15. *Concerning the Holy Mass*, Part 3 (symposium on Maurice de la Taille's theory) in *Blackfriars*, Vol.177, p.171–8, October–December 1925

(ed.) *The Great Victorians*, p.345-54, 1932

39. Preface and closing chapter of M.C. D'Arcy (ed.), *The Life of the Church* (collection of various authors) 1932. The French edition has the title *Christus*.

40. *God the Inevitable* (BBC broadcast 29 May 1932) in W.F. Stead (ed.) *Sermons of the Year*, p.475–85, 1933

41. Introduction to Maurice Leahy (ed.), *Conversions to the Catholic Church*, 1933

42. *Cardinal Newman* in Maisie Ward (ed.), *The English Way*, p.318–28, 1933

43. *Christ the Son of God* (BBC broadcast, 1933) in Leonard Hodgson (ed.) *God and the World through Christian Eyes*, p.117–30, 1933

44. *St Thomas Aquinas* (BBC broadcast, spring 1933) in John Macmurray (ed.), *Some Makers of the Modern Spirit*, p.45–62, 1933

45. *Ernst Troeltsch* in *Dublin Review*, Vol.193, p.13–30, July–December 1933

46. *Dr Orchard's Passage 'From Faith to Faith'* (Part 1) in *Hibbert Journal*, Vol.31, No.4, p.533–41, July 1933

47. Preface to Hubert S. Box, *The World and God*, 1934

48. *Orthodoxy and the New Morality* in *Sidney Dark* (ed.), *Orthodoxy Sees It Through*, p.49–75, 1934

49. *Science and Theology* in *The American Review*, Vol.3, p.129–47 and 370-84, 1934, also in J. Arthur Thomson (ed.), *Science Today*, p.173–98, 1934

50. *The Groups and the Spirit of Worship* in R.H.S. Crossman (ed.) *Oxford and the Groups* (on Buchmanism), p.173–91, 1934

51. *Immortality* in *The Colosseum*, Vol.1, No.4, p.14–18, December 1934

52. *Mirage and Truth*, 1935

53. *The Pain of this World and the Providence of God*, 1935

54. *In What Way is Christ my Saviour?* in *Asking them Questions* (a collection of tracts for boys, Oxford University Press), p.135–8, 1936

55. *Christian Morals* (BBC broadcasts given in February-March 1936 and other papers), 1937

56. *A Roman Catholic View* in H. Wilson Harris (ed.), *Christianity and Communism*, 1937

57. *Revelation*, John Baillie and Hugh Martin (ed.), p.181–224, 1937

58. *Belief and Progress* in (various authors) *Chaos or Catholicism*, p.96–104, 1937

59. *Exegetical Method of History in Modern Times* in Edward Eyre (ed.) *European Civilization*, Vol.6, p.1023–95, 1937

★ Fr D'Arcy also had 15 book reviews in *The Criterion* between March 1928 and October 1938, not listed in this bibliography.

60.   *The Decline of Authority in the Nineteenth Century,* ibid., p.1271–1332

61.   *A Criticism of Marx* in *The Tablet,* Vol.169, No.5068-70, p.913–5, 5–8, 42–4, June–July 1937, (also printed in *Christian Morals,* see above)

62.   *On Liberalism in Spain* ibid., Vol.170, No.5090, p.726, 27 November 1937

63.   *Gerard Manley Hopkins* in Claude Williamson (ed.), *Great Catholics,* p.438–46, 1938

64.   *The Need for a Philosophy* in *The Tablet,* Vol.171, No.5095, p.14–15, 1 January 1938

65.   *The Validity of Religious Experience* (BBC broadcast) in *The Listener,* Vol.20, No.517, p.1255 (8 December 1938)

66.   *St Francis and the Franciscans* in Caroline M. Duncan-Jones (ed.), *An Outline of Church History,* Vol.1, p.94–104, 1939

67.   *The Work of St Thomas Aquinas* (originally BBC broadcasts) ibid. Vol.3, p.21–9, 1939

68.   *The Philosophy of Religion* in K.E.Kirk (ed.), *The Study of Theology,* p.121–46, 1939

69.   Preface to M.C. D'Arcy (ed.) *Thomas Aquinas. Selected Writings,* 1939

70.   *A Christian Society of the Future* (review of John Middleton Murry and Maritain) in *The Month,* Vol.174, No.903, p.205–15, September 1939

71.   *Professor Macmurray's Clue to History* (review of John Macmurray, *The Clue to History*) in *The Tablet,* Vol.174, p.174–6, 5 August 1939

72.   *Philosophy in Present-Day Europe* in *American Catholic Philosophical Association Proceedings* 1939, p.104–10

73.   *Militant Catholicism* (talk given to the National Catholic Alumni Federation Convention held in New York 26–29 October 1939) in *Man and Modern Secularism* (U.S., 1940)

74.   *Catholic Thinkers and Contemporary Thought* in *Thought* (U.S. journal), Vol.15, p.11–14, 1940

75.   *The Nature of Thought,* ibid. p.665–80, 1940

76.   *Henri Bergson* (an appreciation after his death) in *The Tablet,* Vol.177, No.5252, p.29, 4 January 1941

77.   *The Unity behind our Differences* (BBC broadcasts, summer 1941) in E.L.Mascall (intro.), *The Church looks Ahead,* p.79–93, 1941

78.   *No Room for Christianity – on the Nazi Persecution of the Roman Catholic Church* (BBC Home Service broadcast) in *The Listener,* Vol.26, No.656, p.198–9, 7 August 1941

79.   Foreword to John Pick (ed.), *Gerard Manley Hopkins, Priest and Poet,* 1942

80.   *Death and Life,* 1942

81. *Belief and Reason* (six BBC Home Service broadcasts) in *The Listener*, Vol.28, Nos.718–23, October–November 1942 (also as a book of that title, published 1944)

82. *The Effect of the Christian Religion on Civilization* (speech given at Christian Life Meeting, 9 May 1943) in *Blackfriars*, Vol.24, No.280, p.242-6, July 1943

83. *Evolutionary Ethics: an Examination of Dr Julian Huxley's Romanes Lecture* in *The Tablet*, Vol.183, No.5142, p.52–4, 29 January 1944

84. *Gerard Manley Hopkins* ibid. p.308, 24 June 1944

85. *Society and Spiritual Values* (a talk for the PEN commemoration of Milton's *Areopagitica*, 22–26 August 1944) in Hermon Ould (ed.) *Freedom of Expression*, 1944

86. *The Mind and Heart of Love*, 1945

87. *The Parochial and Plain Sermons* in *Newman and Littlemore* (Cowley Fathers), p.50–60, 1945

88. *The Anatomy of the Hero* in S. Schimanski and H. Treece (ed.) *Transformation Three*, p.16–18, 1945

89. *La Religion en Angleterre pendant cette Guerre* in *Etudes* (French Jesuit journal) Vol.246, p.31–8, 1945

90. *The Genius of Newman* in *America* Vol.74, p.34–7, 13 October 1945

91. *The Clown and the Philosopher* in *The Month*, Vol.187 (New Series Vol.1), p.7–16, 1949

92. *'Religio' Medici* (review of broadcasts by Dr Alex Comfort) in *The Month*, New Series Vol.3, No.2, February 1950

93. *Philosophical Pluralism and Catholic Orthodoxy* in *The Month*, New Series Vol.4, No.1, p.41–8, July 1950, also published as *A Comment on Philosophical Systems* in *Thought* (U.S. journal), Vol.25, No. 97, p.288–96, June 1950

94. *No Sting of Death: the Tabernacle of the Most High* (on the doctrine of the Assumption) in *The Tablet*, Vol.196, No.5745, p.388, 4 November 1950

95. *Freedom of Thought* (a debate with Fr Vincent Turner SJ broadcast by the BBC Third Programme, 18 October 1950) in *The Month*, New Series Vol.5, No.2, p.65–86, February 1951

96. *The Nature of Catholicism* (review of Henri de Lubac, *Catholicism*) in *The Month*, New Series Vol.5, No.1, p.46–50, January 1951

97. *'Saint and Mystic'* (BBC Home Service broadcast on Baron von Hügel) in *The Listener*, Vol.45, No.1142, p.97–8, 18 January 1951

98. *Social Writings of the Pope* in *Catholic Mind* (U.S. journal), Vol.49, p.325, May 1951

99. *On Human Love* (BBC Third Programme broadcast on Jean Guitton's *Essay on Human Love*) in *The Listener*, Vol.48, No.1225, p.299 and 302, 21 August 1952

100. *The Power of Caritas and the Holy Spirit* (talk given at Eranos conference at Ascona, 20–28 August 1952) in *Eranos-Jahrbuch*,Vol.21

101. Preface to R. Finnemore, *The Church's Mind on Church Music*, 1953

102. *Japan after the American Occupation* (BBC Third Programme broadcast) in *The Listener*,Vol.50, No.1281, p.455–6,17 September 1953

103. *A Protestant 'Summa Theologica'* (on Paul Tillich) in *The Month*, New Series Vol.10, No.5 p.270–81, November 1953

104. *A Note on Gerard Hopkins* in *The Month*, New Series Vol.11, No.2, p.113–15, February 1954

105. *The Mystery of Evil* in Elizabeth Pakenham (ed.), *Catholic Approaches*, p.13–32, 1955

106. Foreword to Ralph Harper, *The Sleeping Beauty*, 1955

107. *Communism and Christianity*, 1956

108. *The Tactics of Meditation* (BBC Third Programme broadcast on the Spiritual Exercises) in *The Listener*, Vol.56, No.1433, p.386–7, 13 September 1956

109. *N. Braybrooke. The Priest and the Outsider* in *Books on Trial*, Vol.15, p.113, November 1956

110. *The Meeting of Love and Knowledge*, 1957

111. *'The Potting Shed'* (review of New York production of Graham Greene's play) in *The Tablet*,Vol.209, No.6105, p.490, 25 May 1957

112. *Monsignor Ronald Knox* (funeral sermon preached on 28 August 1957) ibid.,Vol.210, No.6119, p.172–3, 31 August 1957

113. *The Varieties of Human Love* in *Saturday Evening Post*, 7 March 1958 and in R.Thruelsen and J. Kobler (ed.) *Adventures of the Mind* (New York, 1959)

114. *The Sense of History, Secular and Sacred* (American title: *The Meaning and Matter of History*) both 1959

115. Introduction to A.R. Caponigri (ed.), *Modern Catholic Thinkers, An Anthology* (U.S.), 1960

116. *No Absent God* (based on Danforth Lectures given at Cornell University, January–March 1959), published 1962

117. *Wrong answer to the problem of evil* in *Catholic World* (U.S. journal), Vol.190, p.81–5, November 1959

118. *God and Mythology* (a chapter from *No Absent God*) in *Heythrop Journal*,Vol.1, No.2, p.91–104, April 1960

119. *Modern Spirituality* in *The Way* (Jesuit journal), Vol.1, No.1, p.1-8, January 1961

120. *Drugs, Brainwashing and this Self* (impromptu talk given in response to previous speakers at the Control of the Mind Symposium at the University of California Medical Center, San Francisco, 28–30 January 1961) published in *The Current* (Harvard, May 1962)

121. *The Influence of Religion on Society and the Individual* (prepared text

for the foregoing symposium, later broadcast by Voice of America) in S.M. Farber and R.H.L. Wilson, *Man and Civilization: Control of the Mind*, 1961, p.164–87

122. *Literature as a Christian Comedy* (McAuley Lecture at St Joseph College, West Hartford, Connecticut) 1961

123. Essay in Suzanne Silberstein (ed.), *Sense and Style: The Craft of the Essay* (U.S.), 1962

124. Preface to Jean T. Wilde (ed.) *The Search for being* (U.S.), 1962

125. *Itinerary to Christ* in *Liturgical Arts*, Vol.30, p.59–60, February 1962

126. *Of God and Man* (collection of 81 sermonettes published in the *Sunday Times*), 1964

127. *Facing God*, 1966 (abridged American edition published as *Dialog with Myself*, part of *Credo Perspectives*, 1966)

128. *The Immutability of God* in *American Catholic Philosophical Association Proceedings*, Vol.41, p.19–26, 1967 (also Chap. 8 in No. 131, below)

129. *Facing the People* (collection of short newspaper articles, U.S.), 1968

130. *Father Martin D'Arcy, who will be 80 this year, talks to Quintin Hogg* (pre-recorded talk broadcast by the BBC on 17 January 1968) in *The Listener* Vol.79, No.2025, p.74–5, 18 January 1968

131. *Facing the Truth*, 1969

132. *Humanism and Christianity*, 1969

133. *The Magnitude of Faith* (Oxford University Sermon as Select Preacher) 1 November 1970

134. *Revelation and God's Architecture* (U.S.) 1976

135. *Christ's Mastery* (7th Annual Hopkins Sermon, preached at Farm Street, 8 June 1975), published by the Hopkins Society, 1975

INDEX

16.   *The Mass and the Redemption,* 1926
17.   *Catholicism,* 1927
18.   *Immanence and Transcendence: A Reply to Professor Alexande*r in *Hibbert Journal,* Vol.25, No.3, p.466–77, April 1927
19.   *The Claims of Common Sense* (paper given 23 May 1927) in *Proceedings of the Aristotelian Society,* New Series Vol.27, p.317–36, also published in *Dublin Review,* Vol.181, p.161–78, 1927
20.   *Irreligion and Religion* (on Bertrand Russell and B.H. Streeter) in *The Month,* Vol.150, p.144-51, August 1927
21.   *The Thomistic Synthesis and Intelligence* in *The Criterion,* Vol.6, No.111, p.210–28, September 1927★
22.   *The Authority of the Expert* in *Thought* (U.S. journal), Vol.2, p.375–91, 1927
23.   *A Critic among the Philosophers* (review of Wyndham Lewis, *Time and Western Man*) in *The Month,* Vol.150, p.511–5, December 1927
24.   *Christ, Priest and Redeemer* (part of the series *The Teaching of the Catholic Church*), 1928
25.   *Knowledge According to Aquinas* in *Proceedings of the Aristotelian Society,* New Series Vol.28, p.177–202 (paper given 7 May 1928)
26.   *Bernard Shaw's 'Intelligent Woman's Guide'* [to Socialism], Part 2 of a collection of opinions, in *The Criterion,* Vol.8, No.31, p.195–201, December 1928
27.   *The Spirit of Charity* 1929
28.   *Thomas Aquinas* 1930
29.   *The Philosophy of St Augustine* in *A Monument to St Augustine,* p.155–96, 1930
30.   *The Meaning of the Mass* (on Maurice de la Taille's theory) in *The Month,* Vol.156, p.302–9, October 1930
31.   *Probability and Certainty* (paper given to international philosophical congress in Oxford, September 1930) in *Philosophia Perennis* (Ratisbon, 1930), Vol.2, p.687–93
32.   *A Modern Form of Thomism* (on Maréchal, Rousselot etc.) in *Clergy Review,* Vol.1, No.6, p.557–75, June 1931
33.   *Is it really Faith?* (review of Gifford Lectures by A.E. Taylor) in *The Month* Vol.158, p.117–27, August 1931
34.   *The Nature of Belief,* 1931
35.   *Christianity and the Modern Mind* in J. Lewis May (ed.), *God and the Universe,* p.103–51, 1931
36.   *Gerard Manley Hopkins* in *Archivum Historicum Societatis Jesu,* Vol.1, p.118–22, 1932
37.   *The Good and the Right* (paper given 11 April 1932) in *Proceedings of the Aristotelian Society,* New Series Vol.32, p.171–206, 1932
38.   *John Henry Newman* in H.J. Massingham and Hugh Massingham